The Women's

The Scarecrow Press, Inc.

WOMEN'S CULTURE

Renaissance of the Seventies

Edited by GAYLE KIMBALL

Metuchen, N.J., & London 1981

About the Cover

FAITH WILDING: *My aspiration as a woman artist has always been to invent a new language of images that can describe the new being of women in the world as well as bring old truths back into new vision. I am trying to learn the lessons of art and nature. The tremendous transformational powers of both move me. On the walls of my studio hang many beautiful dried leaves, buds, flowers, seed pods, and husks. The departed spirit of the plant has left its imprint forever on the form that remains. When I paint this form, I reunite it with the spirit—thus nature and I perform the joyous, complex act of alchemy, which is art. New forms, new worlds, and, perhaps, hope are reborn.*

Library of Congress Cataloging in Publication Data
Main entry under title:

Women's culture.

    Includes index.
    1. Feminism--United States--Addresses, essays,
lectures. 2. Women artists--United States--
Addresses, essays, lectures. 3. Women musicians--
United States--Addresses, essays, lectures.
4. Women authors--United States--Addresses, essays,
lectures. I. Kimball, Gayle.
HQ1426.W6634   305.4'0973   81-9004
ISBN 0-8108-1455-2   AACR2

PREFACE

The origin of this collection of original essays and interviews stems from my Women's Studies courses at California State University, Chico. During classes on the archetypes of women in religion it became obvious that Western history records men's images, projections, fantasies, fears, and ideals. For example, Jungians have fully described male archetypes. But what was women's imagery? What were women's projections on men—obviously not the great mother, not virgin or temptor, but what? Almost no material existed describing the female psyche. Consequently I set out to discover women's approach to creativity from women artists, psychologists, and scholars: their definitions of women's styles of contribution to culture, their themes, approaches, and visualizations.

Acknowledgments are due to the authors of this book for responding so thoughtfully to my questions about women's approach to the arts and to my students for sparking my thinking. My appreciation also goes to Betty Borell; Barbara Kimball; and Jed, Susan, and Philip Suntree for their help. Thanks to Robin Morgan for the use of her phrase "The Women's Renaissance" in the subtitle.

TABLE OF CONTENTS

IV. Literature and Dreams

V. Religion

VI. Organizations

I. DEFINITIONS

WOMEN'S CULTURE:
THEMES AND IMAGES

Gayle Kimball

The first wave of American feminism began with the Seneca Falls women's-rights convention in 1848. The second emerged in 1963 with Betty Friedan's book *The Feminine Mystique*. The third wave is cultural feminism, the conscious emergence of women's culture.[1] This wave is visible in women's creativity, spirituality, and relationships and in feminist organizations. Women's culture draws inspiration from the heart and body as well as from the conscious mind. The focus of this culture is on women's experiences and expression. Women are subsumed in the cultural concept of "mankind"; history, literature, art history, religion, are about male activities, while women remain outside, classed as the "Other."[2] Female muse for the male artist, mother of a son, the woman behind the great man: women were identified according to the men in their lives. Excluded from much of recorded culture, women are now researching their history as well as creating contemporary environments conducive to unhampered creativity, such as women's-studies courses or feminist publishing companies. Cultural feminist endeavors are revealing women's themes and images, as they are different from men's, providing humanity a pluralistic world view more rich and balanced than one seen only through male eyes.

This collection of original essays and interviews explores women's unique culture. These essays are historically possible now because of the essential background of the women's movement, consciousness-raising groups, the rise of a feminist scholarship that considers the study of women vital rather than trivial, and the establishment of women's institutions. In the 1970s women created their own institutions for publishing, bookselling, teaching women's studies, music production, filmmaking, displaying and teaching art, worship, theatre, counseling, rape crisis intervention, refuges for battered women, health care, banking, travel, and farming. The Los Angeles Woman's Building is an example of an organization specifically titled an institution of women's culture—like *Chrysalis*, a magazine of women's culture. Great excitement exists among feminists about the flowering of women's culture, what Robin Morgan calls the new woman's renaissance. Some of the themes that emerge in the women's renaissance are egalitarian use of power; choices in forms of love, sexuality, and family; respect for women's experiences; reclaiming control of women's bodies; and integrative thought processes that include more than the knowledge of the conscious mind.

Growing awareness of women's restrictive sex-role socialization and of the fact that traditional studies of culture do not often include women's contributions has led to the development of cultural feminism. Cultural feminists differ from radical feminists. The latter broke away from the National Organization for Women (NOW) in 1968 over the issue of organizational structure. Radicals wanted to do away with hierarchies as well as all sex roles and gender distinctions. Such writers as Shulamith Firestone and Ti-Grace Atkinson advocated entirely eradicating gender-linked roles of men and women and substituting people not defined in terms of their sex organs or biological functions.[3] So that there would be absolutely no roles determined by gender Firestone advocated a society where brooding devices would birth infants. Another radical feminist, Brooke Williams, defines cultural feminism as "the belief that women will be freed via an alternative women's culture." She believes that this ideology dominated the women's movement beginning in 1974. She faults it for not being sufficiently political or revolutionary, for selling a "happiness mystique." Goddess worship and reading women's novels do not solve men's oppression of women.[4] Her criticism will be responded to later in the chapter.

In contrast to radical feminists, cultural feminists are defining differences between men and the concerns and expressions that characterize women. They believe that women have distinctive experiences and values and that these must be studied as unique contributions to culture. Women have their own social system, according to the sociologist Jessie Bernard. In an interview in which she discussed writing her book *The Female World* Dr. Bernard explained:

> It became suddenly very clear to me that men and women live in different worlds. We all live in a one-sex world ... we have cliches and stereotypes about women, but very little about the world that women live in. So that's what I've been trying to explore—the shape of it, the class structure of it, the group structure of it, the culture of it. . . . The female ethos is one of love and/or duty, one of doing for others. Cooperation rather than competition prevails. I think women are always building up people, women as well as

men. They like to build up people rather than throw them down. It shows in all kinds of research in language and interaction. In conversation, the male style is someone says something and he knocks it down, it's a battle, one-upmanship all the time. Women make a statement and the other women will say "uh-huh" and build it up. They build it up together; instead of it being a battle, it's a cooperative venture.[5]

Perhaps women have greater development of the right hemisphere of the brain and men the left hemisphere: the former is relational, artistic, integrative, intuitive, and imaginative; the latter is analytical, linear, intellectual, and logical.[6] The right hemisphere also controls the left side of the body, devalued in the patriarchy. "Left-handed thinking... encourages sensitivity, playfulness, feeling, openness, subjectivity and imagery in problem solving."[7] However, verbal abilities, in which females excel at an early age, are left-hemisphere functions. Spatial skills, in which males excel, are rooted in the right hemisphere. One cannot make a strict division of hemisphere processes and gender, but there does seem to be a tendency toward different brain development in males and females, females having less differentiation at an early age.[8] Cultural feminists often use qualities associated with the right hemisphere to describe women.

Some cultural feminists believe women have a unique way of thinking that transcends the rational and includes intuition, and draws from the unconscious, from the mystical, and from nature. A persistent theme in cultural feminist descriptions of women's orientation to the world is that it is life affirming, what the theologian Mary Daly describes as "biophilic female energy."[9] This theme stands in contrast to the patriarchal establishment of dualistic vision, which rationalizes rape of the planetary body and of women's bodies. Daly equates patriarchy with necrophilia. A striking parallel in descriptions both of matriarchies of the distant past and feminist visions of an egalitarian future is the perception of women as living in harmony with nature and receiving inspiration by way of their intuition and vision.

Feminist goals for the future are often built on an assumption that there are basic differences between men and women and that women think differently in drawing from a source deeper than the conscious mind or the linear sequential thinking of the left brain hemisphere. Wholeness and connectedness characterize women's thinking. Whether this assumption about women's thinking process is accurate or provable, based on role socialization or genetic and hormonal differences, is not in the scope of this chapter. It is worth noting what qualities cultural feminists claim for themselves, what qualities they value. The "woman is wonderful" school, as Charlotte Bunch calls it,[10] has critics like Bunch who find it unrealistic and a diversion from political activism. However, we do need to know more about what women value, since culture has been male defined for so long.

Women project their own way of relating to nature because they feel that they are more closely allied to it. "This earth is my sister," says the poet Susan Griffin.[11] "Women are daughters/lovers of the earth," says Mary Daly, asserting that female energy is "life-loving." Their connectedness with nature gives women a deeper thinking process. For example, Daly states that male "ecologists such as Barry Commoner can summarize 'laws of ecology,' but it is something else to intuit the deep mysteries. . . ." Daly seems to be affirming the folklore about "women's intuition." She describes men as thinking in a linear way, while women think in spirals, making connections between concepts where men would not be able to see them. Symbols of female ability to make interconnections are "the maze, the labyrinth, the spiral, the hole as mystic center, and the Soul Journey itself."[12]

Her belief that women are "seeking and naming the deep mysteries of interconnectedness" is not unique to Mary Daly. Susan Griffin's book *Woman and Nature* is a prose poem showing parallels in ways men victimize both the environment and women and how women are rooted in nature. Women are close to nature not only because of their joint victimization but also due to some mystical bond: Griffin describes how during the course of writing the book she grew to identify more and more strongly with "voices from nature." These voices inspire some women to be prophets: "Some of us can heal. We can read bodies with our hands, read the earth, find water, trace gravity's path. We know what grows and how to balance one thing against another."[13] Tapping intuition or "sharpening of the senses" is taught to children in Marge Piercy's utopian novel *Woman on the Edge of Time*. Piercy's character explains that "we want to root that forebrain back into a net of connecting."[14]

Another contemporary who believes in the link between women, nature, and mystical thinking is Elizabeth Gould Davis. She believes that women held sway in matriarchies and will regain their influence in the coming Aquarian Age because of their ability to acquire mystical insights. According to Davis, "Throughout the ancient world the tradition prevailed that women held the secrets of nature and were the only channels through which flowed the wisdom and knowledge of the ages." Their special access to mystical knowledge accounted for the "priority of female oracles, prophets, priests, sybils, pythonesses, maenads, Eringes, shamanesses, and so on."[15]

Association of woman with nature is not new; it is also central to other definitions of past matriarchies. In the nineteenth century the Swiss thinker J. J. Bachofen, a man drawing from mythological sources, described matriarchies as societies where women's "kinship with material nature" produced a peace-loving society. People were at one with nature and each other. There were no hierarchies and few laws and taboos because of women's "aversion to restrictions." Child rearing was shared and sexuality unrestrained in that there was no premium on virginity and no illegitimacy. Bachofen also felt that "mystery is rooted in woman's very nature."[16] The transformations that occur in her body led to realization of the transformations of the life cycle and caused women to be the first seers and prophetesses, he believed. In the nineteenth century Marx and Engels drew on the writings of the anthropologist Lewis Morgan to affirm the existence of egalitarian matriarchal societies.

That women are life affirming and peace loving was also the premise of early–twentieth-century feminist Charlotte Perkins Gilman. In her utopian all-female society, described in *Herland*, harmony prevails and the greatest value is placed on motherhood. Gilman theorized that women's historical experiences as mothers cause them to focus on life's immediacy and joy, while the male experience as hunter and warrior taught him to focus on death, the afterlife, and judgment.[17]

In the twentieth century Bachofen's descriptions of matriarchies were continued by Helen Dinar in *Mothers and Amazons* and Elizabeth Gould Davis in *The First Sex*. Women's ties with nature led to her psychic abilities and to her power, say Bachofen, Dinar, and Davis. Dinar joined Bachofen in describing matriarchies as tolerant about sexuality and "almost without laws." Women had control over their own reproduction, as in knowing how to abort. Davis believes that when women had power, the "feminine virtues of selflessness, compassion and empathy" predominated, creating a culture "founded on love and trust, mutual respect and concern, in which all men and women are truly brothers and sisters." Woman was the source of civilization because of her knowledge of the "laws of nature—laws that baffled his dimmer perceptions and rendered him dependent on woman as the interpreter. . . ."[18]

These descriptions of matriarchies are similar to feminist visions of the future that describe societies where people are at one with nature, recognize the inspiration of extrasensory perception, are sensuous, are without hierarchies, and have no taboos on sexuality (except for rape). They maintain no premium on monogamy, illegitimacy, virginity, or exclusive child rearing by the biological mother.

In relation to the environment of the future feminists are concerned with protecting nature and learning from it. In *The Kin of Ata Are Waiting for You*, a fantasy novel by Dorothy Bryant, the kin live simply on an island unknown to the rest of civilization. All their decisions are made on the basis of revelations from dreams. In some unconscious tie with nature, for example, the kin plant vegetables in nonlinear patterns that probably follow underground water sources. A man from our society finds himself on Ata and learns to recognize that through their dreams "they operated with knowledge far deeper than I could ever reach."[19] This search for sources of knowledge beyond the conscious mind is a characteristic of women's culture.

Women's unconscious projections and the themes that recur in their creative expressions have not been carefully studied or even thought to exist differently from those seen in men's work. The only Jungian exploration of the female heroine and her quest for maturity is *Amor and Psyche*, by Erich Neumann.[20] Neumann analyzes the myth as being representative of the female individuation process, but he and the myth's author were males. A study of "the archetypal feminine" and the female rite of passage was finally published in 1980 in Nor Hall's *The Moon and the Virgin*.[21] Men's images or unconscious projections of ideals and fears concerning women have been studied at length by Jungians. Male projections often revolve around two poles, symbolized by Mary, who is selfless and asexual, and Eve, the sexual temptress. Jungians have explored the recurrent archetype of the Good and Terrible Mothers, a major constellation in male imagery.[22] Numerous studies have been written about men's images of women in the literature, painting, film, music, myths, and religion created by men.

Pioneering studies exploring traits of the female psyche were J. J. Bachofen's *Mother Right* (1861, Swiss), Helen Dinar's *Mothers and Amazons* (c. 1932, Austrian), and M. Esther Harding's *The Way of All Women* (1933). Harding explains that a revolution in female consciousness is occurring, so that women are growing beyond naïve, coy, and kittenish postures designed to attract men. Women are evolving from what Harding, using Jungian terminology, names the *anima*, or feminine phase of instinctual relations, to the *animus*, or masculine stage of maturing ego.[23] The latter is characterized by autonomy and ability to work at jobs integrating Logos, as Jung named the male principle of rationality. He defined Logos as objective thinking, while the female element, Eros, represents intuitive skill in relationships.[24] An example of a non-Jungian who defines women in terms of Eros traits is the designer Sheila de Bretteville; she views female values, shaped by centuries of socialization, as "creating relationships, needing and wanting to work with other people collectively and providing nurturing, comforting environments."[25] The final stage of female evolution Harding calls "consciousness," when a woman transcends ego and unites Eros and Logos to manifest altruistic "suprapersonal values."[26]

For Harding and other Jungians women are somehow innately more attuned to Eros than Logos, but the traditional lack of intellectual training for women is enough to explain the differences. Thus Harding, Bernard, Bachofen, Gilman, Dinar, Davis, Daly, Griffin, and de Bretteville all believe that the women's world is a distinctive one, different from men's in its values and way of thinking. This difference may be a result of women's subordinate status, but even if the notion of "biophilic female energy" and spiral thinking is a fantasy, we need to know women's myths as well as we know men's.

An evolution in female consciousness and the documenting of women's culture could occur only with the development of technology, which frees women from the frequent childbearing and lactating that necessitated dependence on a male protector. Taking care of numerous children also left women with little leisure time for thought. The classic example of the good wife is defined in Proverbs 31, in the Old Testament, as one who rises before the others and goes to sleep after they do. She takes care of mundane tasks in order to free her husband to discuss spiritual matters with the elders. Staying at home was also required by women's vulnerability to rape. The author Virginia Woolf imagined that if Shakespeare had a talented sister who might have gone to London to develop her talents in the theatre, she would have become pregnant during an affair with a stage manager and then have committed suicide.[27]

Even as women gained more possibilities for freedom in industrial society, ideologies were promulgated to keep them in their traditional subordinate position. Technology permits birth control, wage-earning jobs that do not require muscular strength, and labor-saving household devices. But the possibility of liberation of women from economic subservience is accompanied by ideological campaigns to keep her restricted from control over her own body, as in the current campaign against abortion. In the nineteenth century the rhetoric used to limit women's power centered on the cult of angelic motherhood as expressed in popular novels, magazines, and sermons. Women were portrayed as too pure and pious to compete with men outside the home in the harsh world of politics and business. In the 1920s the myth of emancipation proclaimed that the flapper was liberated because of a superficial change in mores that permitted her to use alcohol and tobacco and to shorten her skirts. This tactic is best illustrated by the current cigarette commercial slogan "You've come a long way, baby," implying that freedom to smoke is liberation.

Psychology is the ideology of women's oppression in our century. In the 1950s the feminine mystique substituted Freud for St. Paul in order to convince women that they should stay home expending their energies being wife and mother to men, to make up for their penis envy. In the fifties books like *The Power of Sexual Surrender*, by Marie Robinson, told women that fulfillment came through accepting dependency on a man. This would lead to the vaginal orgasm as defined by Freud (Masters and Johnson proved that female orgasms are clitorially based) and to the ultimate satisfaction of motherhood.[28] That the author was a woman, like many of the writers of elementary textbooks about passive girls watching adventurous boys, illustrates that oppressed peoples internalize values of the dominant culture. Women themselves are kept from realizing their oppression because of social myths: gallantry and chivalry, which put women on a pedestal, where there is no room to move; the superficial change in mores, such as the acceptability of women smoking; and the fact that some white women share in white male privilege. This privilege lasts as long as a woman is married to a well-to-do man and does not join the ranks of displaced homemakers. The second wave of the women's movement sought to awaken women to awareness of their oppression, as reflected in their earning capacity being 57 percent of a man's and in their comprising only 10 percent of elected government officials.

In 1963 Betty Friedan's *The Feminine Mystique* named the problem that previously had no name—the malaise of housewives. She wrote that it was not neurotically unfeminine to be unfulfilled by a white wash, a polished floor, and a station wagon full of children. In doing so she was a catalyst in bringing about the rebirth of the women's movement. One of its main tools is the consciousness-raising (C-R) small discussion group, where women realize they are a subordinate class, socialized to be affiliational rather than achievement oriented and to fear success as unfeminine.[29] Preoccupation with physical appearance and charm in order to attract a husband prevents healthy self-identification and saps time and self-esteem. A reaction is seen in the feminist slogan on T-shirts: "Develop Your Brain, Instead of Your Bust."

Yet the notion of woman's happiness as found primarily in her affiliational role as wife has emerged again in the recent movement for *Fascinating Womanhood* and *Total Womanhood*, bestselling books and courses that teach a wife how to keep her man by being seductive, childishly cute, and perpetually cheerful and remaining an angelic domestic goddess. These descriptions of femininity are strikingly reminiscent of nineteenth-century ideology.

Feminists have struggled against the feminine mystique, the fear of success as unfeminine, and *Fascinating Womanhood*. They have organized small C-R groups and such large networks as the National Organization for Women (1966) and the National Women's Political Caucus (1971), whose slogan is "Make Policy, Not Coffee." They have established women's-studies programs (over three hundred programs, five thousand courses). Because of "consciousness raising" women are encouraged to be self-actualizing, and what emerges is the new woman's renaissance.

The rest of this chapter describes the characteristic concerns and themes that are prominent in women's culture of the seventies:

• Anger about women's *powerlessness*, a search for alternatives to patriarchal hierarchical power—such as collective decision making; for some, separatism as a means for gaining control over one's life; and the quest for role models of strong women—both historical and mythical.

• Reaction against romantic love of the Hollywood variety; the monolith of the nuclear family as the only acceptable way of living; and the glorification of motherhood and child rearing exclusively by the biological mother; as well as a concomitant search for *alternative family structures*.

• Respectful description of women's actual lives and *experiences*, as in oral histories, diaries, letters, autobiographies, and women's traditional crafts.

• Reclamation of *sensuality*, health care, control over contraception and birthing, and free choice in sexual preference.

• Emphasis on knowledge lodged in the *unconscious*, the right brain hemisphere, spirituality, and the occult.

• Concern for *wholeness* and overcoming duality.

Power

Power is of primary concern to women because women have suffered from a lack of it. A popular corrective visual image is a fist in the female Venus symbol (♀).[30] A paucity of strong role models has denied women a model of female power. One needs a tradition to react with, to rebel against, to build on; women creators have often had to work in a vacuum without knowledge of the struggles and successes of previous women. Women, therefore, are digging into both the historical and the mythological past and also creating science fiction in order to have both a history and a clear goal for an egalitarian future. The "amazon," an image often found in feminist literature, is an alternative to the patriarchy's passive madonna. The existence of an ancient matriarchal society is defended by Helen Dinar, Elizabeth Gould Davis, and Evelynn Reed and fictionalized by the novelist Monique Wittig.[31] A symbol of the matriarchy, Sagaris, the double-edged axe, was the title selected for a feminist summer university held in Vermont in 1975 and in Minnesota in 1977. It is also frequently used in feminist jewelry. Most scholars do not believe that matriarchies existed, including UCLA archaeologist Pat McDonald, who did fieldwork in eastern Europe.[32] Such feminist scholars as Susan Rennie, however, do believe that they existed. What is important are the attributes that women ascribe to matriarchal culture, because these reveal female images.

Mythological goddesses provide a rich source of inspiration for women, as in Buffie Johnson's paintings or Louise Bogan's poem "Medusa." "Hera" and "In Goddess We Trust" are slogans found on buttons and shirts. The goddess is an image of strength for the artist Mary Beth Edelson, who explains:

> If woman is the head, the natural head, then all of civilization has to be turned around. . . . The first time I did ritual photography outdoors, I was specifically thinking of speaking with the goddess. I wanted to project my body as myself and something greater than myself. We are the goddess. Each one is a goddess and in the process of becoming a goddess; what I experienced was immense energy and power. [33]

When God Was a Woman, by Merlin Stone, documents the sovereignty of the goddess in ancient times. [34] In her public talks about the goddesses Stone makes their names a kind of litany of female awesomeness.

Biblical women have been another source of image making for women. Martha Graham's dances about Judith and Eve exemplify this, as does her use of heroines of Greek mythology like Clytemnestra. Judith's beheading of her enemy is a common theme in Renaissance paintings by women.

"She Is Risen" and "The Christa" are slogans that provide an image of a female messiah (Ann Lee was a model of an actual female messiah for the Shaker religious communities). Negative religious images of women have been reversed, so that Eve, witches, and Lilith are celebrated in feminist rituals and literature as strong knowledge seekers, independent and wise. A radical feminist group called WITCH (Women's International Terrorist Conspiracy from Hell) used guerilla-theatre tactics to hex multinational corporations, using the witch image. Feminist Wicce (witchcraft) is practiced in covens throughout the United States. The goddess is celebrated as high priestesses and crones lead the nymphs and maidens in rituals.

Women are researching other foremothers as role models. Joan of Arc and the Virgin Mary have long been images adopted by women in mental institutions as figures to copy. [35] The artist Judy Chicago's "Great Ladies" series honors historical women, such as George Sand. Her large-scale multimedia work *The Dinner Party* includes abstract images of mythical and historical women produced on thirty-nine plates on a triangular table thirty-nine feet long. The names of nine hundred and ninety-nine other women are written on floor tiles below the dinner table. Chicago recognized that our images of historical figures were mostly male, as in the painting of *The Last Supper*. Viewing *The Dinner Party* feels like making a pilgrimage to a sacred shrine, making it the Notre Dame Cathedral of women's culture. Films document women's leadership; for example, women active in labor disputes are the subject of *Union Maids*, *With Babies and Banners*, *Harlan County, U.S.A.*, *Salt of the Earth*, *Blow for Blow* (about French women), and *Norma Rae*.

Other creative women are doing self-portraits and using autobiographical material as an exploration of their own identity and strength. Examples include the self-portraits that the sculptor Marisol Escobar frequently employs in her art or the self-portraits of photographer Imogen Cunningham. Putting on and taking off masks and looking into mirrors are other recurring images of self-discovery in women's art.

"The Future Is Female" proclaims a shirt slogan. Science fiction writers are creating positive roles for women that go beyond well-known science-fiction images of sex objects like Wonder Woman, Supergirl, and the Bionic Woman. In a collection of science-fiction short stories titled *Women of Wonder*, however, many of the female authors do not venture far from traditional emphasis on women in love or women as mothers. Several stories center on women as victims; others focus on women as professionals—usually nurturing physicians. In *More Women of Wonder* there are greater numbers of strong women: a warrior, a crew member of a spaceship, a leader of an anarchist world revolution, and in the third collection, another physician, a noble turned bandit, and a women's army.[36]

In *The Left Hand of Darkness* Ursula LeGuin describes an androgynous society where beings alternate gender during periods of estrus so that politics are affected, for example, when the king becomes pregnant.[37] LeGuin's culture is without male dominance, so that it does not fight major wars or divide people by sex roles, and options are freely available as to monogamous or promiscuous relationships, with emphasis being on the present rather than striving for future glory. The lack of dualities in sex roles effects oneness with others and with the present.

Joanna Russ's *The Female Man* is one of the earliest feminist science-fiction novels. In it she creates a "gyandrous vision" of female power.[38] She describes an all-female society called Whileaway. Its women delight in the full moon, the solstices and equinoxes, the flowering of trees and bushes, "the planting of seeds, happy copulation, unhappy copulation, longing, jokes... acquiring new shoes, wearing same, birth, the contemplation of a work of art, marriages, sport, divorces, anything at all, nothing at all, great ideas, death. . . ."[39] The emphasis on nature, sensuality, and acceptance of seeming opposites are characteristic female themes. Another society that Russ describes in her novel separates warring men and women. Her character Jael, a female assassin, expresses her rage and enjoys her power to commit violence against men.

Marge Piercy creates a feminist utopia in *Woman on the Edge of Time*, which describes a future society where there are no roles based on sex. Parenting is assumed by a group of three adults given the nurturing of an infant created by mechanical means. Males and females are able to nurse their child due to injections of hormones. Children live in a special building of their own, cared for by skilled teachers, while all adults live alone. They select a small core of close friends and lovers. No premium is placed on monogamy or heterosexuality, but rather on personal inclination. Education is gained through working with adults in actual job situations, so there is no segregation by age. The society recycles and lives simply in small towns in harmony with the earth. Language is without gender: "per" replaces the pronouns "his" or "her." The heroine, Connie, who time travels to this future society, is told, "Our dignity comes from work. Everybody raises the kids, haven't you noticed? Romance, sex, birth, children—that's what you fasten on. Yet that isn't women's business anymore. It's everybody's." Piercy's is the most developed portrayal of radical feminist goals for the future. Her goals and those of other well-known feminists are documented in a videotape on *Feminist Visions of the Future*.[40]

Anger about patriarchy has led some women, usually lesbians, to advocate separatism from men. A quarantine of the disease of romantic love, and a resulting separation of men and women, is suggested by Professor Sally Gearhart. The quarantine would last until men and women learn independence and learn to overcome jealousy, possessiveness, and expectations that the other person will satisfy all one's needs.[41] She portrays the separation of men and women in her collection of science-fiction stories *The Wanderground*: men are confined to cities because outside them they are impotent, and machines do not work. Their loss of power resulted from nature's rebellion against men's violence.[42] Women must create their own institutions because of men's "metaphysical cannibalism," according to Ti-Grace Atkinson and Jill Johnston.[43] Issues of separatism have occurred on a less grandiose scale in performing women's music. The Olivia Records performers would prefer to play to all-women audiences because "we should not have to expend energy to neutralize the vibes of men." Olivia "strongly advocates separatism from men, as a long-term transitional strategy,"[44] although they currently perform for mixed audiences.

A less revolutionary solution to gaining power is the movement to train women in assertiveness, taught in small counseling groups and through numerous books. From all spectrums of political framework women are working for utilization of their strength. Anger is a common theme, as voiced by Rita Mae Brown in her collection of poetry *The Hand That Cradles the Rock*.[45] Anger erupts at the violence done to women; as a result, not only is literature created, but women form rape crisis centers and refuge centers for battered women.

Women want neither to duplicate the male hierarchy nor to reverse it to gain power over men. Rather they are developing a form of decision making that is based on consensus. Radical feminist groups, such as the New York Feminists and the Redstockings, experimented with rotating leaders selected by lot and allocating tokens, which equalized the number of times each person spoke in a meeting. A NOW chapter selects leaders by lot, with group power to approve or veto the selection; offices are frequently rotated and decisions must be cleared with the whole group. Leaders are often called "facilitators" rather than "chairpersons," illustrating the role of the leader as equal in power to all group members.

The Los Angeles Woman's Building is a pioneering center of women's culture built around the nucleus of the Feminist Studio Workshop school for artists begun in 1972 (San Francisco also has a Woman's Building). Its leaders find that major decisions are best made by using the C-R technique of eliciting contributions from each member, going around the circle of participants to find a consensus. Each woman voices her opinion without interruption. They believe, however, in the necessity of leadership and are wary of "the tyranny of structurelessness," as described perceptively by the political scientist Jo Freeman.[46] Olivia Records, Iris Films, and the Feminist Health Centers are examples of feminist business collectives that also share responsibility. Some feminists have experimented with living communally and attempting to do away with heads of households and sex-stereotyped tasks. For example, "The Furies" (Washington, D.C., 1971 to 1972) was one of the first feminist collectives. Most feminist organizations try to share power and decision making. They also attempt to be aware of the impact of class background, racism, and homophobia on ways of behaving.

"Sisterhood Is Powerful" expresses the effort to find power through unity with other women. A newly emerging sense of bonding with other women—"Uppity Women Unite"—opposes the competitive jealousy about other women's attractiveness to men that many women are taught as teenagers. The phrase "Sisterhood Is Powerful" was introduced by radical feminists, used as the title of the poet Robin Morgan's collection of feminist essays, and expanded to "International Sisterhood Is More Powerful" by the International Tribunal on Crimes Against Women (Brussels, 1975) and the Copenhagen conference in 1980. Another example of the frequent use of the sisterhood theme is *Sistercelebrations*, the title of a book describing feminist religious rituals.[47] Valuing other women, supporting their efforts, and organizing reform groups like NOW and the National Women's Political Caucus are results of the second wave of the women's movement.

Friendship among women is emphasized in women's culture; this is the theme, for example, of the French actress and director Jeanne Moreau's film *Lumière*, about the relationship of four women actresses. Moreau explained the necessity for a woman's perspective: male directors, "although at times close . . . were still in a man's world. There were doors to be opened. Only a woman who had lived such a life could bring out the mysterious patches."[48]

The formerly "mysterious" aspects of women's experiences as friends are also viewed in other films about women: *Julia, The Turning Point, Girlfriends,* and *Nine to Five.* Sisterhood is a departure from the old emphasis on Mother and Son. The feminist theologian Mary Daly explains that

> radical feminism releases the inherent dynamic in the Mother-Daughter relationship toward Sisterhood, which is thwarted within the male-mastered system. The Mother does *not* demand self-sacrifice of the Daughter. Rather, both demand of each other affirmation of the self and of each other in an on-going personal political process which is mythic in its depths. . . .[49]

The relationship of mother and daughter is reexamined in *Of Woman Born,* by Adrienne Rich, who writes about motherhood from both a historic and a personal view. This examination of women as kin also occurs in *My Mother/My Self, The Mother Knot, The Reproduction of Mothering,* and *Sisters.* The connections between women as friends, as mother and daughter, and as sisters are all being explored.

Intimate relationships between people are significant political or power issues. "The Personal Is Political" is another slogan contributed by radical feminists. A major contribution to personal freedom is the realization that power is exercised in the choice of who does household tasks, in the dependencies of romantic love, and the perpetuation of the myth of the vaginal orgasm—as well as in the deliberations of Congress or the White House. The women's movement looks carefully at the locus of power in personal relationships and in the family. Its goal is egalitarian relationships and choice in lifestyles.

Alternatives to the Nuclear Family

Many men and women find women's subordinate status rooted in the nuclear family because of its rigid separation of female and male roles.

As the family was defined in the nineteenth century, middle-class women stayed home while their husbands had wage-earning jobs outside the home. Marriage made "man the master and woman the slave," observed Elizabeth Cady Stanton. The domestic role of women also serves the interests of capitalism, according to contemporary socialist feminists, by providing a cheap reserve labor force and soothing and pacifying wage earners. Women conserve capitalist values of consumption, competition, and obedience to father and boss. Women are made symbols of the objectifying of sexuality, whose outlet can be sought in buying power sources like cars. Advertisements invariably show cars with a sexy woman draped over them. Despite the impact of capitalism, films show that isolation in the home is bad for women's mental health: examples are *Diary of a Mad Housewife*, *A Woman Under the Influence*, *Alice Doesn't Live Here Anymore*, and *An Unmarried Woman*. This same point about the negative impact of traditional marriage on women's mental health is made by the sociologist Jessie Bernard in *The Future of Marriage*. *The Hazards of Being Male* and *The New Male* relate the harmful effects of sex roles on men, as described by Herb Goldberg.

Romantic love is the cement used to make women stick to the nuclear family structure, pouring their energies into men while men create culture, according to radical feminist Shulamith Firestone. "That need for loving like a/ screaming howl in the soul,/ that's the drug that hangs us and/ drags us down/ deadly as the icy sheet of slag/ that froze your blood"* is Marge Piercy's portrayal of Janis Joplin and romantic love in her poem "Burying Blues for Janis." In *Combat in the Erogenous Zone* Ingrid Bengis reveals her struggles with her push-pull attraction to and resentment of predatory males, and her experiments with alternatives of lesbianism and celibacy; similar themes are found in *Kinflicks* and *The Woman's Room*.[50] Women are rejecting the romantic and passive images of Cinderella, Sleeping Beauty, and Snow White waiting for the prince. This is of benefit to men who are rebelling against expectations that they rescue and protect women.

The monolith of the family should be fragmented and its functions—sexuality, work, reproduction, and socialization of children—be independent of each other, according to the British Marxist feminist Juliet Mitchell.[51] The basic unit of society should be the individual adult, not the family, advocates Jo Freeman, a political scientist. Women's visions of the future family include a variety of living arrangements, as in Joanna Russ's short story "Nobody's Home," which describes a family of eighteen adults with two triplet marriages, a

---

*"Burying Blues for Janis," from *To Be of Use*, by Marge Piercy. Copyright © 1969, 1971, 1973 by Marge Piercy. Reprinted by permission of Doubleday & Company, Inc.

quad, and a marriage of eight.[52] Living in an extended family or commune, as a hermit or single, with or without men, as well as group responsibility for child care, are alternatives suggested by Cynthia Washington.[53]

Today those women who decide to marry are often challenging tradition by keeping their own surnames, writing egalitarian marital contracts, keeping separate banking accounts, and sharing housework evenly. Others are remaining single longer or perpetually, living in groups, practicing serial monogamy, building extended families, relating exclusively to women, and in general rethinking the myth that the typical family has a wage-earning husband, a housewife, and two children. The two-paycheck family is in the majority; this is the most revolutionary social change of the century, believes Caroline Bird, since a paycheck gives women more autonomy and influence in her family.[54]

Women's Experiences

Women's experiences are named and seriously portrayed in women's research and creations. Women are "beginning to make the image which corresponds to our bodies, sensibility and experience . . . a new language altogether against isolation, against silence, against suppression and madness."[55] Bodily functions of menstruation, childbirth, and sexuality are portrayed in women's art and literature. So are objects associated with traditional women's roles, such as food and other items found in kitchens, and women's clothes and jewelry. *Womanhouse* is a pioneering example of using women's lives as the subject matter for art: Judy Chicago, Miriam Schapiro, and their women students at California Institute for the Arts produced this group project in 1972. They converted an old house in Los Angeles into an art piece, each room reflecting female activities and captivity in the home. They created a flesh-colored, nurturant kitchen whose walls were covered by forms that resembled gradients from breasts to fried eggs, bathrooms filled with makeup and menstruation paraphernalia, a linen closet containing a mannequin captured in the shelves, a movie star's bedroom, a bride, and performances of one woman perpetually ironing and another putting on and taking off makeup. A film, *Womanhouse*, documents this feminist collaborative art piece.

Art critic Lucy Lippard defines other female art images that reflect women's experiences:

> Images of veiling, confinement, enclosure, pressures, barriers, constrictions, as well as of growth, unwinding, unfolding, and sensuous surfaces are common. Others are dealing with organic "life" images and others are starting with the self as subject, mov-

ing from the inside outward. All of this work, at its best, exchanges stylistic derivation for a convincing insight into a potential female culture.[56]

Authors Karen Petersen and J. J. Wilson add the following to this list of female imagery found in art: mirrors (narcissism or introspection), doubling (two parts of the psyche), and antiwar themes.[57] *Ms.* magazine included a useful article on "What Is Female Imagery?" in the May 1975 issue.

Women's films also reflect attention to women's lives. The second International Festival of Women's Films included many films about women, for example the Swedish film *The White Wall*, a story of a divorced housewife; from the United States *Not a Pretty Picture*, about rape; a French film, *Nathalie Gragher*, about a young girl; and a Norwegian film, *Wives*, about three women who meet at a school reunion. Many women's films center on life as we actually live it and not on action-packed stories of races, crime, chases, fights, rapes, and assassinations.

Women's lives are no longer seen as trivial but rather as valid content for art. The artist Mary Beth Edelson writes, "As I research our past, I encounter enormous stumbling blocks. I feel right in my gut that our history has been erased, stolen, lost, or not thought important. I'm mourning our lost history, and creating in rituals a meditative oral history from the inside."[58]

Another manifestation of interest in the daily experiences of women is the use of their journals, diaries, letters, and oral statements in the study of history and literature and as a form of creative expression, as in the diaries of Anaïs Nin. "Today women are talking to each other, recovering an oral culture, telling our life stories, reading aloud to one another the books that have moved and healed us, analyzing the language that has lied about us, reading our own words aloud to each other," explained Adrienne Rich.[59] Journal writing and "visual diaries" are part of the curriculum of the New York Feminist Art Institute, which opened in 1979. Women researchers often write in the first person, are less formal, use less jargon, cite their own experiences, and acknowledge their own class and race bias, according to a study by Bonnie Woods.[60] From the halls of academia to artists' studios women are referring to their personal experiences in the content of their work.

Women's Bodies

At the core of the female experience is the woman's body. Judy Chicago suggests that men and women relate to their environment differently;

men with projective imagery and women with inner-space imagery. The neo-Freudian view that "anatomy is destiny" was developed by the psychologist Erik Erikson, who found that boys' play patterns were phallic, building towers that thrust and fall. Girls built inner spaces, such as rooms.[61] Of course, boys are given erector sets and girls, doll-houses. How great a part biology actually plays in the socialization process is a subject of debate among scholars, but our bodies are bound to influence our perceptions.

Erotic imagery occurs frequently in the work of women artists, without objectivizing or degrading the subjects or viewing them as mere design forms without intelligence. Louise Bourgeois, Louise Sharp, Lynda Benglis, Juanita McNeely, Joan Semmel, Sylvia Sleigh, Judith Bernstein, Martha Edelheit, Anita Steckel, Lenore Fini, Judy Chicago, Mary Frank, Carol Schneemann, and Hannah Wilke are examples of women creating erotic art. "Women are more interested in sex and in sexual relationships. And women are discovering themselves. It is therefore not surprising to find that their work is often biomorphic, sexual, narcissistic, and mythic."[62]

Central core imagery, likened to the female genitalia and sexuality, frequently occurs in women's art and even in women's music. Concerning the circular cyclical form, composer and musician Kay Gardner finds that "the forms from one [female composer] to the other are so similar as to be startling to me . . . the climax in the middle, with the structure following the climax same as that leading up to it, only backwards." She relates this to women's multiorgasmic sexual expression. The pianist Sally Piano verifies that women's musical "patterns go around, and around, and around, rather than building up to a certain point, then crashing."[63]

Regaining their sensuality is critical for women who have been viewed as virgins or whores and been taught that sex appeal was their main tool for success, who have viewed their bodies as belonging to men and been burdened by neglect of the clitoris—"the joy button," as the novelist Alix Kates Shulman refers to it.[64] Masturbation and the beauty of female genitals are celebrated by Betty Dodson in her paintings, photography, and sexuality workshops. She shows slides of female genitals, noting the heart shape, the mother-of-pearl colors, and the range in design from baroque to Swedish modern.

Female sexual fantasies are researched and reports published, such as Nancy Friday's books, as are semiautobiographical novels focusing on sexuality, such as *Fear of Flying*, by Erica Jong. *The Hite Report* updates the importance of direct clitoral stimulation for orgasms and reveals women's disappointment with traditional sexual practices. "Don't Fly Me, I'll Fly Myself' and "Fly You" are button slogans that proclaim the female desire for independence from being sexual objects.

Also lesbians and bisexuals have "come out of the closet," gaining support to make their sexual preference known. Lesbian presses publish journals, poetry, fiction, and sociological studies. Such filmmakers as Barbara Hammer portray women loving women. Others advocate a period of celibacy for women as a means of establishing independence.

An image that is selected by the Feminist Health Centers to signify women taking control over their bodies is Wonder Woman, shown in a poster brandishing a plastic speculum, which is used in self-help vaginal exams, and a small cowering physician representing the American Medical Association. Women are experimenting with safe birth control, including such techniques as keeping track of vaginal mucus and body temperature. Many women are rejecting the risk-laden Pill and returning to the diaphragm and cervical cap.

Groups like MOTHER are advocating techniques of midwifery that are beneficial to mother and infant. Health activists are challenging hospital delivery practices: Carol Downer and three other women of WATCH were arrested in Florida in April 1977 for inspecting a hospital maternity ward. Downer was previously arrested in Los Angeles in 1972 for practicing medicine without a license when she informed women they could treat vaginal yeast infections with yogurt insertion. Women are learning about their bodies from books like the widely read *Our Bodies: Our Selves,* put together by the Boston Women's Health Collective. The Feminist Health Centers have written a more recent book, *Women's Health in Women's Hands,* with photographs of women's reproductive organs at various stages. Their publications are causing changes in medical practices and in understanding of female health care and sexuality.

The Right Hemisphere of the Brain

Women have easier access to the unconscious, according to Jungian psychologists Carl Jung and Erich Neumann, M. Esther Harding, and the neo-Freudian Erik Erikson. That women have tended to develop the attributes of the holistic right brain hemisphere is demonstrated historically by their affinity for mysticism and prophecy. Numerous Catholic saints, like Teresa of Avila and Hildegard of Bingen, have been mystics. And in America Anne Hutchinson, Sarah Edwards, Ann Lee, Sojourner Truth, Elizabeth Seton, Mary Baker Eddy, and Kathryn Kuhlman, among others, demonstrate women's aptitude for mystical expression. This affinity of women with the mystical may be explained by the fact that they were not educated to develop their rational abilities or their egos and were, therefore, more open to unconscious inspiration. "Woman's intuition" is a truism that is perhaps based on her isolation from the academic world or may be due to different brain-hemisphere development; it may be a result of the socialization process or may be tied to the evolutionary history of the traits required by motherhood.

Whether or not these theories are accurate, women are indeed manifesting an interest in the spiritual and the occult. *Women's Mysteries*, by M. Esther Harding, and *Moon, Moon*, by Anne Kent Rush, are examples of books about women's rituals and mythology connected with the moon, whose cycle corresponds to the female menstrual cycle and is a common symbol of matriarchy. This feminist interest in the occult was observed by Susan Rennie and Kirsten Grimstad in their travels to gather information for *The New Woman's Survival Sourcebook*. They found most interest in spirituality existing in the Southwest and the West Coast, including exploration of psychic phenomena, ESP, dream analysis, astrology, rituals, Tarot, I Ching, Wicce (feminist witchcraft), natural healing, and yoga. Women, they noted, are realizing that they "in particular are the repository of powers and capabilities that have been suppressed, that have been casualties of western *man*'s drive to technological control over nature."[65]

Womanspirit is an Oregon-based center for women's spirituality that produces a magazine of the same title. One of its leaders, Ruth Mountaingrove, explained: "We are making a new culture for women... our culture is being born, ours is alive, exciting, a celebration... there we take our own power—power to name, to define our own morality and strength. Power to love our bodies, "the mother" in each other, and to be aware... of the treasure to be had in our alliance with the earth."[66] Feminist rituals are also occurring in establishment churches, as described in *Women and Worship*.[67]

Women have been viewed as the "Outsider," so they are aware of the dualities of the patriarchal view that splits conscious/unconscious, humans/nature, spirit/body, friend/stranger. A frequent theme in women's work is wholeness. This is symbolized as androgyny by such writers as Virginia Woolf and Carolyn Heilbrun or by the psychologist Sandra Bem and Jungian analyst June Singer.[68] Some feminists think that the "andro" swallowed the "gyn" and prefer the concept of "gynergy," or female power. Artists are using the theme of combining female and male characteristics: Lynda Benglis posing nude sporting her controversial huge phallus as an announcement of a gallery opening in *Artforum*; performance artist Eleanor Antin assuming the role of the bearded king; or the short story of "Baby X," whose parents will not reveal its sex.[69] A symbol adopted by feminists for metamorphosis from fragmentation as well as resurrection from powerlessness is the butterfly. Another common theme in women's art is combining fragmented pieces to make a whole, as in quilts and quiltlike themes in art.

Part of woman's contribution to wholeness is an emphasis on joy and life affirmation or "playful celebration." High priestess Z. Budapest explains that women's values are pagan, "pleasure-oriented, joy and feasting prone, celebrating life with dancing and lovemaking. Working in harmony with Mother Nature, we discover and recover the All-Creatix, the female power without whom nothing is born nor glad."[70] The themes of life affirmation, oneness with nature, and joyful relations among equals occur frequently in women's culture.

Conclusion

The concept of women's culture is controversial in the women's movement. Some feminists criticize it as being apolitical. All feminist women's creations and organizations, however, are parts of a woman's culture that functions with aims, styles, and images different from patriarchal culture. Women provide alternatives to hierarchical power and to thinking in dualities, which lead to rape of environment and women and to suppression of emotion, the unconscious, and the sensual. Karen De Crow, the fourth president of NOW, warned against the concept of women's culture, equating it with separatism, in her farewell address to the Detroit NOW convention in 1977. She stated that women should not build exclusive record companies, restaurants, and so on, because they provide a false security and replicate the existing male separatist world. She advocated total integration as the only viable tactic. She warned against "pie-in-the-sky" retreat to mysticism. Radical and socialist feminists also criticize cultural feminists for retreat from the reality of political struggle.

The warning against retreat from confrontation is valid. However, the equation of women's culture with separatism or political apathy is not accurate. Most feminists are not permanent separatists. Cultural feminists do recognize that separation, as in C-R groups, can be a necessary part of the creative process whereby we vitalize our interior lives. If her language uses the pronoun "he" as the norm, if deity is personified as Father and Son, if painting and song lyrics depict women as decorative and sexual objects, if her modes of viewing the world are shaped by male perceptions, a woman cannot form an accurate or positive self-concept.

To realize that the personal is political and to identify with strong role models are potentially revolutionary. A concrete example of the strength of women consciously identifying and creating women's culture is the Los Angeles Woman's Building. That it is entirely women directed is a proving ground for feminist theories put into practice.

Outreach through degree programs in art, extension courses, and summer programs pass on their experience with feminist leadership, power, education, and creativity.

Women have themes, concerns, and experiences that often make their work different from men's and therefore a rich part of the human fabric. As Carl Jung saw, the western world is suffering from barrenness because of the dominance of masculinity and, thus, the structures of the conscious mind, ego, and intellect, without the balance of intuition and emotion. Theodore Roszak also describes the twentieth century as the triumph of masculine dominance, which has led to wars, "the tyranny of cerebral organization, the grinding obsession with productivity, the alienation that comes of the need to dominate."[71] Formation of a women's culture will require us "to question everything. To remember what it has been forbidden even to mention. To come together telling our stories. . . ."[72]

The feminine Eros principle must provide balance if the western world is to survive as the technological rape of mother earth threatens life itself. Women's culture is a key to human survival. Awareness of women's culture is so new to us that the definition of its values and styles and the building of its institutions only began again in the 1960s and 1970s. The realization that women often compose paintings, music, and architecture differently, structure organizations differently, have different religious and spiritual beliefs and rituals, is a far-reaching discovery. Its applications vary from pragmatic advice as to how to succeed in the business world by understanding male games and rules, as in *Games Mother Never Taught You*,[73] to academic analysis of the different worlds of men and women by the sociologist Jessie Bernard, to belief that the integration of women's culture is necessary for the preservation of the planet.

We are witnessing a potentially revolutionary proliferation of women's culture: films, music, magazines, presses, books, and bookstores; coffee houses, theatre groups, and credit unions; health clinics, women's centers, caucuses in academic societies, and women's-studies programs; shelters for battered women, centers for displaced homemakers, political caucuses, minority women's groups, and international feminist groups. The third wave of the women's movement provides an upswelling of the talents of half the population previously silenced by the patriarchy. We are fortunate to be born in this era of the woman's renaissance.

The chapters that follow trace the characteristics of women's culture in the visual arts; music; literature and dreams; religion; and organizations. In each area well-known creative women were interviewed as a primary source, and feminist scholars drew from their research to write overviews. Authors were asked to think about how women's themes in their field were different from men's. Reader responses are requested. Please address them to Gayle Kimball, Women's Studies, California State University, Chico, California 95929.

Notes

1. Ann Pride (Editor of KNOW Press). Speech to National Organization for Women Conference, Philadelphia, October 1975.

2. Simone de Beauvoir. *The Second Sex*. New York: Vintage, 1952, p.S7.

3. Shulamith Firestone. *The Dialectic of Sex*. New York: Bantam, 1971. Ti-Grace Atkinson. *Amazon Odyssey*. New York: Links, 1974.

4. Brooke Williams. "The Chador of Women's Liberation: Cultural Feminism and the Movement Press," *Heresies*, 3, 1 (Issue 9), 70, 71, 72.

5. Jessie Bernard. Interview, May 1979. Jessie Bernard. *The Female World*. New York: Free Press, 1981.

6. Robert Ornstein. *The Psychology of Consciousness*. San Francisco: Freeman, 1972, pp.52, 65.

7. Noel Birkby and Leslie Weisman. "A Woman Built Environment," *Quest*, 2, 1 (Summer 1975), 15.

8. Corinne Hutt. *Males and Females*. Baltimore: Penguin, 1972, pp.85, 86.

9. Mary Daly. *Gyn/Ecology: The Metaethics of Radical Feminism*. Boston: Beacon, 1978, p.352.

10. Jessica Benjamin and Lilly Rivlin. "The deBeauvoir Challenge: A Crisis in Feminist Politics," *Ms.*, 7 (January 1980), 51.

11. Susan Griffin. *Woman and Nature: The Roaring Inside Her*. New York: Harper and Row, 1978, p.219.

12. Daly, pp.400, 401, 410, 414.

13. Griffin, pp.xvi, 175.

14. Marge Piercy. *Woman on the Edge of Time*. New York: Knopf, 1976, p.132.

15. Elizabeth Gould Davis. *The First Sex*. New York: Penguin, 1972, p.32.

16. J. J. Bachofen. *Myth, Religion and Mother Right*. Princeton, N.J.: Princeton University Press, 1967, pp. 80, 85, 87.

17. Charlotte Perkins Gilman. *Herland*. New York: Pantheon, 1979. (Written in 1915.) *His Religion and Hers*. New York: Century, 1923.

18. Davis, pp. 336, 345. The Foundation for Matriarchy, in New York City, works to promulgate "a society in which the mother-child bond is not alienated."

19. Dorothy Bryant. *The Kin of Ata Are Waiting for You*. Berkeley, Calif., and New York: Moon Books and Random House, 1976.

20. Erich Neumann. *Amor and Psyche*. Princeton, N.J.: Princeton University Press Bollingen Series, 1956.

21. Nor Hall. *The Moon and The Virgin*. New York: Harper and Row, 1980.

22. Erich Neumann. *The Great Mother: An Analysis of the Archetype*. Princeton, N.J.: Princeton University Press, 1972. Robert Bly. *Sleepers Joining Hands*. New York: Harper and Row, 1973, p. 31 ("In mother consciousness there is affection for nature, compassion, love of water, guilt and care for the dead, love of whatever is hidden, intuition, ecstasy."). H. R. Hays. *The Dangerous Sex*. New York: Pocket Books, 1966. Wolfgang Lederer. *The Fear of Women*. New York: Grune and Stratton, 1968. Ann Ulanov. *The Feminine in Jungian Psychology and in Christian Theology*. Evanston, Ill.: Northwestern University Press, 1971.

23. *Anima* is defined by Jung as female qualities of emotion, intuition, access to the unconscious. *Anima* is the name for the contra-sexual femaleness in the male, governing his moods. *Animus* stands for male rationality and intellect and is the name for the masculine qualities in a female, governing her opinions. Carl Jung. *Two Essays on Analytical Psychology*, Bollingen Series II, Vol. 7. New York: Pantheon, 1953, p. 205. Ulanov, pp. 36–41.

24. Jung, Vol. 7, p. 208. Ulanov, p. 155.

25. Faith Wilding. *By Our Own Hands*. Santa Monica, Calif.: Double X, 1977, p. 39.

26. M. Esther Harding. *The Way of All Women*. New York: Putnam, 1970, p. 22.

27. Virginia Woolf. *A Room of One's Own*. New York: Harcourt, Brace and World, 1957, p. 50. (First published 1929.)

28. Matina Horner. "Why Bright Women Fear Success," in *The Female Experience*, Carol Tavris, ed. Delmar, Calif.: Communications Machines, 1973.

29. Marie Robinson. *The Power of Sexual Surrender*. New York: Signet, 1959.

30. The Venus symbol is the astrological sign for the planet Venus. Mars symbolizes masculinity.

31. Helen Dinar. *Mothers and Amazons*. New York: Anchor, 1975. Davis. *The First Sex*. Evelyn Reed. *Woman's Evolution*. New York: Pathfinder, 1975. Monique Wittig. *Les Guerillères*. New York: Avon, 1973.

32. Pat McDonald. "The Equality of Women in Prehistoric Europe." UCLA, unpublished paper.

33. Mary Beth Edelson and Arlene Ravin. "Happy Birthday America," *Chrysalis*, 1 (February 1977), 51.

34. Merlin Stone. *When God Was a Woman*. New York: Dial, 1976.

35. Phyllis Chesler. *Women and Madness*. New York: Doubleday, 1972, p. 26.

36. Pamela Sargent. *Women of Wonder*. New York: Vintage, 1975. *More Women of Wonder*. New York: Vintage, 1976. *The New Women of Wonder*. New York: Vintage, 1978.

37. Ursula LeGuin. *The Left Hand of Darkness*. New York: Ace, 1969. Her book *The Word for World Is Forest* portrays women as governors and hunters and men as mystics and seers (New York: Berkley, 1976).

38. Joanna Russ. "Reflections on Science Fiction," *Quest*, 2, 1 (Summer 1975), 44.

39. Joanna Russ. *The Female Man*. New York: Bantam, 1975, pp. 102–103.

40. Piercy, p. 243.

41. Sally Gearhart and Peggy Cleveland. "On the Prevalence of Stilps," *Quest*, 1, 4 (Spring 1975), pp. 52–64. A fifty-minute color videotape is available from CSU/Chico for $250, along with five other tapes (women's health, careers, family, male/female relationships, and parenting).

42. Sally Miller Gearhart. *The Wanderground*. Watertown, Mass.: Persephone, 1979.

43. Atkinson, p. 39.

44. *Plexus*, 3, 3 (June 1976), 3.

45. Rita Mae Brown. *The Hand That Cradles the Rock*. New York: New York

University Press, 1971. "The fruitful interchange of dream and reality, the awareness of the strangeness of fact, the authenticity of fancy: these often constitute the special strength of women as writers, the positive result of the social alienation they suffer. The 'negative' result is their anger: a response to impotence, a source of energy. Neither fancy nor anger solves social problems. Both may lead to personal resolutions of dubious value—to indulgent self pity, to passivity, masochism, narcissism as postures of defense so rigid that they prevent growth. But both can also provide means for growth" (Patricia Meyer Spacks. *The Female Imagination*. New York: Avon, 1975).

46. Jo Freeman. "The Tyranny of Structurelessness," in *Women in Politics*, Jane Jaquette, ed. New York: Wiley, 1974.

47. Arlene Swindler, ed. *Sister Celebrations*. Philadelphia: Fortress, 1974.

48. Jeanne Moreau. Quoted in "The Feminine Eye," *Plexus*, 3, 10 (December 1976), 10.

49. Mary Daly. "The Qualitative Leap Beyond Patriarchal Religion," *Quest*, 1, 4 (Spring 1975), 26.

50. Lisa Alther. *Kinflicks*. New York: Signet, 1975. Marilyn French. *The Woman's Room*. New York: Summit, 1977. Chesler, p.286. Dinar, pp.13, 25, 107, 214.

51. Juliet Mitchell. *Woman's Estate*. New York: Vintage, 1973.

52. Joanna Russ. "Nobody's Home," in *Women of Wonder*, Pamela Sargent, ed.

53. Cynthia Washington. "Concrete Playgrounds on My Mind," *Quest*, 2, 1 (Summer 1975), xx.

54. Carolyn Bird. *The Two Paycheck Marriage*. New York: Rawson, Wade, 1979, pp.xii, xiii.

55. *Art: A Woman's Sensibility*. Introduction by Deena Metzger. Miriam Schapiro, director. Valencia: California Institute of the Arts, 1975, p. 1.

56. Lucy Lippard. *From the Center*. New York: Dutton, 1976, p.7.

57. Karen Petersen and J. J. Wilson. *Women Artists*. New York: Harper Colophon, 1976, pp.1–5.

58. Mary Beth Edelson, in *Chrysalis*, 1 (February 1977).

59. Adrienne Rich. *On Lies, Secrets, and Silence*. New York: Norton, 1979, p.13.

60. Bonnie Woods (Ohio State University). Talk on "Feminist Inquiry." First National Women's Studies Association Conference, San Francisco, January 1977.

61. Erik Erikson. "Inner and Outer Space," in *The Woman in America*, Robert Hilton, ed. Boston: Beacon, 1964, p.51.

62. Maryse Holder. "Another Culture: At Last a Mainstream Female Art Movement," *Off Our Backs*, 3, 10 (September 1973). Also Joan Semmel and April Kingsley, "Sexual Imagery in Women's Art," *Woman's Art Journal* 1 (Spring/Summer 1980).

63. Kay Gardner. Letter to Ruth Scovill, February 17, 1977. Ruth Scovill interview with Sally Piano, August 1976.

64. Alix Kates Shulman. *Memoirs of an Ex Prom Queen*. New York: Bantam, 1972.

65. Susan Rennie and Kristen Grimstad. *The New Woman's Survival Sourcebook*. New York: Knopf, 1975.

66. Ruth Mountaingrove. "Clues to Our Women's Culture," *Womanspirit*, 2, 6 (Winter 1975), 49, 50.

67. Sharon and Thomas Neufer Emswider. *Women and Worship*. New York: Harper and Row, 1974.

68. Virginia Woolf. *Orlando*. New York: Signet, 1960. (First published in 1928.) Carolyn Heilbrun. *Toward a Recognition of Androgyny*. New York: Harper Colophon, 1973. Sandra Bem. "Androgyny vs. the Tight Little Lives of Fluffy Women and Chesty Men." *Psychology Today* 9, 4 (September 1975), pp.58–62. June Singer. *Androgyny*. New York: Anchor, 1976.

69. Louis Gould. "Baby X," *Ms.*, 1, 6 (December 1972), xx. Gilman, *His Religion and Hers*. Mary Daly, *Quest*, 1, 4 (Spring, 1975), 35.

70. Z. Budapest. *The Feminist Book of Lights and Shadows*. Venice, Calif.: Luna, 1976, p.3.

71. Betty and Theodore Roszak, eds. *Masculine/Feminine*. New York: Harper Colophon, 1969, p.103.

72. Betty Harragan. *Games Mother Never Taught You.* New York: Warner, 1977.

73. Rich, *On Lies, Secrets and Silences,* p.13.

Gayle Kimball *is coordinator of Women's Studies at California State University at Chico. Her Ph.D., in Religious Studies, is from the University of California at Santa Barbara.*

DEFINING WOMEN'S CULTURE

Interview with Robin Morgan

Robin Morgan is a feminist-activist. Based in New York City, she is a
poet, essayist, lecturer, and editor. Some of her published works are
Sisterhood Is Powerful, Monster, Lady of the Beasts, and Going Too
Far. She is a contributing editor of Ms. magazine.
    In her interview she defines women's culture as a "new women's
renaissance" arising from the feminist movement, revolutionary and
vital for the preservation of the planet. It expresses the half of human
experience not much heard of previously with "tremendous energy,
passion, and a quality of daring to speak the unspeakable." She
characterizes her own poetry as shaped by her female experience, as an
example of the emerging women's creativity, and compares it with male
poetry.

GK: *I'd like to ask you to define women's culture.*

RM: I think it means different things to different people. I think most
of the time the phrase "cultural feminism" is used pejoratively; at
least I've heard it used that way by people who would call themselves socialist-feminists, as if they were criticizing "women's culture" as the feminist form of cultural nationalism or as a retreat
from political action. To me, culture and politics are inseparable.
I was an artist before I became a feminist, and I feel that I found
my fullest aesthetic expression *as* a feminist and also found my
most far-reaching and important political expression as an artist. I
think that a political revolution that does not take seriously its
artists, and does not see the aesthetic vision as inseparable in

integrity from all political action, is by definition a patriarchal revolution. And most of the revolutions we've seen in history have been precisely that.

I do think, on the other hand, that there is a way in which people can certainly use the arts in a fake way—as a sort of an ivory-tower retreat from reality. But that is rarer than many would have us believe. Certainly, where genuine artists are concerned, it's very rare. Mere survival for an artist is usually so desperate that it *is* a radical existence. People who play and dabble with art—that's a different thing; but they are usually people who play and dabble with politics, too.

To me, "cultural feminism" is, in a sense, almost meaningless. Feminism in itself is so profoundly revolutionary that it would be the first really integral culture the world has known. By that I mean what I sometimes also call the new women's renaissance—there is an explosion of sensibility, creativity, accessibility, complexity, exploration, philosophy, and arts. This is occurring out of the feminist movement. It's of enormous importance not only to feminists and to women in general but to the arts in general, and eventually to all people.

GK: *What are the characteristics of that renaissance, and why is it also important to men?*

RM: It is unlocking the creative energy of more than half the human species, that part which has been kept forcibly imprisoned for most of patriarchal history, with rare and notable exceptions. They were usually there to prove the rule and were allowed to publish or exhibit or perform only in a kind of look-at-the-dancing-dog sense, or they were permitted to succeed at a cost no one should have to pay. In general, the artist in the patriarchy usually has had to pay for expression at an enormous cost—even the male artist. But what happens to the female artist is something almost *in*expressible—in fact, it's called silence, as Tillie Olsen and others have pointed out.

What happens when you begin to unlock all that human energy is something quite extraordinary; it's comparable, in a sense, to Elizabethan England, with its incredible flowering of science and the arts, or to Renaissance Italy, where they began to have a political vision that overlaps with the metaphysical one. This creates an atmosphere of daring, of reaching out, not only in language but in subject matter. For example, recently I've been rereading Dante and rerealizing what an enormously political act it was for him to write in the vernacular, in Italian instead of

Latin, which was the elite language. That was part of the beginning of a Renaissance temperament—which was also influenced by the Provençal poets who had flowered under the hegemony of Eleanor of Aquitaine. You get a whole legacy of creativity any time there have been women in power, a kind of ripple effect created because there's been a tiny droplet of that suppressed energy released.

Now, today, you have the beginnings of a waterfall, hundreds and hundreds of thousands of women who will not be silenced any longer. What that may mean is a lot of mediocre work, a lot of even crappy work—but mostly a lot of *work*. And out of that can come works of real greatness, of lasting value, works that can push the space that we have considered literate out farther. After all, half of all human experience has not really been expressed much or clearly or loudly or subtly—and now that can be said.

GK: *What I want to get at is the characteristics of that female expression. In your book of essays* Going Too Far *you write about "metaphysical feminism" and concepts like "passionate thinking"; could you continue with that in terms of defining the characteristics of this female renaissance?*

RM: That's individual preference, to a certain degree. I know what I'd like them to be and I know those characteristics that I respond to most strongly. I think, even objectively, one might say: tremendous energy, passion, and a quality of daring to speak the unspeakable. That's almost like a "first-phase" explosion. What I'm looking forward to is a point when the daring can express itself in greater complexity because the basic things already have been said. Then one can begin to look at the interstices. What I was saying in "Metaphysical Feminism"—what I've thought about even more since—is that there is a life-urgency need for us to refuse simplification. It's not even the desire for complexity; it's the flat refusal to reduce and simplify that is so much at the heart of the thinking that has been destroying the species—the either/or thinking.

As feminist art begins to refuse polarities, not only in writing but in the visual, performing, and musical arts, it permits a third approach, beyond the simple either/or. The more that happens, the more there begins to be no area into which we cannot reach. One concrete example: the birth of the New England Women's Symphony. It's enormously exciting to me, not just because the musical director is Kay Gardner, who is a fine musician and who has studied with Antonia Brico, but because NEWS is going to be playing serious women composers—dead and alive, known and unknown. Now, I—as a good supportive feminist who comes out of 1960s consciousness and likes rock (in its place)—have for ten years been dutifully schlepping myself to women's-music events and hearing warmed-over versions of rock, albeit with feminist lyrics, and sometimes with a different beat. But now, at last, I need no longer be a closet lover of classical music—whether Bach, Mozart, or Sibelius, Clara Schumann or Anna Magdalena Bach. Finally the woman's movement has come to a point where we are able to accept and affirm serious women composers as well. These musicians are not merely trying to make it in the men's world; they're not saying, "Unless I've performed at the Philharmonic I'm nowhere," nor are they trying to be female Mick Jaggers. Something is beginning that hasn't existed before. I find that enormously exciting. I think, too, that it will "up the ante" on what we dare from each other and it will begin, I hope, to raise our standards of excellence.

GK: *What's interesting to me is that Kay Gardner says that women's musical form is different. Women's composition goes in circles and not in the sharp climax and anticlimax—like the form of female sexuality.*

RM: In terms of the cyclical thing, I don't know. I myself love refrains; but on the other hand I have to confess that I love refrains in Homeric poetry and all down through the ages. I don't know that I am addicted to refrains because I am a woman. I do know that sometimes in the graphic arts I get dizzy from the circles as if it's a whole new political correct line—that unless you're painting in circles, you're not a Real Feminist Painter—you *have* to have that "vulva space" in there somewhere. Still, I think that might be a phase necessary to go through before we take on the world.

I certainly find language being used that was not usable five or ten years ago, ranging all the way from the obvious references like a tampon and dishtowel to experiences that can be expressed in no other way but by language that has not been considered poetical, like "toothbrush." In other words, the focus of a woman's world—which is perforce, in many situations, very home centered—means that in order to speak of that experience language has to be used that was hitherto not considered usable in a poem.

GK: *Is it fair to say then that now women are dealing with the immediate and focus more on the reality of things as they are?*

RM: Yes, I think so. So much that I almost long for us to get past this phase. This is where I get very greedy, and I can tend to make people angry. I'm never satisfied, carp, carp, carp—whatever we have is not enough. I think we are definitely dealing with the immediate, and I think that is important, inevitable, and to be affirmed. What I find myself longing for, as well, is also getting beyond that to a point where we can take on all of the general subjects that for so long have been the purvey of the ruling class of artists, who have been men. In other words, because it was their subject it was considered the only subject—the philosophical issues, life and death issues.

Then you get more than half the human species, which has been aesthetically disenfranchised, bursting out. Of course the first thing it bursts out with is what it has not been permitted to say exists, which is dishcloths and Pampers, vulva shapes, lesbian love poems. It is of enormous importance because this is in fact the very path of the human experience that has been denied. But if only that persists, and meanwhile men are speaking of the other, then we still have a lack of integrified art, of integrity. It's the old thing that Virginia Woolf called for as well—the longing to be at a stage where we do not *have* to write as partisans. I may not live to see that—none of us may. I may not live to see men writing just as concretely about dishcloths *et al.* and using those as constructively and symbolically and metaphorically as women have been forced to do. I know a few men who are doing that now; Kenneth Pitchford is one. Of course, a lot of work has gone into him—by me *and* by him! In general, though, these are not such common poetic subjects for men as I would like them to be.

I think of myself and other women artists whose work I love and respect *as* "women artists" now, in history, because that is where we are placed. I think it would be a lie to say, at this point in history, "I'm just an artist." Obviously, I am writing and those artists whose work I respect very much are painting or dancing or composing out of both a female and an aesthetic sensibility, and the two begin to be interdistinguishable. But I do think that ultimately the aim is for that not to have to be the case, so that one could in fact be merely an artist without any prefixes—black or woman or whatever—because there would not be a ghetto sensibility.

GK: *What about in your own poetry or your own prose, do you find that there is indeed a style that's different, say, from your spouse, Kenneth Pitchford, or another male poet, simply because you're a female—besides using domestic imagery?*

RM: I hate to fall into the trap of exception, but I find a much clearer difference with almost any other male writer one can think of than with Kenneth, mainly because in the, at this point, sixteen years we have lived together we have influenced *each other* so damned much that sometimes one of us is quoting a line from the other in a poem, and we literally don't know where it came from. But I think, in general, I focus more on specificity of a relationship and then out from that into the archetype. I think Kenneth's approach—I may be being very unfair, I'm thinking of one or two poems in particular—is more from the archetype into the reality of the relationship, which is nice because then we sort of meet.

I think most men are dealing only with the archetype or even stereotype and not with the reality at all, and I think that that has been true of most male artists for a very long time. What makes the seventeenth-century metaphysical poets in England so interesting *is* their concretion, their specificity, their comparative lack of fear of dealing with the smell and touch and feel of life, including that of real women.

GK: *So you think the seventeenth-century metaphysical male poets parallel women's genre?*

RM: More than any other group, than any other male "school" that I can think of over the centuries. Certainly what happened with the moderns—I mean the post–Pound/Eliot/Williams school in American and British poetry since the nineteenth century—really has been disastrous for women. It's been a movement away from emotion, away from passionate thinking, except insofar as Eliot would look back longingly at the metaphysicals now and then. It has been incredibly objectifying of and denying of women specifically and of life-affirming qualities in general.

GK: *What about the obsession with love that you talked about that's been women's reality? Do you think that, too, will change as we become more whole?*

RM: I know feminists whom I respect who would instantly answer that by saying, "God, I certainly hope so. I hope this obsession with love will go down the tube." Maybe this is a sign of my unsalvageability, but I would answer "No." Maybe I'm an unregenerate mystic, but I hope in fact that the obsession with love is catching—to men. I think unless the whole species begins to be obsessed with it, on a philosophical as well as a practical level, we're doomed. How can one love; how can one *not* love? The tensions expressed therein, the ethical and the moral aspects of what love entails between individuals, between groups, in terms of building human societies, in terms of raising children, in terms of dealing with the old, in terms of race or class or age divisions—at some point (at the risk of sounding really frighteningly mushy) it all does come down to that. But I do not mean a Hallmark card kind of love. I'm talking about a fierce, cleansing, purgative, revolutionary kind of love that demands change—profound change.

GK: *And the change is along the line of passionate thinking?*

RM: Yes. It may sound trite, but it's really quite strange: one does not get involved in a struggle quite as debilitating as this one with so little reward for so long a time—that is, one's whole life—unless there's something motivating that even goes beyond anger and that gets involved with hope. And hope gets involved with (a very cranky, sometimes) love—but a love nonetheless. If I didn't believe the human species was capable of these changes, I would not be doing this, and I can say the same of every feminist I know, no matter how filled with rage she is at any given moment. It's ironic because Ché Guevara, who did a lot of killing in his time, said something like, "At the risk of being ridiculous I must say that a great revolutionary is motivated by profound feelings of love." He could get away with this, of course, because he was very "macho," but for a woman to say that is to run the risk of being thought Mary Worth.

GK: *When do you think consciousness of women's culture began?*

RM: We have to develop a whole historic approach to this, the same way we do toward feminist movements in general. They come in waves and they have been going on for thousands of years. The whole Provençal poetry period of Aquitainian France was a major women's culture—it's just that it happened to be seven hundred years ago. This wave? Well, I can best think in terms of my own history—*Sisterhood Is Powerful* in '70 and *Monster* in '72; although I had been a poet already for fifteen years, I remember feeling nervous about giving readings from the *Monster* poems. Although I was known as a poet as well as an activist, and people were supportive of that in the women's movement, I remember feeling faintly embarrassed, almost as if to give a poetry reading instead of a speech was not real, bona fide, political, grown-up behavior. But by the time 1972 was over I no longer felt that. So to me, I would say it began somewhere in the early seventies.

GK: *What institutions and people do you see as the nucleus of women's culture? Where are the key centers, people, and focal points?*

RM: I know where they are considered to be—and I tend to mistrust them all. Not because good people aren't there but because they're so localized. They tend to cluster in New York and Boston, and in San Francisco. There is a visual-arts cluster in Los Angeles, and in New York as well. That depresses me to an extent because it seems that those are the old centers where the male power structures have always had their schools. I know good stuff coming out of the Midwest; I know good stuff coming out of the South.

There is certain material you read and you suddenly sit straight and the hair on the back of your neck stands up and you think, "My god, this is a real poem"; that comes from almost anywhere. It's strange how those women are able to get in touch with "women's culture" through books, through whatever they can find. And there is a bit more of it available now than there was even fifteen minutes ago.

GK: *Can you name names and institutions that you think are pivotal?*

RM: I think that all the feminist publishing ventures ranging from KNOW to the Feminist Press to Shameless Hussy to Daughter's Inc. are very important as alternatives. I think that organizations like the Feminist Writers' Guild, Women's Ink, and the new publication *Feminist Review of Books* are excellent ideas. They are none of them perfect. But the freedom to fail ought to be part of this, too. The first issue of the *Feminist Review of Books* was, touchingly, a storm of orchid throwing. Everybody was reviewing everybody else and loved everybody else. I hoped that that would work its way through in the next two or three issues—and it has, successfully; now we can get down to some decent, serious feminist criticism. But it's understandable why once you have your own space you tend to celebrate it for the first period.

I guess I didn't want to focus that much on the institutions or on the individual people so much because I don't want to set up yet another hierarchy. To the extent that it exists it is remarkably unhierarchical if you compare it with male structures. People really do try to help each other get grants, get funding, get publicity, and get published. There is a network that goes on of women helping women, and that is not centered on either coast.

For example, since I've been a contributing editor of Ms. I've shared an office with Yvonne, who is not only a superb poet but also the poetry editor and who receives more individual, unsolicited submissions of poetry than any other poetry editor in this country. That tells you something about the way women are writing. It is true that a lot of the stuff that comes in is written by women who have never written anything before. Some of it painfully shows. A lot that comes in is cathartic; but mostly it is just *there*. Yvonne staggers in; you can hardly see those little feet move under those huge packages. Certainly it means that Ms. is a clearinghouse for women, some of whom don't know that any other feminist publications exist. There's great care taken to try to steer people to other places, other alternatives, where they might get published. That kind of network is to me the major cultural institution. It is not focused on either coast. It is really beginning now—and especially since the International Women's Year conference at Houston—to serve, function, and vibrate all over the place.

GK: *What do you think men's roles are in women's culture? Is it a separatist kind of thing, or where will the other half fit in?*

RM: I think that there's a period where it's separatist and it needs to be separatist. By that I mean women are writing for each other, and that's hard enough, God knows. Even Virginia Woolf said that she would try and write just for herself or for other women—only to find that she was nonetheless writing as if there were men in the next room overhearing her, so she was still writing as if for their approval. That continues to happen, I think, but less and less. It is necessary in order that we discover and develop our own voices and that we try to unlearn what Honor Moore has called the "Male Approval Desire Syndrome." I do hope this is a phase, though, mainly because I think that what women have to say as artists, as cultural beings, and as political sensibilities is capable of transforming the entire species, and has to. There comes a sort of suicidal point if we insist only on talking to ourselves and on leaving outside and "unaffected" all those who happen to have power, money, munitions, matériel, and the means of ending the planet. That makes me nervous, but I don't think it will happen. I think there are men who are eager to hear what women have to say. In fact there are *some* men who are literary transvestites of a sort, who will immediately rush into print, saying, "We know better than women what it is that women really want." We've seen *that* happen at different times, but lately there are better signs, even in the context of the current fierce right-wing backlash against feminism. This new "homework" that's getting done is not only because individual women are struggling with those men but because those women are saying, "I'm tired of telling you this for the fourteenth time; here, read this and *then* talk to me."

The wonderful, exciting danger of the painted word or the printed photograph or picture or the record is that it can reach ears that one didn't even necessarily intend for it to reach. That can be terrifying. It means a responsibility for the serious artist, and I think that ultimately we will be speaking to—not as primary audience but as an addendum audience—men as well as women. The burden rests on *them*; for too long it has rested on us. We were shouting and screaming and they weren't even paying any attention. Right now our main concern is that we are speaking, period. And that we are speaking to each other. Their concern has to be to try to listen.

GK: *Do you foresee that women's culture will phase out?*

RM: Yes, but in the way that the communists speak of the withering away of the state, or when I said that the job of a good feminist revolutionary is to make herself extinct because she's no longer needed. This "phase" may be one that lasts for twenty, thirty, fifty, a hundred, or a thousand years; when I'm speaking historically I don't mean a season. I'm certainly *not* saying that women have to stop talking to each other now and begin to address ourselves to men. I don't want to be misread that way.

GK: *What would you like to see in a kind of an excursion into the future, an ideal view?*

RM: The more I think and live through this, the more it seems to me a really profoundly religious revolution. That's such a dangerous thing to say—it can be so easily misunderstood as meaning not political, not economic, or not practical—none of which I mean. I mean a religious revolution in almost a scientific sense, in that it seems to me the next step in human evolution. I don't mean by that that we have simply to evolve into it by gradualist means. I do mean revolution; the feminist revolution is the stage that will finally propel the human species into another evolutionary curve, that itself will reach out into the universe and so alter existence as we know it. So "religious" is the closest word I can use to describe it, even though it's a word that I abhor in terms of organized religions. Still, all that's a very far leap that none of us will live to see. In the immediate future I'll settle for the ERA, mobilizations against pornography, more women writing and composing and painting, reproductive freedom, a decent economic system . . . a few basics like that!

GK: *Religious revolution involves love, overcoming dualities, peace: those kinds of things that seem so abstract as to be almost meaningless. Is that the direction of the revolution?*

RM: That's the direction, but it's a synchronous direction, along with all the other directions. In other words, when you read it back to me that way, although you're being accurate, it still sounds to me like a sort of love-peacenik kind of we'll-just-evolve-into-happiness. That's all very well, but it also is going to take arm twisting in the back rooms of legislatures, it's going to take getting out on the streets again, it's going to take arrests, it's going to take its own form of real confrontation. It is, after all, a battle about power. But power in *all* senses of that term. I refuse to let us settle for power the way that the male left or right settles for power. That's why I keep harping on the metaphysical uses of power. On the other hand, if our politics are solely up there in the visionary ether, while we are starving to death and being clitoridectomized down on earth, that too will fail. Lately I have been finishing speeches with the phrase, "I wish you power—and the grace to use it well," which is my attempt to try to say the two things together, in synthesis.

II. THE VISUAL ARTS

WOMEN'S IMAGERY/
WOMEN'S ART

Sandra Roos

During the decade that I have taught courses on women's art my students and I have noticed the consistent appearance of certain types of imagery. We have seen what could be roughly categorized as either *centric images* or *synthetic juxtapositions* uniting two or more opposing qualities in one form. Although sometimes very abstract looking, this imagery is notably rich in biological-experiential associations. We have never been totally successful in evaluating the import of these images, however, possibly because we have looked for a single meaning when in fact several interrelated meanings have been present. The task of articulating their overall significance and character was greatly aided when I began to compare them with art from other cultures and time periods, noting overlapping themes and using the mythology of these cultures for insight. Corroborating these findings with my own responses to contemporary works has given me the essentials for a working definition of women's imagery that posits centric and synthetic imagery grounded in primary life experiences.

In this essay I shall focus on prehistoric and twentieth-century art, looking at some of the implications of prehistoric art and then surveying a number of the more important modern and contemporary artists who use women's imagery and seem to share some of the attitudes of the earlier period. Beginning with centric imagery, many twentieth-century women have added to their iconography images of synthesis. This parallels a general process of expansion in which women, starting with the more traditional medium of painting, have reached out to include a fuller range of materials and a wider kinesthetic as well as intellectual breadth in their work. The unique qualities of these more recent manifestations of prehistoric themes will be as much the subject of these pages as the points of affinity and continuity between the two periods.

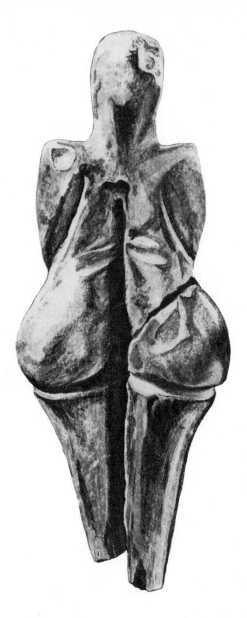

Back view of female image from Dolni Věstonice (Moravia)
East Gravettian or Pavlovian
fired-clay
Drawing by Jean Brooks

Women's Imagery/Women's Art   43

During prehistoric times art abounded with naturalistic and abstract female forms, and early, female-related experiences provided a major component of the mythologies that arose around the worship of the Goddess. The forms echoed the themes of the myths, and we find each used to articulate metaphysical as well as psychophysical issues. Early naturalistic examples of this dual potential of female imagery are the paleolithic "Venus" figurines. One can neither respond to them as erotic figures, nor yet deny their sexuality. Starkly symmetrical, devoid of individuality, they become a synthesis of the sexual and the nonsexual. Their balanced shapes and regular, smooth stone surfaces invite an intellectual as well as emotional response. A synthesis of opposites, an experience of wholeness, is communicated by means of the single female figure. Our reasoning minds might insist that this is a fallacious symbol, though: how can totality be suggested by only one sex? Our feeling minds might retort, the female not only gives birth, unlike the male, but can reproduce in her womb a male likeness as well as a female one. Can she then not be considered both male and female, the original unity? And should not her image suggest this duality—and this unity?

In prehistoric times the female image was the symbol par excellence of this fusion of opposites. A fascinating example, somewhat different from the ones just described, is a staff discovered at Le Placard, France, which resembles the torso of a female with an exaggerated vulva and circular womb perforation. But it also suggests a phallus, and the staff could have been used to break the hymen of young girls during puberty rituals. Many of the "Venus" figurines have similar dual associations, and their round, phalluslike heads may have been used in a like manner. They were originally painted red ochre, the color of blood and the symbol of the life force. Woman herself became the symbolic expression of the sacred energy that animated all life and also governed death—the transformation of life. Her image conveyed this holistic message: it became a symbol of process and unity synthesizing within its boundaries a wide range of polarities.

A more abstract symbol of holism, although still incorporating concrete associations, is the circle. Circles, perforations, and disks, as well as circular ritual sites (Stonehenge, *c.* 1900–1300 BC, being a later and larger-than-usual example), were widespread in prehistoric times, and scholars believe them to have originated as abstract womb or vulva images. In paleolithic times circles were carved on cave walls or rock fragments within the caves and are thought to have paralleled the symbolism of the caves themselves as sacred wombs and markers of ritual sites. But, although they can be sexually symbolic, circles also demand nonsexual interpretations. As abstract shapes circles communicate feelings of harmony, simplicity, and unity. They indicate oneness and infinity and over the years have come to be identified with the idea of pure being. But even the most esoteric interpretations of the circle can be traced back to mythologies that saw the original circle as the cosmic womb out of which all life emerged.

The circle as Original Center and Source, as Being before Becoming, precludes most everyday notions of physicality and sexuality. But as physical beings we quite readily juxtapose metaphor with abstraction and liken the idea of original oneness with our experience in the womb; and when life emerges out of this oneness we relate it to birthing and personify the source as female. Such a juxtaposition of idea and image fits in with our childhood feelings of woman as all-powerful and unlimited Source. Rather than contradicting our early experiences, abstractions and conceptualizations of these images seem to expand them and add a quality of transcendence.

Although the circle was the primary abstract symbol of feminine completeness, the life- (and death-) giving energy aspect of the female was also expressed by the spiral, an image that appeared rather late in prehistoric times in conjunction with the neolithic Goddess religions. The spiral and its relative, the labyrinth, speak more specifically to the process of coming into life than does the circle, the latter making reference more to the primordial unity and source of this process. The double helix is the most complete form of the spiral, and implies both expansion and contraction, energy and entropy, life and death. Both spiral and circle contain a center, which is the point of beginning (or the point of end). This still/active center is not only where the process of coming into existence begins, it is also where one must return to rediscover one's roots and the original experience of wholeness. The spiral can serve as a symbol for one's individual journey through life, first expanding outward through physical maturity and complexity, then contracting inward toward the center and the ultimate meaning of the journey. The final contraction is death, and the significance of the spiral is that ego consciousness must die, at least temporarily, if the source of life is to be grasped. The rebirth that follows brings with it a new state of consciousness and ego awareness, and a new spiraling outward.

Another abstract form appeared late in prehistory and was also associated with the Goddess. Pattern, which is not really one image but a series of contrasting and repeating juxtaposed images, has been associated with women in almost every culture and time period. An interesting use of pattern in conjunction with a figure of the Goddess is a clay deity from Yugoslavia, which also incorporates concentric circles and spirals in a particularly powerful abstraction of the female form.

Although sometimes including female figural stylizations within its own format, pattern is usually too abstract to rely on female-related associations for its meaning. Its import, though, is surprisingly similar to the work we have already discussed, and formally pattern can function as both synthetic and centric imagery. Shapes oppose each other dualistically to be absorbed in the (seemingly) unending flow of the pattern. And, though composed in a linear and sequential manner, in the shrines where they were frequently found they would encircle and enclose the worshiper within the sacred space. The unifying message of patterned image is notably explicit when it was used to decorate the ceramic vessels that had come to replace the cave as metaphor for the Goddess. Patterned circles would often ring the walls of the containers, leading the eye to the central void of the interior. In vessel or shrine actual physical interior space was used in combination with the rhythm of patterned imagery to mesh together past and present experiences into new living wholes.

Other forms, such as plants, animals, and the moon, were also used instead of the female figure or its abstractions to convey similar holistic statements. And they became female symbols or images by association. This is true even of the Greek cross, the Greek swastika, the Christian fish, and other symbols that today have no feminine associations but in neolithic and early historic times were emblems of the Goddess and, as adjuncts to her image, were also intended to convey ideas of unity with duality. Cyclic change and regeneration were part of this meaning, and often references to the seasons or the cyclic waning and waxing of the moon and other processes were made to enlarge the reference system of the Goddess and her related images. What determined the feminine content of these images and ideas was more the state of holistic consciousness conveyed or alluded to than the female form itself. Context and the way forms were rendered became particularly critical in defining meaning. Line, shape, surface, and other formal means were all used in addition to image associations to specify content—a content that, however, invariably had holistic implications and was always grounded in basic life experiences.

Instead of using figures or symbols of the Goddess, contemporary artists have emphasized forms abstracted from the female figure, in particular the womb shape. Like all centric shapes, womb imagery has certain iconic power in the way it arrests our focal vision and manifests itself in a perceptually clear and contained manner. This has been emphasized in contemporary art as well as modified through the use of formal means and new materials so as to alter the iconic impact and bring in additional psychological nuances and associations.

The psychological content of womb imagery has been of special significance to many contemporary women. Some artists have used their tools to express the unique psychobiological experiences of women, objectifying certain fleeting internal sensations and responses in their work. Our most important womb experiences, however, may not be as women experiencing our own biology but as infants in the wombs of our mothers. Many psychiatrists believe that these prenatal, as well as early-childhood, memories are a major source of a number of unconscious impulses and attitudes. They are experiences obviously shared by women and men and can be plumbed and relived in interrelationship with other feelings when we view womb imagery.

As women—and men—our responses to womb imagery are part of a larger response pattern we have toward the female in general. To understand the breadth of these responses we need to keep in mind that the female is a unique creature: she recreates life in ways we still do not fully understand, an ability that has elicited awe for millennia. For us as children she is our first experience of warmth and sustenance and offers us our first concrete sense of total oneness and belonging with another. She is also usually the cause of our first experiences of deprivation, pain, and aloneness. In our total dependence on her she can seem superhuman, provoking in us emotions ranging from delight to despair. These early responses and emotions often carry over into adulthood, deeply coloring our more mature experiences.

Female images can tap these feelings, allowing us as adults to explore and understand them as we reexperience their intense urgency from a safer distance. As art imagery the female figure (and its aspects) can do even more. Through the combined use of meaningful form and association it can bring together a variety of experiences in new ways. It can provide a synthesis and transcendence of piecemeal past experiences in a way that pure intellectual reflection cannot. The emotions of childhood can be metamorphosed, providing access to new areas of meaning. Transformed into art, female and female-related images can provide concretely accessible forms for otherwise intangible, difficult-to-grasp feelings and thoughts.

Though important for both men and women, the experiences that women's imagery evokes are of special significance for women, since images relating to women are in a sense self-images and raise questions of self-identity. Exploration of female iconography has added dimensions for both women artists and women viewers, and it is not surprising that women have created some of the most meaningful art in this area: a special probing of the psyche, a unique journey into the inner regions of the self.

The female figure and other images referring back to female-related experiences, such as the spiral or pattern, have become empty of content to many in a time when we live on the edge of our consciousness and rarely seek our center. Nor do we as a culture feel the urge to plumb our depths to find and express a sense of wholeness and relate this to the world around us, possibly because we feel our world to be splintered and beyond reintegration. The reintroduction of women's imagery into our century's art seems to indicate a new optimism and a return by some to an earlier sensitivity where life is viewed as process, an interplay of related—not antithetical—forces. Women's imagery has become again a means of focusing upon this interrelatedness, drawing upon a richness of experience and association available to everyone. This new art has new experiences to add to the old, and new methods have given it a breadth of nuance not found in the past.

II

One of the first twentieth-century artists to be recognized in the context of women's imagery was GEORGIA O'KEEFFE (b. 1887), who, however, was quite disturbed by the sexual interpretations of her art—and for good reason. Freudians and pseudo-Freudians began labeling and explaining her work in the most superficial and demeaning manner, insensitive to the throbbing stillness they radiated. The flower was her favorite theme for many years, a constant source of reflection during a time when she was forced to live in crowded city conditions or with her husband's relatives. She made her flowers big so that even busy New Yorkers would take time to see what she saw in them. She tenderly waited with them through their metamorphoses and traced their various personalities. Their deep interiors were sometimes soft and dark as velvet, with a deep red glow, other times billowing and palpitating as they unfurled; sometimes gently curved, other times stark and linear with angular rhythms.

Through O'Keeffe's painting we relive the awe with which our earliest ancestors must have viewed the first blossoms of the seasons. Before even the leaves appear on the trees, while all is still gaunt and colorless, the first buds burst forth and new life comes out of seeming death and emptiness. Thanks to Georgia O'Keeffe we cannot see flowers again without experiencing some of the wonder she felt, wonder that must have also motivated our ancestors when they first fashioned the image of the flower and made it a sacred symbol of the Goddess.

EMILY CARR (1871–1945) found her energy in the caverns of the Canadian forests, whose rugged terrain and tangled undergrowth presented a tortuous maze that defied penetration. In Carr's first paintings the walls of her forest were impenetrable and opaque; but as she listened to the heartbeat of the forest she discovered the tree of life that stood at its center, solitary yet not alone. No flowers clung to its branches, but its roots seemed to descend to the very core of the earth and radiate the energy of the whole planet. The tree stood as a sentinel before the rounded open spaces behind it. Only occasionally did it bend aside to allow one to be swept into the swirling, arcing darkness of the forest interior.

The journey to the interior was not a frightening one for Carr, just as it had not been for O'Keeffe. Each discovered the vast and welcoming embrace of the sky waiting for them when they eventually emerged. For Carr this embrace was an experience of great animation and energy; for O'Keeffe, one of imperturbable calm. Carr painted the sky dancing above the sea or caressing tender young saplings. O'Keeffe, later in her life, would look at the Blue (as she called it) through the holes of the heavy sun-bleached pelvis bones she picked up on her lone walks through the desert:

> . . . when I started painting the pelvis bones I was most interested in the holes in the bones—what I saw through them—particularly the blue from holding them up in the sun against the sky as one is apt to do when one seems to have more sky than earth in one's world—
>
> They were most wonderful against the Blue—that Blue that will always be there as it is now after all man's destruction is finished . . . [Lloyd Goodrich and Doris Bry. *Georgia O'Keeffe*. New York: Whitney Museum of American Art, 1970, page 25].

O'Keeffe's interior world was expressed through the landscape of her exterior world through forms she saw around her. Yet she felt free to change these exterior images and colors in order to fit her interior mood more precisely, just as she believed that what *she* saw did not necessarily have to resemble what other people saw. This is also the attitude of HELEN FRANKENTHALER (b. 1928), a more abstract American painter whose work nonetheless parellels that of the older master to a surprising extent. Frankenthaler shares O'Keeffe's love of landscape and also, to a degree, her sense of rhythm and color. Frankenthaler's artistic consciousness unfolds and expands in the manner of both O'Keeffe and Emily Carr. Her painting *Interior Landscape* is tighter, more constricted than O'Keeffe's flowers, however. And within it one senses an anxiety to break free from its enclosing walls, to burst out like a flame. In fact the expansiveness of her later works (such as *Magic Carpet*) comes almost as an orgasmic release. But, although one feels a new space and openness in many of Frankenthaler's more recent paintings, there is also a sense of precariousness, of a battle not yet finished.

The great French innovator SONIA DELAUNAY (1885–1979) was one of the first artists to believe that color and rhythm could express the interior world in the same way as the more recognizable metaphors of nature were able to. She recognized in the radiating circle and spiral the

Helen Frankenthaler, Interior Landscape
1964
acrylic/canvas, 104¾" × 92¾"
San Francisco Museum of Modern Art,
Gift of Women's Board

same life-force energy that our forebears did and used it to unify the conflicting tensions of the horizontal and vertical. Her use of color was inspired—and inspiring. She realized the way colors seemed to move to the eye and effect parallel movements in the psyche. She may have been familiar with Annie Besant and C. W. Leadbeater's idea on color and psychic projection published in the book *Thought Forms* at the beginning of the century. If so, this must have only verified her own intuitive sense of the meaning of color and ability of the mind to communicate through pure form.

Rhythme Couleur, Opus 1541 is a particularly interesting late work by Delaunay. We find here, as in her other paintings, bisected concentric circles played off against squares and rectangles. But, as in so many of her other paintings, square and circle interact in a twisting fashion to create a spiraling tension pressing out (or pulling in?) from the center. Spiral and circle, movement and repose, overlap in one singularly expressive work. It is important to note that Delaunay believed that her message of form and color should not be limited to the small audiences of art galleries, and in both word and work she insisted that textile and clothing design could be arenas of creative expression as valid as the traditional painted canvas—an idea increasingly put into practice by younger artists today.

It was the power of color itself that prompted the Greek-born sculptor CHRYSSA (b. 1933) to turn to neon in the early sixties after settling in New York. Chryssa was responding to other urgings as well, the most important being that her images should exist in tactile, three-dimensional space—and that their color should be intrinsic to their forms in the same way the color of the flower is intrinsic to, and cannot be separated from, the flower itself. The rhythmic movement of life was also an element of the imagery that surfaced in her mind, but she was dissatisfied with the illusion of movement that was produced by colored paint on a canvas. The molded forms of neon tubing animated by the flickering quiver of colored gas presented to her mind's eye the right form for being. Thus the wings of the *Clock of Morning Birds from Iphigenia in Aulis by Euripides* give concrete form to the cavernous spaces only alluded to in the canvases of Carr and O'Keeffe; and *Clytemnestra* exposes to real space the pain and hope of a thousand births and a thousand deaths.

Clytemnestra was an ancient Greek queen who killed her husband and his mistress to revenge his killing of her daughter at the outset of the Trojan War. She was in turn killed by her son, the most infamous deed that could occur during the neolithic period. But times were already changing, and her son was vindicated and the patriarchy affirmed—and the struggle for women's survival begun. It can be no accident that Chryssa chose this theme for these important pieces, just as it was no accident that one of her early clay pieces alluded to the neolithic Goddess icons of the Greek Cycladic islands. These figure-based pieces were departures from her works based on signs and letters and give an important perspective to the latter. The religions and icons of old have been subverted by media images and consumerism. But the feelings behind them are similar; and once we recognize and get in touch with their power, we can divorce them from their consumer references and take advantage of them to discover more about ourselves.

The deep transparent voids of Chryssa's pieces are echoed by the works of her American contemporary, LEE BONTECOU (b. 1931). Although Bontecou, like most painters, begins with canvas, she cuts and shreds her materials, painstakingly tying them together with metal threads so that they protrude from the wall like large hungry mouths. The throats behind the mouths are hard to discern, lost in the shadows of the canvas and sometimes shrouded in a cushion of thick, soft velvet. We reach in hesitantly, not sure of what we will find. Or we are barred from reaching in by cagelike grids, heavy drawn zippers, or jagged sawblades that evoke menacing smiles. Reminiscent of *vagina dentata* imagery found in many parts of the world, they also bring to mind the protruding breasts created in Çatal Hüyük, Turkey, over eight thousand years ago, breasts whose soft and rounded forms reveal boars' heads or vultures' beaks nestled in their interiors. Once again the theme of life and death, death and life, repeats itself.

It is interesting to compare Bontecou's womb-mouth canvas constructions with the (ostensibly) flat painted canvases of BRIDGET RILEY (b. 1931). The English Riley has an uncanny knack for making flat surfaces come alive and appear to extend into the space between observer and wall. Early canvases, such as *Blaze*, share not only the central imagery of Bontecou's constructions but also the latter's more aggressive moments: two-dimensional surfaces bristle at us in a no-man's-land uncomfortably close to where we stand. Although actually a series of patterned concentric circles, each circle expands and contracts to create a twisting motion, rhythmically advancing from center to edge and back again. A similar spiraling progress can also be found in some of Bontecou's pieces from the mid-sixties that use smaller openings and emphasize a linear winding of bulbous protrusions leading to the almost hidden central locus.

As Riley matured as a painter her images softened, and most of her recent work takes us laterally across their surfaces into some distant space rather than focusing us in the manner of *Blaze*. Uniform and repeating lines, hypnotizing in their reiteration and as large as we are, carry us into space away with them. But they go nowhere and eventually bring us back to ourselves in hovering stillness. Such must have been the effect of the patterned walls of the sacred neolithic shrines. Once entered, the encircling, pulsating color helped one forget the concerns outside, quieted the mind, and allowed for reflection on what was within. The patterns actually created the experience of integration to which the symbols in the chambers alluded.

There are many artists like Riley who have worked with patternlike

Lee Bontecou, Untitled
1961
canvas and welded metal
Collection of the Whitney Museum of American Art, New York

repetitive units and tensions/countertensions within their work as well as centric imagery. Equally sensitive to the effects of both is LOUISE NEVELSON (b. 1899), whose boxed and stacked assemblages form huge walls in which the boxes become variegated motifs in a metered environment of pattern. Vertical versus horizontal, surface versus interior, are each part of the cadence that gives Nevelson's walls, totems, and boxes their special vitality. The boxes, as well as a series of chests she created during the sixties and seventies, were direct outgrowths of a painful soul-searching she experienced when her son was at war and she feared for his life—and her own sense of self as a woman and artist. The pieces were usually painted black to emphasize the ambiguity of their shadowy recesses; some are overpowering, threatening, while others are inviting and embracing. This is also true of the walls, where the boxes lose some of their individual character to become part of a flow of point and counterpoint as both our focal and peripheral vision tug at our psyche for recognition. But our response to Nevelson's work is not only visual; hers are environments to be experienced with the total body as we walk into the spaces, touch the walls, and feel their size next to our own. They are vessels to enter, either actually, as in the walled rooms, or through our imagination when the opening of the tiny chambers beckon to us.

A dynamic synthesis of opposites also marks the works of two other sculptors, BARBARA HEPWORTH and EVA HESSE. Hepworth (1903–1975), British, often utilized the framework of the female form; the American Hesse's mature works completely departed from it. Hepworth shared Nevelson's desire for total physical involvement with her work, and many of her large pierced slabs are reminiscent of the perforated life-sized stones used in ancient British ritual sites as part of rebirth ceremonies. The squarish, semiopen bronze sculpture at UCLA invites one to crawl through its circular entrances and sense the spaces within as well as without. Smaller pieces of marble or wood are firm, smooth, and meant to be grasped, caressed, and experienced in their total mass and texture.

Barbara Hepworth was the first modern sculptor to take a heavy, opaque material and pierce through it to reveal its inner recesses. The marble in *Image II* has been slightly hollowed out to reveal an open, interior core. This inner space is echoed by an ovoid recess midway between the inner and outer layers. Lines ring this recess, connecting other lines and suggesting an almost spiraling movement from outer silhouette to inner center. *Image II* also has a slight suggestion of the human torso. Its soft contours and womblike associations contrast subtly with the hard material and sharp, precise lines. Intellectual control corresponds to biological process here in a way typical of all of Hepworth's sculpture.

Hepworth's life and work were an exploration of the dialectic between inner and outer experiences and the subtle paths that connect the two. She lived by the ocean, watching the tides ebb and flow, the moon wane and wax, the seasons slip by to return again and again. Sometimes she imagined that she became the hills, rocks, and seashore, other times she stood aside and listened as an observer. Through her work she found harmony in even the most dissonant. She lived to work, and the life she found in her work was richer than most even dream about.

Hepworth's long peaceful life contrasts sharply with the painful and much too early demise of Eva Hesse (1936–1970). The play of opposites that flowed smoothly through Hepworth's veins coursed abruptly, sometimes harshly, through Hesse's. Hesse's world was the city, where harmony was harder won and found its forms in absurdity and paradox. The shallow, bandaged, and empty space of *Hang-Up*, for example, gives no refuge but instead extrudes a long, thin, erratically bent wire. Absurd, but not absurd, is how Hesse described it, and it reminds one of the equally unusual hanging hoops and sausagelike shapes that crowded her studio during the sixties. In her notebooks she described the tensions she felt: "1. Mother force: unstable, creative, sexual, threatening my stability, sadistic—aggressive. 2. Father, Stepmother force: good little girl, obedient, neat, clean, organized-masochistic" (Robert Pincus-Witten. "Post-Minimalism into Sublime," *Artforum*, November 1971, page 36. Illustrations of Hesse's works I have mentioned can be found in this issue. See also Lucy Lippard. *Eva Hesse.* New York: New York University Press, 1976).

These tensions find resolution in rather unique ways. In Hesse's sculpture *Laocoön* the snakes of the goddess Diana have been transformed into bandaged wires that subvert and make ridiculous the sturdy, right-angled structure that represents Laocoön; yet Laocoön is not subdued, and they meet to form an unsteady alliance. The same uneasy pact is found in pieces like *Contingent*, where the geometric planes become limp and viscous as cheesecloth squares are immersed in fiberglas or latex, the "ugly," unaesthetic materials in which Hesse found her beauty and harmony. Unlike *Hang-Up*, such works as *Contingent* or *Expanded Expansion* do not focus our attention. Instead they share the rhythm and sense of horizontal extension into space that marks the best of pattern, though they do not extent into infinity as Hesse might have liked them to. And as individual pieces they offer an aesthetic, psychological counterbalance to her more iconic objects, giving her total oeuvre a quality of breadth and completion.

In some pieces, such as *Right After*, Hesse stretched our sense of gestalt, or wholeness, almost to its breaking point. She believed that order could be found in chaos, and this is where she chose to find it. She played aggressive feelings against receptive ones, rational against intuitive, and in the process often created works of art that were hard to decipher as such. The very activity of making art became part of her end product—process itself became a type of form. And in recognizing that materials and processes could communicate feelings as easily as forms or objects, she helped to redefine art and direct it back into the world of ritual from which it had originally sprung. This of course was the direction that both Nevelson and Hepworth were moving toward when they emphasized physical involvement with their objects and made them part of the environment.

Though Hesse's mottled surfaces and twisted ropes may give telling evidence of the activity involved in making her pieces, they are still objects and, as such, are still static and reflective in nature. Many women artists of the sixties and seventies abandoned objects altogether, or used them only as tools, depending for the most part on their bodies to convey their ideas. Sometimes gropingly, they created new rituals, often too personal to be clearly communicated, yet as they probed deeper into their own psyches they came surprisingly close to a ground shared by us all. The Italian-born GINA PANE (b. 1935) has been notably successful in this regard, although there continues to be much objection to some of the materials and ideas found in her works. Fire, milk, blood, and pain are the primary tools she uses to explore mother-child tensions and her own self-awareness as a sexual, feeling adult in an anesthetized society. Broken mirrors, roses, lace, black cloth, and even a mannequin are a few of the many other objects that augment her basic vocabulary. Much care is spent on the photodocumentation of the performances. She juxtaposes a number of photographs, often repeating the same image, to create beautiful patternlike effects that exist in an uneasy tension with their sometimes repellent content.

The impact of performance art like Pane's usually rests on its ability to charge our space and bind us to the energy of the performer—an extremely challenging task. Other women artists choose instead to create the equivalent of a ritual site, building structures that direct our movements and attention, making us the performers and evoking in us directly the experiences at hand. In both cases the impact can be unusually powerful due to the dynamics of the work's actual presence, its reality occupying our own space and time dimension. An example of the latter type of art is the work of ALICE AYCOCK (b. 1946). Inspired by prehistoric and early historic religious sites and buildings, as well as sources ranging from literature to psychology and anthropology, Aycock's works are a mine of evocative imagery and experience. *The Beginnings of a Complex . . .* brings together several of her themes in one pieces. A labyrinth of subterranean tunnels and structures and stairways that lead nowhere provoke both comforting and frightening experiences, each coexisting with the other. Even when she is not using enclosing spaces, her work takes us on a lived journey into some hidden part of the self, where fear and hesitancy must be overcome to continue or emerge unscathed. *Circular Building with Narrow Ledges for Walking* makes this process more explicit in the imagery itself. It consists of a seventeen-foot reinforced concrete circular wall with a ladder leading over the edge. Once we vault the wall we find a tiny ledge with steep stairs that twist precariously down the interior face of the wall into the deeper level below. *Circular Building,* like most of Aycock's work, depends to a large extent on our own fears and curiosities duplicating hers for the piece to be effective. It is amazing to what degree this does indeed happen.

Aycock's works are usually situational reenactments of personal experiences, expertly intermeshed with the old mythological tales with which she is so familiar. Her structures communicate the content-feeling of these experiences and myths without actually recounting the story. Many artists working in real time and space actually tell stories in their works, introducing a narrative quality usually associated with more linear, rational modes of consciousness. These are the most difficult, since there seems to exist a natural tension between thought and image, and it is very easy for one to overwhelm the other. A separate body of conceptual art evolved during the seventies that concerned itself almost exclusively with examining how these different responses operate in our minds. Artists working in this area would often set up structures within which spontaneous responses to situation or images could be compared with learned ones. Although all images (including words) come about originally as intuitive responses to inner experiences, most of the images we use today are learned, that is, their meaning has been passed on to us by others and has not been independently rediscovered by each user. The original experience that produced each image remains dormant, its depth and nuance deliberately held at bay to allow the more abstract reasoning process to take place instead—a process that prefers logical precision in its imagery and aims to be clearly understood by all.

Although all good art embodies both kinds of consciousness (including the art we have already discussed) conceptualists have focused on the interplay between the two modes of thinking in their art in a much more self-conscious manner. Other artists, while not strictly conceptualists, have also chosen to juxtapose apparently different systems of though or articulation in their work. An example of the latter is JUDY CHICAGO (b. 1939), one of today's better-known proponents of feminine imagery. Chicago has incorporated text into her centric imagery, sometimes on the paintings themselves, other times on the walls where they hang. In this way she believes it is possible for those more familiar with verbal imagery to use this linear mode as a catapult toward a more nonsequential understanding of her metaphors—and vice versa. In the past she has also relied on performances and other more ephemeral activities to communicate her ideas. More recently she has taken to china painting, making plaques and oversized sculptural plates (see pages 66 and 67), as well as small ceramic figurines, activating in her own psyche many of the old symbols of the Goddess that she has realized through the equally ancient medium of ceramics.

Close to Chicago's figurines are the tiny works molded in plaster or carved in marble by LOUISE BOURGEOIS (b. 1911). Bourgeois, born in France but later settling in America, brings us back, perhaps more so than any other artist mentioned so far, to the formal imagery found in earlier times. For this reason she seems to be a fitting conclusion to the spiraling trajectory of this essay. Her smallest pieces are especially intriguing. Like ritual objects, they are meant to be held, and some have an almost magical/fetish quality to them. Her relationship to her objects is intense and personal, and she projects onto them her own personal interpretations of masculine/feminine qualities. Many of her objects physically reflect a dual identity and have a rough hermaphroditic quality to them, not unlike the prehistoric "Venus" figurines and artifacts. In 1975 she scattered some of these small pieces on the floor of a cavernous latex environment that she called the *Destruction of Father*. This was a life-sized version of similar smaller pieces she had executed in other materials, all exploring her own psychological experiences of sexuality and their cultural counterparts.

Although her materials are often traditional, Bourgeois has experimented with most of the new substances with which Hesse was so involved, and both shared a concern for "becoming" as well as "being" and a fascination with duality and paradox in general. Bourgeois is particularly interested in the transformations that certain materials undergo, like plaster, which is soft and malleable when wet but then hardens to an impervious, harsh consistency. She delights in using this brittle plaster as molds for softer resinous pieces or impressionable wax for casting "finished" bronzes. As to the bronzes, she admits liking the process involved more than the solid artifacts that result, and for this reason most of her works remain in their original plaster or wax format or are carved into marble, a material that she feels contains the artist's energy long after the form is finished. This sense of presence is important to her because she also feels that art is not just something to be sold on the market or to make one famous—it is the living projection of a probing mind.

Bourgeois and the other artists I have mentioned are only a few of the sensitive minds that are redefining the feminine experience as well as women's imagery. As they develop their intuitive and receptive sensibilities, they begin to feel in a more integrated manner and make imagery that reflects this integration. They discover both rational and irrational responses and find expression for both, probing the bonds that tie them together as they unfold in the mind.

The female image has served for millennia as the metaphor for this unity in duality, this synthesis. And although it may suggest receptivity or deep space, it suggests much more; it is activity and surface and the light of the reasoning as well as the intuitive mind. It is life before the duality of masculine and feminine was conceived and the synthesis that must grow out of this duality. It is an image that seems to spring out of sexuality but at the same time goes beyond the sexual. And though the female biology has provided the most pervasive metaphor for this holism, it is not the metaphor that counts in the long run but the state of mind that it expresses. And the vital power of this consciousness rests in its ability to discover symbols wherever they may be—to recognize in the world around us the images of our own interior thoughts. It rests in the wonder and joy we experience as we begin to comprehend life in all its magnitude.

Sandra Roos *teaches philosophy of art and art history at California College of Arts and Crafts, as well as a course on women and art. Her M.A. is from the University of California at Berkeley.*

Louise Bourgeois, Femme Couteau
1969/70
polished marble, 26" long
Collection of the artist
Drawing by Jean Brooks

A FEMALE FORM LANGUAGE

Interview with Judy Chicago

Judy Chicago helped found the woman's-art movement when she taught
a group of women art students at Fresno State College in 1970. The next
year some of the students went with her to California Arts near Los
Angeles, where with Miriam Schapiro she established the Feminist Art
Program. Together with the students they produced the first feminist
collaborative art piece, Womanhouse, documented in a film by Johanna
Demetrakas of the same title. Chicago was the first to articulate the
concept of a recurrent female imagery in art, such as an inner space or
central core, found in the works of artists like Georgia O'Keeffe, Barbara
Hepworth, and Lee Bontecou (as well as her own work). She documented
her observations of women's imagery and her struggle as a woman artist
in her book Through the Flower. From 1974 to 1979 she worked on The
Dinner Party, a large multimedia piece that is a symbolic history of
women in Western civilization. Two books by Chicago (published by
Anchor/Doubleday) translate the information in the visual piece into
another form, one that combines words and images and resembles
traditional illuminated manuscripts.

GK: In terms of the central-core–imagery idea, the earliest example
that I can think of is in the early nineteenth century—Sarah
Peale's watermelons and other fruit. Can you see where it has
operated before then?

JC: The earliest places where it operated is in women's early architecture, in yurts and in kivas and in pithouses. If you look at the
early dwellings that women made, huts, architecture was in fact a
female occupation and still is. All tepees were made by women; it
was women's work, and you see central-core imagery there. You
see it in baskets and pottery. In women's art you see it in less pure

Judy Chicago

form—I mean in women's mainstream art as opposed to women's indigenous art. You see it in blankets, you see it in quilts, needlework, you see it in china painting, you see it in any women's indigenous art. And you see it crop up in women's abstract art much more than in realistic art because when a woman is making an abstract image, she is forming her own image as opposed to

A Female Form Language 61

reproducing reality. She is dealing with an interior reality, and so you see the impulse. Which is why I believe that it wasn't until the development of abstract art that women's sensibility could in fact begin to manifest in "high" art as opposed to women's indigenous art forms.

I also feel that women are potentially better abstract artists at this moment because one of the reasons that a lot of men's abstract art is so boring is because it is not centered in the self. It doesn't come from an interior place; it's objective and formalized, so much of it. Women are actually connected to themselves more deeply than men; we have been allowed that, ironically, as a result of our oppression. This results in women often bringing a level of personal content to abstract art that's much richer, at least to me. Everybody who says you can't tell the difference between a Noland and a Chicago is uninformed. An informed viewer could tell the difference; a profound difference.

GK: *Do you think that as men and women transcend rigid roles their art will become more similar? Or do you think that the body phenomenology is so basic that there'll always be those different approaches to seeing life?*

JC: I'm not sure, because I'm not sure how much is physical and how much is cultural. We'd have to live in a nonsexist society, and we're a long way from that. Who knows if there's not actually some inherent propensity for men to be more objective and women to be more subjective? You see, if that is a possibility, it just suggests all the more the necessity to wed objectivity and subjectivity so that neither sex is as extreme as each is now. And that means a dual sex solution to everything.

GK: *It seems that your use of female imagery has evolved: you started out with an emphasis on female sexuality and biology; now the butterfly is more a symbol of resurrection. It's more spiritual, and so it seems like there's a transmutation.*

JC: I think that's definitely true; what I wanted to do was to universalize from a female form. Now what is the hallmark of our femininity—the vagina, right? I took a vaginal form and I started to transform it step by step, working with it and developing it until it began to be a metaphor for a much, much larger spiritual reality.

GK: *Which is what? Wholeness?*

JC: Wholeness, and also anthropomorphizing the world in terms of the feminine. In my series *The Womantrees* the forms look like some sort of strange animals and beetles or butterflies, and then they also appear to be trees or caves. I'm very interested in transformational imagery and transforming the feminine.

I have also addressed myself to other aspects of the feminine—the terrible mother, the terrified girl, the manipulator, the coward, the one who wishes to be provided for but does not wish to take responsibility—I think that's also there. But most of my images affirm women—I'm interested in affirmation—but I'm also interested in all aspects of life.

GK: *So that the main images that you've worked with in making a female mythology are butterfly and flower shapes, concepts of flying, mother goddesses, and using female materials?*

JC: Yes, and also I think there's a dialogue between flight and compression that's very strong in my work because the desire to fly, to be free, in human beings is in conflict with the desire to retreat from life. And, since women are encouraged to retreat from life and are in fact rewarded for retreating from life, there is a continual push-pull-push toward being oneself and realizing one's power and then terror of the consequences of power in terms of what the world tells you—you see, it's not popular to be powerful if you're a woman.

In my porcelain triptych (*Did You Know Your Mother Had a Sacred Heart?*)—derived from Virgin Mary imagery—one can see the positive/negative imagery in my work. Someone said the forms were painful, like tears. I think this is true—there is that type of iconography in them. There is also beauty and delicacy.

Mary is actually one of the few holy female images that we have, even though she has been very destructive to women. This has been a post-Renaissance development. I mean, Mary was a much more positive force during the Middle Ages. She was the mediator between the people and God, because people couldn't relate to this masculine God, and she was much more a carryover of early mother goddesses. She is the only remaining representative of the mother goddess, as diminished as she is.

This work is part of my attempt to reconstitute Western civilization in terms of the feminine, from top to bottom. There's a recurrent flying phallus in art but no counterpart for the flying cunt; in other words, an active feminine principle. We have many images of an active masculine principle from the beginning of Greek times. We have a male godhead with no comparable female godhead. We have images of male power with no comparable images of female power.

GK: *Just a father, the concept of God the Father.*

JC: God the Father, male sexuality without a counterpart of female sexuality. That doesn't just mean I want to see role reversal, it means an understanding of what the female principle is, and what the female spiritual principle is, and what female eroticism is because my erotic images are not like male erotic images. They are not dehumanizing, they are tender; they are about contact. What is erotic to me is the level of contact. I think that is one of the main things in my work—the slow building of an image structure that can in fact take the same world and look at it differently and image it differently—recreate it in *our* own image and likeness as women.

GK: *You've used Erich Neumann's* The Great Mother *and his concept of the good mother and the terrible mother and the great round, etc., but they are all male projections.*

JC: When I addressed myself to negative images of women, I turned those images around. For example, in *The Dinner Party* Kali represents the terrifying aspect of the feminine. I felt it essential to deal with what I think is the reality of species bondage, which has to do with the fact that we bear children. Women will always, on some level, mythologically represent the life force in a way that the male will not, and in some ways that is inherently terrifying.

It is within the nature of the human condition to fear life at some levels and to fear death. So to some extent the female will stand for that always. I think that we can embrace that rather than run away from it, understand that it is a part of our life experience and separate the mythological from the real. One is not, as an individual, responsible for that: one is, as a member of a species, connected to that. By acknowledging that I think we can diffuse the terror that surrounds it. Our connection to the life process can be seen as a part of the ecstasy of existence and the complexity of life.

GK: *Do you see any female counterpart to a Great Father image?*

JC: Unfortunately, the Great Father as he has been projected is a god of wrath and judgment and destruction and power. He's enforced by all these violent films that are in fact images of the Great

Father pounded into our brain: Clint Eastwood, the enforcer, the great wrathful god. If you read the Revelations of St. John in the Bible, it's fascinating in terms of how the image of God, Jehovah, connects to our whole structure of the male role and what is expected of a male.

GK: *Could you describe* The Dinner Party *and why you did it, and why you gave so many years of your life to it?*

JC: *The Dinner Party* is either the greatest thing I've ever done or the biggest white elephant. The project is a three-part work: (1) a piece that deals with women's history; (2) two books; and (3) a wonderful film by Johanna Demetrakas. *The Dinner Party* exhibition tells the story of women's history through china painting and needlework and through a mythological rewriting of history.

GK: *Who are some of the mythological and historical women represented?*

JC: First, female goddesses and then actual women. Each figure stands for a different aspect of the feminine or relates to a particular period of Western history that was significant. It presents history in terms of the feminine as opposed to the masculine form. It addresses the fact that you can read history and never see a woman's name.

GK: *How was the bulk of the labor done on such a mammoth project?*

JC: The first two years I worked myself, and by the time the piece was done almost four hundred people had participated in the work.

GK: *Can you give an example of the new way* The Dinner Party *presents women's history?*

JC: The way I dealt with witches and witchcraft would be a good example. Now witchcraft has generally been presented as a strange, not understandable, outbreak of hysteria throughout Europe. But I don't think that's what it was at all. The burning of witches was consistent with the closing of the guilds, the ending of female education, the dissolution of the convents, the taking over of women's property. It all happened in the same three hundred years. Between 1400 and 1700 around six to nine million women were burned at the stake. Every woman who dissented, who didn't submit to the growing restrictions on female

66   *The Visual Arts*

A Female Form Language   67

options, was burned alive. And by the seventeenth century women were essentially silenced and male power was firmly established and institutionalized. The seventeenth century was a low point in women's history.

GK: *What kind of visual image on a dinner plate did you make to correspond to witchcraft?*

JC: I made an abstract portrait of Petronilla de Meath, the first woman who was burned at the stake in an authenticated witch trial. The image combines iconography from witchery with the form language I use. It is not a literal image but a symbolic one based on historical research.

GK: *How is this different from a historical account of women's history?*

JC: It's art. It's imaginative. It's not written like dry history. And it's not scholarly. What's the difference between the *Odyssey* or the *Iliad* and history?

GK: *If you had a chance to go to a seance, who would you choose to talk to of the thirty-nine women who are on the plates?*

JC: I would pick Eleanor of Aquitaine and Theodora of Byzantium. I bet she was a real toughie—I think she and Justinian had a real on-the-money relationship, one of those where it was an equalized relationship.

GK: *You frequently talk about female values. How do they work in the way decisions were made in* The Dinner Party *project?*

JC: It wasn't an authoritarian structure. There was a hierarchy and a chain of command, but within that structure it was very loose and open and fluid, too. People could move up and down the scale of leadership based on how much responsibility they took, not based on any a priori delegation. There was plenty of room—a person could move in and out of roles and positions and responsibility in a manner that's not possible in traditional structures, where you're frozen into a role based on your sex or race or class. That doesn't happen in the work structures I create. People change roles; the typist ended up doing a million other things. Someone came in one day a week and ended up working full time and taking control over a whole area, and in so doing learned a lot about her own power.

And also there was a lot of room for creative input and energy. There was an atmosphere of honesty—one that emphasized growth and reality as opposed to dissembling. There was consciousness raising once a week and our open session once a week. It took some people awhile to get over being intimidated by me; even though I don't think I'm an intimidating person, they still thought so. As people became more comfortable they became able to challenge me, and that opened up a real dialogue. And that's what I wanted. I wanted an alternative to the mythology that surrounded me in the world; that surrounds every woman of power. The world tries to suffocate us with stereotyped images of us—to make us seem terrifying rather than wonderful.

The Dinner Party structure was also very good for the men. It was a nonsexist structure, so a man who came into it could begin to see himself acting as a male, rather than a person. He could feel the discrepancy between his ability to be a person and his role conditioning, which is not available anywhere else. Men are generally reinforced in the male role in the world.

GK: *What kind of images do you see used by other women artists?*

JC: So many women are so encased in the art world, and the art world is basically so boring. One woman I talked to was only interested in other artists; she was so fenced off. I don't see that much art that interests me, generally. I find art that's directed to the art world boring, whether it's by men or women. I feel peership with writers and not artists. I look to pre-Renaissance sources for my own stimulation. I look outside art often, to the decorative arts, to design.

GK: *Do you think it's fair to say that you're the first person who began to talk about female imagery in women's art?*

JC: Yes, Lucy Lippard wrote about it in *Ms.*—the first in this, the first in that. Being the first doesn't matter; it's being the best.

GK: *Is there anything else you would care to say about women's imagery in art?*

JC: I think that the problem is not women's imagery in art. I think there's a tremendous amount of it. I think the problem is its relationship to the rest of the world and the whole position of art in society and women's limited sense of their own power so that women can't see how powerful their work could be. They've accepted the limited role of the artist, or they have internalized a fairly powerless self-image as women. Both together reinforce each other. Or, as one young woman artist said, "Well, I'm basically selfish. I just like to do my work and that's all and I don't give a fuck about anything else."

I believe in the power of art, the whole notion of art reaching out to large audiences, like in the Middle Ages, when most people were illiterate. They couldn't read or write, but they knew how to read the images in the Church. They all understood visual imagery: they were literate visually. We live in a society that is visually illiterate, and I feel that women's imagery has to address itself to that. And if women make images that do not address themselves to larger issues, who will care about art? So you make these images—if they can't act in the world to change the way women are seen, to give new input to the world and to address the whole structure of alienated values, who cares if you make those images? The question is, why aren't women addressing themselves to getting the work out there? I'm primarily interested in new images reaching a larger audience, as I believe

Did You Know Your Mother Had a Sacred Heart?
1976
china-paint on porcelain, 18" × 55"
(photo by Diane Gelon)
Photo courtesy of The Dinner Party, © *Judy Chicago 1978*

images can change the way we see ourselves and *that* can change the world. Artists need to address themselves to making art that is relevant to people's lives without sacrificing quality.

GK: *Elaborate on the notion of a future world where there is both women's inner-core imagery and men's projective imagery. What would you see as a more ideal future for men and women?*

JC: The first thing that would result is that both men and women would be able to be in contact with the projective and interior reality, simultaneously. That would be the first thing that would happen—that it would break the schizophrenia of the sexes. Both would be able to experience holistically their full potential. What we have now is a division by gender that allows most people to only experience reality from their side of the gender split. And for those of us who cross over, it's clear how much richer life is if you can be both a man and a woman simultaneously. That's called being a person.

HUMOR IN CALIFORNIA UNDERGROUND WOMEN'S COMIX

Dolores Mitchell

In the Winter 1976 issue of *Inklings*, the Greenwich, Connecticut, Museum of Cartoon Art journal, President Mort Walker writes that of the thousands of cartoonists represented in the museum's collection fewer than twenty are women, most of whom are not humorists but illustrators of love and adventure tales. He asks if women are "afraid to laugh at themselves? Do they take life more seriously? Are they too interested in projecting an image of beauty and culture to become involved in comedy?" He speculates that perhaps women don't release their hostilities through humor as readily as men do.[1]

Walker does not speak of the growth of underground "comix" by women artists in California starting around 1970. The women's movement provides an audience responsive to the satire in these books and has surely helped release the feminine barbed pen from earlier inhibitions by encouraging both the acknowledgment of hostile emotions and the questioning of current ideals of beauty.

Walker also made no mention of the long history of exclusion of female caricaturists by male editors and artists. As recently as 1950 women found it difficult to join the National Cartoonists' Society. *Editor and Publisher*, a trade journal, writes of a battle of the sexes

> over whether the lipstick set would get into the stag stronghold. Despite a referendum last November that came out 6 to 1 in favor of admitting women as members, cartoonists Hilda Terry and Barbara Shermund, who had been approved by the membership committee, got blackballed at the all-male gathering.[2]

They were finally admitted.

Joyce Farmer, who draws underground comix in California, comments: "Women cartoonists usually have a hard time finding outlets for their work. We are women oriented, and the mass-media editors seem incapable of understanding our nonmasculine orientation."[3] B. Tyger of the San Francisco Academy of Comic Art concurs: "Women have not always been welcomed into the profession with open arms."[4] Notable exceptions, publications in which women cartoonists were encouraged as early as the 1920s and 1930s, include the socialist journal *The Masses* and *The New Yorker*. Some editors felt that women artists had a knack for drawing women in styles and situations that would attract female readership. These artists experienced far more editorial pressure than is present in the underground-comix situation.

When newspaper comic strips first developed at the turn of the century, their humor was often outrageous and even ribald. But with syndication, and as advertisers and editors became more responsive to the prejudices of the mythical "general reader," the freewheeling fun was thwarted. The earlier spontaneity was restored as underground comix developed in the 1960s in New York, aided by fast, cheap photolithographic presses that were sometimes run by artists' co-ops.

Women cartoonists benefited by this development, although some were dissatisfied with images of women in these comix. Joyce Farmer writes:

> Women in humor comics are often the butt of the joke in traditional "mother-in-law" or "dumb Dora" manner. *Mad* frequently indulges in this type of "humor." Women featured in underground comix written by men do not have such simplistic images. It may *seem* that Robert Crumb or S. Clay Wilson are using women as sex objects but often the intent is pure satire. Many other underground cartoonists are not so sophisticated and do indeed use women to fulfill their most macho and sadistic sex/violence fantasies.
>
> Lyn[5] and I began cartooning as a direct reaction to the image of women in the most popular underground comix, ZAP. We intended to create a total human who happens to be female. Consciousness-raising experience had shown us that we, as women, often hold male-oriented, mass-media images of ourselves and what we "should be."

Cartoonist Trina Robbins first worked in New York, but states that "the beginning of 1970 saw a mass exodus to San Francisco, which remains the underground cartoon capitol of the world."[6] Of some twenty comix I have studied by women artists published in California between 1970 and 1976 I will deal only with those sections that emphasize humor, although there is considerable variety to the books, with at least a third of their space devoted to adventure stories, science fiction, or sexual fantasy.

The most conspicuous trait shared by earlier cartoons by women and current underground women's comix is the reversal of male and female ratios of characters in comparison with such art by men. Throughout its four-hundred–year history the caricature has been drawn primarily by men, and men have been the chief targets for derision. In 1974 I studied several California collections of caricature and comic-strip art dating from the seventeenth century to the present in order to develop an exhibition of caricatures of women.[7] Women were present as major or minor figures in only one-quarter of the thousand works I examined. By contrast, females make up from 75 to 100 percent of the character cast in most cartoons by women artists, whether in the 1930s or today.

Also shared by the early and recent women cartoonists is the great emphasis on humor based on clothing, cosmetic, and hair styles, and household furnishings, especially in the more private rooms of the house: bedroom, bathroom, and kitchen.

In the 1920s and 1930s Helen E. Hokinson's cartoons in *The New Yorker* depicted rich middle-aged women trying to talk knowledgeably

Joyce Farmer
"The Menses Is the Massage,"
from Tits & Clits Comix
1972

about welfare, voting, and the League of Nations, while draped in furs and topped by whimsical cloches and turbans. Their plucked eyebrows, cupie-doll mouths, and pouter-pigeon bodies provided humorous contrast with their mock-serious expressions. In Marty Link's "Bobby Sox," still published, although the artist is a generation older than the twenty- and thirty-year-old women who draw the underground comix, we laugh at teenaged "Emmy Lou" as she tries on a slinky black dress while wearing old loafers. Emmy's mother, in her slip, seated before a mirror with a mudpack on her face, is depicted as a modern version of the traditional age-and-vanity theme. We are encouraged to chuckle at the incongruity of this middle-aged mother trying to look beautiful.

Underground comix artist Lee Marrs states: "Women do have a tendency to deal more directly with everyday events, details, atmosphere. They often work from the specific to the general, and their work has a personal orientation."[8] In Marrs's "All in a Day's Work" we follow the job-hunting misadventures of a plain, thirtyish, bespectacled typist who changes from demure Peter Pan–collared blouses to a braless halter, and finally goes topless as she attempts to blend into various work milieux.[9]

Artists draw strength from their experiences, and most women have been indoctrinated since childhood to be sensitive to nuances of appearance. They learn early from parents, peers, films, and fashion magazines what kind of purse and gloves can be carried with a casual (but not cocktail) outfit, beyond what length a skirt looks dated, and how to deduce a man's bank balance from whether his haircut looks as it it cost $35 or $3.

Didi Glitz, a character created by underground cartoonist Diane Noomin, exploits society's tendency to judge respectability by costume. She robs a bank wearing a glamorous modacrylic wig, heart-shaped sunglasses, a tent dress to disguise her pregnancy, and sexy white boots. Then she slips into a washroom and emerges wearing a maternity smock, a sweet bow in her hair, and carrying two large Macy's shopping bags. She is as good as invisible.[10]

In underground comix by women clothing, accessories, and furnishing delineate a wide variety of lifestyles, from those of working women to middle-class parents to commune tenants. In one strip a boss wears a vested suit, his foreman a shirt and tie, and the janitor a shirt without a tie—a visual presentation of their comparative status. The artists' skillful pens fabricate quilted "Mao" jackets, fad shark-tooth necklaces, palmtree-stenciled sequined skirts, eyelet-trimmed slips, and the clutter of bedrooms with glasses hanging from lampshades, piles of pantyhose, and scattered bristle curlers.

A teenager with an underdeveloped figure wears overly sophisticated clothing. Her high-heeled shoes and bobbysocks clash, but, after all,

she can't afford an entire cohesive ensemble, and so a few emblems of sexual maturity must do. A husbandless mother tries to rejoin the singles scene by dressing as a teenager in a miniskirt, knee-high boots, and a backcombed hair style ten years out of date.

There is, then, some continuity in the work of earlier and current women cartoonists, but there are also elements of divergence, as when current artists emphasize themes that were only hinted at before, parody earlier images, and work openly with their personal experiences.

The recent work tends to be overtly autobiographical; in earlier cartoons by women creator and characters maintain separate identities. If one looks through a group of clubwomen cartoons by Helen E. Hokinson, no single woman emerges from the group who impels one to say: "Ah, and there is the artist herself!" Frequently, as can be seen by comparing the photos or drawings of the artists that appear on the inside covers of many underground comix with their respective strips, the heroine's features are based on those of the artist. Roberta Gregory's cat points to an image of her artist mistress and tells us: "She's Frieda."[11] As cartoonist Joyce Farmer states: "We are the characters and they are us, and I, at least, feel too close to them to judge their image."

In the beginning or end of many books the artist, through words and images, communicates directly with the reader, asking for responses to stories, or presenting personal viewpoints. Trina, in "A Visit with the Artist in Her Own Studio!!," draws herself saying to us:

> I know my work puts some men uptight. . . . Hey, man, if you're taking it personally it was probably meant for you. I admit to a lot of genuine hostility! I'll start liking you better when you start liking women better. . . . On the other hand, what I get from a lot of women is accusations of sexism, because I draw beautiful women and I think they're beautiful! I insist on the right to be a feminist and still wear pink satin![12]

In a similar format, Roberta Gregory greets us with "Hi, folks! I'm the lady artist (and writer). . . . I really want my sisters to . . . understand what was going on through my head at the time."[13]

Images of handwritten diaries and snapshots often accompany stories, and the ages of the main characters generally match the twenty-to-thirty bracket of the artists, or are of the adolescent period of their recent memories. Because these artists draw so heavily on their personal experiences it may be decades before many older women appear in their pages. Scarcely any women over forty are seen, except for an occasional mother oppressing a teenaged heroine. By contrast, middle-aged and even older women were drawn frequently by earlier women cartoonists, and when developing my exhibition on caricatures of women I noted that when male artists did caricatures of women it was most often to poke fun at aging women, who although they had lost both beauty and the ability to reproduce, still retained their vanity.

The autobiographical bias of this art, and the use of females for most of the characters, create dilemmas. As women the artists have been socially conditioned to aspire to beauty in appearance and poise in behavior; yet the comic artist's forte lies in debunking the ideal and the heroic. A further complication: the women's movement, of which these artists are keenly aware, calls for an appreciation of variances from the ideal. If earlier comic artists got laughs from accentuating nature's mistakes, as the following quotation from a seventeenth-century definition of caricature suggests, and there no longer *are* mistakes, only infinite, fascinating variety to hips, noses, weights, colors, and mannerisms and mores—what's to laugh at?

> Nature takes pleasure in deforming human features; she gives one person a thick nose and another a large mouth. If these inconsistencies and disproportions have in themselves a comic effect, then the artist . . . can accentuate the impression and cause the spectator to laugh.[14]

WITH PUBERTY
CAME UGLYNESS
AND GUILT......

Aline Kominsky
"Goldie A Neurotic Woman,"
from Wimmen's Comix 1
1972

Some women underground-comix artists simply play it straight. Their books are not funny but are designed to show the admirable qualities of the antistereotypical. Other women artists still find humans, including themselves, imbued with a heavy portion of the ridiculous and continue to exercise a comic sensibility whose task is to keep us modest. As Lee Marrs says, "Humor can be more effective than preaching in getting people to achieve new insights." One might add that before new ones can develop, old, outmoded ideals have to be demolished, and laughter can shatter them. Nevertheless, there is a tension present in much of the underground comix by women because of the fine line demarcating laughter that denigrates an image, such as that of a teenager with fat bulging in her sweater and jeans, and humanizing laughter inspired by a recognition of universal problems.

The artists do debunk themselves. As Roberta Gregory expands on her motivations for creating her characters, her cat puts her down by telling us her mistress is too longwinded. For the first five boxes of "A

Visit with the Artist in Her Own Studio!!" Trina depicts herself loung-
ing langorously at her drawing board as she is offered cocktails by male
hands. In each box she is glamorously attired in a different style in a
parody of reader-designed fashions worn by certain earlier comic-strip
heroines ("Trina's Art Deco Velvet Gown Thanx to Judy Gross, Ozone
Park, Queens"). In the fifth box the voice of Trina's little girl, who
demands to be taken to the potty, intrudes into this world of romance,
leisure, and high style. In the final box we see the real Trina, a harried
mother in patched jeans and shirt, her work and fantasy interrupted by
reality.
Lee Marrs says:

> We get asked, why not develop a real superheroine? But we think it
> is most important to develop from an outgrowth of our own honest
> feelings, and I don't believe in superheroines. I am interested in
> the process women go through to get it together. The ins and outs
> and ups and downs. Some women want all of us to concentrate on
> completely new positive archetypes, but I did what I was closest to.
> I was a *fat* kid.

The ideals still have power to attract, however, as the many Walter
Mitty–type fantasies in the books suggest, although the heroine is usually brought back to plain reality by the story's end. In these fantasies
the heroine temporarily becomes more glamorous, assertive, wealthy,
daring, or powerful. Lee Marrs's Pudge, Girl Blimp thinks that she has a
chance to act in a film and imagines herself transformed into a tall,
slim, beautiful blond, but reverts to her short chunky self as she is
rejected even for a porno-flick cast. She consoles herself for lack of
closeness to her parents with the fantasy that she is a Martian transplant.

Trina, in "Why I Left New York," is enraged when a street-corner
hood makes an obscene remark as she passes him. She imagines herself
transfigured into a powerful woman in a flying cloak, with bulging eyes
and fangs. "Pow," she punches him in the nose. The final box shows
her back to normal, with a satisfied look on her face as she wipes her
hands, while the hood remains standing against the building with a
smug air. [15]

Michele, in "Monday," gives us a young woman typist who daydreams that she is queen of the jungle, liberating her coworkers as they
are led through the brush in neck chains by the boss. She is struggling
with a tiger as the coffee-break call comes, whereupon she joins the
single file of the colorless typing-pool workers. [16]

In another "if only I could"–type fantasy Diane Noomin's Didi Glitz,
upon being rejected by the butcher who impregnated her, and turned
down for a loan because she has no husband, decides to gain instant

*A: AH YES. HERE, WE HAVE THE "REAL-ME" SYNDROME. WITH MOST EVERY HUMAN, IT'S DIFFERENT. BUT THERE ARE UNIVERSAL TRENDS. FOR A WHILE BACK, IT WAS CHARLES LINDBERGHS. ALSO JACKIE ONASSIS... THIS COULD BE A JANE FONDA.. A DESIRE TO BE OTHER, MORE GLAMOROUS, EXCITING THAN THEIR ACTUAL SELVES.
B: WHY DON'T THEY BE THEIR ACTUAL SELVES?
A: IT'S HARDER.

Lee Marrs
"The Screen Queen,"
from The Further Fattening Adventures
of Pudge, Girl Blimp, 2
1975
© 1975 Lee Marrs

wealth by robbing a bank. She succeeds; takes a cruise, during which she gives birth; checks into a foreign luxury hotel as a rich widow; and toasts crime, love, and liquor as the men line up.

Closely related to fantasies of this sort is the theme of pretending, or the contrast between inner feelings (the desire to revolt) and outward actions (conformity). In Lyn Chevley's "The Perfect Wife and Mother" the wife says all the right positive things as she helps her husband off for work and child off to school: "Bye darling. I love you too. Don't work too hard and have a good lunch." Then as the door slams: "They're gone now. I'm alone at last and safe from interruptions. Thank goodness for some privacy. Now I can pluck my chin in peace!"[17] In another comic a shy teenager hides her insecurity by pretending she is tough and dressing like a hooker.

One finds an obvious rejection of the imagery of certain earlier media strips, including some by women, in parodies by women underground cartoonists. Joyce Farmer:

> What do I say about the usual image of women in comic art? Simpering and ineffective. And Wonder Woman? An adventure hero, except for a few details, who may as well be male. The "straight" comic publishers, e.g. Marvel or D.C., make their female characters merely a cartoon reflection of the media image of women. Comic women are shown as dependent on men for their fulfillment and security. Whatever small gains in the status of women are allowed by the "straight" companies is diluted further by the universally male staff writers, whom I know from personal acquaintance to be quite unliberated.

Similarly, in response to the question "What kind of traditional images of women do you find in popular strips?," Lee Marrs states:

> The same stereotypes as in movies and books. Also there are very few women, and when they are there it is to scream and get rescued or they function as chairs. When the women's movement became visible in the sixties, D.C. and Marvel Comics sent down editorial policies to use more women. But those women simply acted like men or were girlfriends of superheroes.

In "Breaking Out" Carole depicts a rebellion of female characters from older strips, drawing each in its original style.[18] When Porky Pig comes home and demands that Petunia cook dinner, although he is unwilling to listen to her talk about her day, she shouts: "Cook your own dinner, Porky, I'm splitting! That was the last straw. I'm going to make a new life for myself. Goodbye!" In addition to humor through the incongruity of a stereotyped character behaving in an atypical way, there is humor in seeing a hitherto supporting character take center stage, much as when Rosencrantz and Guildenstern present Hamlet from their viewpoints.

Juliet Jones drools: "You're one of the most fascinating and exasperatingly mysterious men I've ever met . . . sigh sigh." But in the next box her true self (we suspect the cartoonist has left the room) speaks: "???Who put these inane words in my mouth: How long must I be this mindless simp, kept docile under the shadow of an eraser???" If these formerly predictable characters can change, the reader may also be able to break out of entrenched patterns—this is a message easily deduced from such stories.

A number of satires are aimed at television ads and women's romance and home magazines that seek to manipulate desires for commercial ends. The cover of *Manhunt!* (1973) uses these "come-on" titles based on sex, fear, and guilt: "Can This Marriage Be Destroyed?"; "Fat Was My Badge of Sin!"; "Dr. Reuben Ruined My Sex Life"; "My Love Was a Real Sucker... of My Blood!"[19] The inner-cover ad promises instant magical enhancement of sex allure for $11.98, as a three-breasted woman illustrates an "Add-a-Breast" kit. There is a clip-out coupon and testimonials: "Tits are my business as a wet nurse. . . ." The back inner cover is a Maidenform bra parody: "I dreamed I lost my maidenhood in . . . ," and in the illustration a blond frantically searches old shoes, drawers, and the space under her bed.

The satire continues in other books, as in a "Miss Universal Udder" contest for goats and a "Virgin of the Month Club," which offers teen-aged boys to lascivious women readers. In "The Neighborhood Know-it-All" women gang up on a pest who tries to make them feel guilty for their lack of obsession with kitchen-floor wax buildup and keeping a spotless house.[20] An outside perspective on the bizarre nature of many things we accept as normal is provided when Trina's Amazon Queen visits our civilization, dons a bra as headgear, and uses feminine hygiene spray to kill mosquitoes.[21] The latter product is singled out in a Lee Marrs spoof in which the spray cans are filled with heroin in a plot to addict and subjugate women.[22]

Much humor in these books is based on the contrast between ideal, socially conditioned expectations, and the disillusioning reality that characters encounter. This often involves appearances, as in the contrast between a beautiful model wearing an advertised brand of makeup and the incomplete transformation of a comic character who wears the recommended false eyelashes and lipstick but has a huge nose, or who puts on a padded bra but has a thick waist and elephantine legs, or who has elegantly polished nails on big, wrinkled fingers. A teenaged girl looks at *Playboy* while sitting on the toilet and compares herself with the pictures of models: "I know I'm not normal. My nipples aren't pink."[23] Another women muses: "I'll probably never get another man. I look like a 50 year old Jewish businessman."[24]

The most frequent departure from a physical ideal in these books involves fat. Episodes at a fat farm draw humor from depicting women in leotards who can't touch their toes or sit straight because of huge tummies, who try to wedge into clothing many sizes too small, and who go on uncontrollable eating binges. A slim or normal-sized woman usually shares the panels to provide contrast. Some episodes suggest an eventual acceptance of being heavy. The heroine may meet a fat man who also loves to eat; or a man from another country, where plump women are considered beautiful; or she may go to a woman's group where figures are compared and an attempt is made to approve of weight differences. In some cases the resolution of conflict is not very satisfactory, and once in a while the heroine loses weight.

This conflict between real and ideal can involve behavior, as when a girl's storybook concept of love must be reconciled with back-seat-of-a-car reality. The sex positions of inept teenagers are comical, and sex organs appear ludicrous rather than sensuous. In an antiromantic episode in the lives of Chin Lyvely's "Perfectly Permeable Peters Sisters" one of the girls evaluates a sexual encounter: he was "Great, just great! Devastatingly handsome, well hung... except that he has crabs, clap, a bladder infection, a flare-up of eczema and garlic breath!"[25]

Postmarriage disgruntlement is a theme with a long tradition in caricature, as in Hogarth and Daumier. The one fat Peters sister daydreams of marrying and sees herself and boyfriend framed in flowers "in a fantastically beautiful organic wedding in a meadow with birds and sunshine."[26] Her sisters refuse to be bridesmaids until she experiences the reality of living with her boyfriend for a week. It is a disaster. He is a messy musician, their cats fight, and he expects her to cook for his combo. In the final box she cries and is consoled by her sisters: "Sob, he threw me out 'cause I'm fat."

Aline Kominsky's autobiographical character marries a nice, quiet Jewish boy.[27] They both go to college, yet she must cook while he worries about his exams. In an assertive moment she tells him off but soon begs for forgiveness, humbling herself in an attempt to relate to him more closely. He takes her act of homage for granted, and she has maneuvered herself back to box one of their relationship. Given an overview, we can indulge in the laughter of the gods: the reasons that communication cannot occur are plain to us, even as the heroine struggles to make contact with her mate.

Some stories focus on incongruous juxtapositions of the heroic and the antiheroic, using normally separate value systems that curdle when combined. Lee Marrs, in "Cyberfenetics—the Relationship of People to Their Machines," proposes the everyday housewife, looking frazzled, her face unmade and rollers spilling from her hair, as the heroine of the future, able to lead humankind into "a whole new world—in true symbiosis with the machine."[28] She is shown in heroic battle with the elements, water and fire, as the polar-bear spirit of the icebox she is struggling to defrost barrages her with icecubes and the lion spirit of her oven attacks with flaming tongue. In the style of Soviet Realism posters three valiant housewives ascend a mountain peak armed with vacuums, mops, and silverware while a glory of sunrays fills the sky.

A reversal of expectations creates humor in some of this art: in Shelby's cover for *Wimmen's Comix* 4 a Princess holds a frog and says: "Can't see turning a perfectly good frog into a prince!" On the back cover we see her rescuing a prince from a dragon. More laughter generated by surprise occurs when women behave in ribald or aggressive ways. Joyce Sutton (Farmer) depicts a woman striding unabashedly into a men's toilet because she needs paper and shocking a man using the urinal.[29] Children can be unexpectedly salty as they play with vibrators and make racy remarks in French.

Lesbian strips exploit the humor of embarrassment, as when a woman discusses a sex problem with her gynecologist and he is startled to learn that she means sex with another woman, or as when bystanders are dismayed to see women hugging each other.[30]

There is similar humor in revealing what goes on in private rooms of the house, where humans, caught off guard, do not display their cautious, poised, public selves. Here we have the humor of Tampax dilemmas, awkward intercourse, potty ponderings, gynecologist exams. Joyce Farmer writes that "as we wrote, our bawdy sense of humor took over and we satirized every (previously unmentionable) facet of our female lives. Birth control, sexual gratification, menstrual periods—nothing was sacred!"

Not even the women's movement, which is generally depicted in these comix as a positive force, is sacred. Sharon Rudahl, in "The Two Timer or How I Got Purged from My Women's Group," satirizes the jargon of yeast infections and the hypocrisy of gossiping about nose jobs when self-acceptance is supposed to be a goal.[31]

Many of the foregoing themes are incorporated in the continuing adventures of Lee Marrs's "Pudge, Girl Blimp."[32] We follow both her physical journey as a teenaged runaway to the city of her dreams, San Francisco, and her spiritual journey into adulthood, topics traditionally associated with "coming into manhood" novels, like *Tom Sawyer*. Suspecting she is a Martian, and rejecting her detached businessman father and nagging mother, she is hopeful that the future will be good, despite her past failures with high school peers because of her fat. She is full of the high expectations society has encouraged, especially that sex will be glorious, and is determined to rid herself of the secret shame of being a virgin at age seventeen. On one cover she exclaims: "Oh wow! Off to my first job!! Maybe my boss will be single . . . and he'll take off my glasses and say. . . ."

Pudge's image is that of the wanderer, with cast-off, ill-matching, but functional clothing: a warm army jacket, walking sandals, knapsack, suitcase. She decorates herself with symbols of identity that belong to other identities: an IKE button, a Normal Community Marching Band T-shirt, travel labels that were probably on the suitcase when she bought it at the Salvation Army. At least she has a rightful claim to the women's symbol around her neck.

She strides along smiling, eyes big with excitement and glasses, oblivious to a claw hand reaching out behind her, a monster chasing a woman on the fire escape above her, and the long line in front of an unemployment-compensation office, which includes mortarboard-wearing college grads, Nixon, and a machine-gun–carrying Tanya. She is some seventy-five pounds overweight, short, with frizzy hair and protruding teeth. She eats a banana while carrying a hero sandwich and pamphlets on nursing, computer programming, and beginning welding.

Hoping to be raped, she goes to Golden Gate Park at night, only to be arrested by a female officer posing as a male attacker. She moves into a crowded Haight Ashbury tenement and pulls an unconscious male into her room but is foiled by a police drug raid. On her release, fearing she has contracted VD from a jail toilet seat, she goes to a free clinic, but is rejected even there as not belonging when to the doctor's question "What are you on? Grass, speed, coke?" she answers inappropriately: "Well, I did have a coke at lunch."

She goes to a woman's talk group and begins to understand that society has unreasonable standards of perfection. At that point Marrs could have opted for an easy resolution, with Pudge achieving maturity and solid self-acceptance. Back in her room Pudge says that she sees herself: "as an independent person. It's just a start, but I know who I am." But Marrs chooses irony, and in the next box Pudge continues: "I'm a failure. A washout. A nothing!"

Michele Brand
"Monday,"
from It Ain't Me Babe
1970

Yet Pudge has resilience, curiosity, and hope. The issue ends as she looks forward to a date with a plainclothes cop who has just raided their house.

Marrs employs a polyphonic storyline and style that demands more reader involvement than the usual fast-scan comic strip. There are numerous asides and subplots, as in a police station scene in which a boy scout is cross-examined as a drug-pusher suspect. The art abounds in local and topical detail, suggesting that the artist has roamed San Francisco with a sketchbook. Cablecar men turn a trolley. Hare Krishna chanters line up in front of the Powell Street Woolworth. Japanese children fly kites in Golden Gate Park. Hubcaps are robbed in daylight hours. An old person holds up a younger one. Businessmen talk about shares. A six-year-old crosses the street carrying a machine gun. A police station mug shot is titled: "Wanted for chronic impertinence." Bulletin-board notices offer: "42 kittens free," "Lithuanian Film Festival—'Two for Nausea,'" "Sincere Pisces seeks acrobatic goldfish."

In "Pudge" and other women's comix heroines struggle to be true to themselves in a world where pressures are great to do otherwise. Their imagery of adventurous exploration of life, and capacity to bounce back from its blows, is in marked contrast to William Manchester's description of "a lady" during the 1932–1941 period in America, from his *Glory and the Dream*:

> Being a lady had certain advantages. Men opened doors for her, stood up to give her a seat on buses and streetcars, and removed their hats when she entered elevators. . . . Her activities in public were circumscribed by convention. A middle-class lady could neither smoke on the street nor appear with hair curlers. In her purse she carried cosmetics in a small disc called a compact, but this, too, could be produced only in private or a ladies' room. She never swore or told dirty jokes. (Sometimes she wondered what a lesbian was. But whom could she ask?) Advertising copywriters saw to it that she had enough worries anyway: halitosis, B.O., undie odor, office hips, paralyzed pores, pink toothbrush, ashtray breath, colon collapse, pendulosis, and athlete's foot.[33]

Notes

1. Mort Walker. "Forum: Do Women Have a Sense of Humor?," *Inklings* (Winter 1976), 10.

2. "Cartoonists Society Excludes Two Women," *Editor and Publisher*, February 11, 1950.

3. Joyce Farmer. Letter to D. Mitchell, March 2, 1976. All other quotations in this article from Farmer are from this letter. Farmer signs her artwork Joyce Sutton.

4. B. Tyger. Letter to D. Mitchell, February 4, 1976. The San Francisco Academy of Comic Art (2850 Ulloa St., San Francisco, CA 94116) is a library and research center that contains newspapers, periodicals, comic books, and other sources for the popular arts.

5. Lyn Chevley (Chin Lyvely).

6. Ed Ward. "Profile: Ed Ward Interviews Intrepid Trina Robbins," *Comix Book* (Box 7, Princeton, WI) 5 (July 1976), 47.

7. "Women Libeled: Caricatures of Women," an exhibition, Art Gallery, California State University, Chico, March 19–April 5, 1974.

8. Lee Marrs. Telephone interview by D. Mitchell, March 12, 1976. All other quotations in this article from Marrs are from this interview.

9. Lee Marrs, in *Wimmen's Comix*, 1, (Last Gasp, Box 212, Berkeley, CA 94701) 1 (1972).

10. Diane Newman (she signs her work Diane Noomin). "Didi Glitz She Chose Crime," *Wimmen's Comix*, 4 (1974).

11. Roberta Gregory. "Lady Artist Comix," *Dynamite Damsels* (Box 4192, Long Beach, CA), 1976.

12. Trina Robbins, in *Fight Girl Comics* (Print Mint, 870 Folger, Berkeley, CA), 2 (1974).

13. *Dynamite Damsels*, 1976.

14. F. Baldinucci. *Vocabolario toscano dell'arte del disegno*, Florence, 1681.

15. Trina Robbins. *Comix Book*, 4 (1976).

16. Michele Brand. "Monday," *It Aint Me Babe* (Last Gasp, Box 212, Berkeley, CA 94701), 1970.

17. Lyn Chevley (Chin Lyvely). *Tits & Clits Comix* (Nanny Goat Productions, Box 845, Laguna Beach, CA), 1972.

18. Carole, in *It Aint Me Babe*, 1970.

19. Cover by Lee Marrs.

20. Lee Marrs, in *Wimmen's Comix*, 4 (1974).

21. Trina Robbins. "She," *Fight Girl Comics*, 1 (1972).

22. Lee Marrs. "Mei-Lin Luftwaffe Aerial Infant," *The Further Fattening Adventures of Pudge, Girl Blimp*, 1 (1973).

23. Diane Newman (Noomin). "The Agony and the Ecstacy of Shayna Madel," *Wimmen's Comix*, 3 (1974).

24. Aline Kominsky. "More of the Bunch," *Twisted Sisters* (Last Gasp, Box 212, Berkeley, CA 94701), 1976.

25. Pandoras Box Comix (Nanny Goat Productions, Box 845, Laguna Beach, CA), 1973.

26. *Ibid.*

27. Aline Kominsky. "More of the Bunch," *Twisted Sisters*, 1976.

28. Lee Marrs, in *Wimmen's Comix*, 4 (1974).

29. Cover of *Tits & Clits Comix* (Nanny Goat Productions, Box 845, Laguna Beach, CA), 1972.

30. See *Dynamite Damsels*.

31. *Comix Book*, 4 (1976).

32. Lee Marrs. *The Further Fattening Adventures of Pudge, Girl Blimp*, (Last Gasp-Eco Funnies, Inc.) 1 (1973); (Star Reach Productions, Box 385, Hayward, CA) 2 (1975).

33. William Manchester. *The Glory and the Dream*. New York: Little, Brown, 1974, p.62.

Selected Bibliography

Becker, Stephen. *Comic Art in America*. New York: Simon and Schuster, 1959.

Berkman, A. "Sociology of the Comic Strip," *American Spectator*, June 1936, pp. 32–36.

Boime, Albert. "The Comic Stripped and Ash Canned," *Art Journal*, Fall 1972, pp. 47–52.

Bruere, Martha Bensley, and Beard, Mary Ritter. *Laughing Their Way: Women's Humor in America*. New York: Arden, 1934.

"Cartoonists Society Excludes Two Women," *Editor and Publisher*, February 11, 1950, p. 3.

Clarke, Gerald. "The Comics on the Couch," *Time*, December 13, 1971, pp. 70–71.

"Comics Getting Back to Basics," *San Francisco Chronicle*, May 15, 1975, p. 2.

Davidson, Sol M. "Culture and the Comic Strip." Doctoral dissertation, New York University, 1959.

Hiller, B. *Cartoons and Caricatures*. London: Studio Vista, 1970.

Hofmann, Werner, *Caricature from Leonardo to Picasso*. London: Crown, 1957.

Irvins, William M., Jr., *Prints and Visual Communication*. Cambridge, Mass.: MIT Press, 1969.

Johnston, Laurie. "Women's Liberation in the Comics," *New York Times*, February 3, 1973, p. 34.

McCord, D. F. "Social Rise of the Comics," *American Mercury*, July 1935, pp. 19–25.

Murrell, William A. *History of American Graphic Humor*. New York: Cooper Square, 1938.

O'Sullivan, Judith. *The Art of the Comic Strip*. College Park: University of Maryland, Department of Art, 1971.

Quennell, P. "Comic Strips in England: Future Folklorists Will Find in Them the Mythology of the Present Day," *Living Age*, March 1941, pp. 57–63.

Schulz, Juergen, ed. *Caricature and Its Role in Graphic Satire*. Exhibition catalog, Brown University, Department of Art, 1971.

Spiegelman, Marvin. "The Content of Comics: Goals and Means to Goals of

Comic Strip Characters," *Journal of Social Psychology*, April 1953, pp.97–102.

Walker, Mort. "Forum: Do Women Have a Sense of Humor?" *Inklings: Journal of the Museum of Cartoon Art* (Greenwich, Conn.), Winter 1976, p.10.

Dolores Mitchell *teaches art history at California State University, Chico. Her Ph.D is from UCLA.*

GODDESS IMAGERY IN RITUAL

Interview with Mary Beth Edelson

M*ary Beth Edelson is an artist with a holistic approach to art. Positive, self-affirming images of women with sacred, humorous, and intangible motifs are frequent focuses for her public and private rituals documented in nature with extraordinary photographs. Her themes include collecting stories and myths of our time, and fire transformations. Recurrent images in her installations, sculptures, drawings, paintings, performance, and books are the Goddess with upraised arms, magical caves, and flying rocks. Her images are exuberant celebrations of free contemporary women. Edelson is an active participant in women's culture and a member of the AIR Gallery in New York City, where she lives.*

GK: *Please discuss the imagery of emergence in your paintings.*

MBE: I've been working with a liturgy, or ritual performance, of the feminist movement. How we look, how we feel, the sounds and movements that tell our story. Within this story, or liturgy, emergence and rebirth are stages that carry us along: they are preparatory stages. More often than not I have used a passage—a doorway, gate, or cave—as a symbol leading to emergence. In the late sixties I often painted an open flower in the foreground of my canvases nestled between rocks. The hard-soft positioning of the rock and flower appealed to me, as did their dramatically different relationship to time—the rock seemingly eternal and the flower transitory. Spread-eagle, the flower was exposed and pointing toward you, so that the viewer was confronted by openness. The open flower is also a symbol of the woman who is not beholden to anyone, her own woman.

GK: *That relates to the virgin goddesses, who are also described historically in those same kinds of terms. Your image for the passage was going through the rock forms?*

MBE: The image for the passage was a journey through water; water that was tightly bound on all sides by slate-grey walls. The high color had drained out of the work, and the water could potentially engulf you, swallow you up. The walls were territories that were unfriendly, uninviting, and unknown, with diagonal, wavy lines that indicated a field of energy but also limited your access to the passage. In later paintings the passages became more open; you could see through and beyond. Light as possibility appeared on the horizon. Those paintings came directly out of dream images of a journey state. My dreams helped me with the passages because, when I mustered the courage to pass through them, the experience was one of elevation: walking on air, bouncing—a celebration of victory over external limitations.

GK: *It seems like going through a birth canal. Is there that kind of imagery going on?*

MBE: Yes, it's like a birth canal and it's also like going down into your own personal depths. I thought of the parameters as walls of the mind. I was going down into a watery way that was my unconscious, getting down and wallowing around in that liquid mass, losing myself in a creative adventure to see what emerged. I stopped doing those paintings very suddenly; signaling, I guess, that I had emerged from the dark passage and was ready for something else. Perhaps because the paintings were so specifically working through these stages, I felt I must give them up in order to go on. In any case, I developed an aversion to painting. I felt negative about that act. (Although now I think I could go back into it with a fresh mind.)

The other aspect of that negativity was communication. I had to get out of the isolation of my studio and into a broader context, associate with other people and not just my canvases. Some color then came back into the work, and I began participating with other people, using images that had to do with transformation and emergence works that said "becoming" and, finally, "I am." The *Woman Rising* series—"Sexual Rites," "Earth Rites," and "Moon Mouth"—were emergence pieces. I manifested the "I am" position in private photographic rituals by standing with my legs apart, firmly planted on the ground, and with my arms lifted in the stylized pose of

Mary Beth Edelson
"Moon Mouth,"
from Sexual Rites/Woman Rising *series*
1973

the Goddess with the upraised arms. That, to me, is a powerful
and assertive female stance that says, "I am strong, continuous:
I am here and I am not going away." It also says I have gone
through an emergence, I am becoming—still evolving, but "I
am."

GK: *Meaning one in oneself?*

MBE: Yes—complete. Concentric circles that I draw on my breast
and on my womb also relate to that wholeness as well as act as
a ritualistic signifier; that is, we don't usually go around painting our bodies—this is a peculiar act. I felt I needed to employ

an astonishing act to alert my body to be receptive to communications with nature, Goddess, cosmic forces, etc.: that I was in fact inviting and calling on these energies to visit me. The images that I work with now are exploring and defining images. I'm not trying to say "I am"; I'm saying "we" are.

GK: *What are you finding from your definition process?*

MBE: That women need images to relate to that are strong and positive. When I was active in the civil-rights movement, I remember the power of the slogan "Black Is Beautiful," understanding what that reassurance meant for people who had grown up without mainstream positive images of themselves. It is the same for women now. We need to overstate to realize our full confidence.

While we are on images, we can also talk about the many images considered by the *Heresies* magazine collective as we defined ourselves. Those discussions represent a true collective, or collection of images coming from a number of women deeply involved in feminism and visual images. One of the most difficult decisions for the *Heresies* collective was to pick a name for the magazine and to pick an image for the first poster. We literally spent months discussing those two subjects. We explored the open flower, which is used by many feminists as a symbol of emerging woman. We considered the pink rose— because of its color and also because it is the name of women. We were interested in layered meaning. Another image that stayed with us for awhile was the rock. We identified with a rock: the solidness, the attachment to the earth, the rock as a foundation and as a marker on the landscape, its relationship with mountains, caves, crevices, and the Great Round. We talked about the cyclical, living aspects of rocks and that they have an inner core.

The teapot was explored. Women sit around a teapot and share. We noted the teapot's warmth, comfort, vessel aspects, the nourishing aspects, and the roundness of it, and its pouring out.

We talked about drawing Amazon-like women, and considered all working on the same drawing together; one of us drawing the head, another the eyes, etc.—to make a truly collaborative drawing.

We finally settled on the fan for our poster. We liked that image because it opens and closes, because it is composed of a series of fragments, strips of multiple images that made room for all of our ideas, and because we could actually make the

Mary Beth Edelson
"Goddess Head,"
from Calling series
1975

poster itself into a real fan. That took a slew of hand folding,
but we did it anyway.

Some women in the collective have continued developing
these images.

Goddess Imagery in Ritual 95

GK: *Do you see any kinds of images in women's work that indicate a women's sensibility?*

MBE: We've all been trying to figure that out for some time now. We do know that we have made a significant contribution to "mainstream" art history by introducing "the personal" approach as a valid realm of art making. Women are more interested in multiplicity, cycles, and layering. This interest affects the *way* we make art and the *kind* of art we select to make. Because many of us can tolerate working with a number of entities at one time, we are more likely to devise cohesive, integrated life systems during our art-making process. This integrating process is not only more satisfying to the individual but is more likely ultimately to interest a wider audience. We also appear to be more capable of and more interested in integrating artwork into the non-art community. But we still can't answer that question fully. Many feminists like myself have analyzed political images, weaving women's history and our contemporary culture into our work. We always hope to intuit feminine images, but I recognize that, for a time anyway, desire may develop our images rather than an unconscious feminine source. Time should relax us, and the answer to that question may then be clearer.

GK: *What I'm interested in is ritual and how that works in your art now, how you came to it, and when you began it.*

MBE: The ritual came to me as a personal rite, performed first with my children and later documented in the early seventies. I was setting aside a particular time, saying to them, "This activity that we do now is special. This time and these gestures I hope will make a lasting impression upon you. So we are going to act it out. We are going to ritualize our behavior and document ourselves with photographs. The photographs will stand as a record of the unity and wonder that we experienced."

GK: *What kinds of concepts were you dealing with?*

MBE: I was trying to tie them to the earth, to help them understand in a direct way that nature was not something outside of them. We laid on the earth together, touching. We felt ourselves part of the earth and part of each other. Turning over, we felt, through our bodies, connections with the earth and the sky. With trees, we hugged the trunks, circling the base with our

Mary Beth Edelson
"Whale Jump,"
from Calling series
1975

bodies and weaving our arms around each other, encompassing and merging for a moment, mother and child become one
again—one with each other and one with the earth. With both
my son and my daughter, we gathered sticks and branches,
breaking them to symbolize breaking away from weaponry,
violence, and the use of force in our lives, and then providing
another use for the sticks. We built a series of human-scale
concentric circles on the ground, adding leaves, white sand,
bark, flowers, and birdseed to the sticks. Working from the
nature that was around us, we developed the mandala. It was a
spiritual act of respect for nature.

Goddess Imagery in Ritual 97

GK: *The first times you documented your private rituals without your children they were also done in nature. What concepts were you working with then?*

MBE: The first time I documented my private rituals with myself my purpose was to use my body as a stand-in for the Goddess, and also to get in touch with my greater self. The stylized poses that I took were my way of calling on the Goddess; my way of getting Her attention, identifying with Her, and slipping into Her body. I was calling on energy and on Spirit. My concepts were centered around emergence, gaining confidence and power, and then congratulating ourselves and celebrating. They were rituals of becoming. During one ritual I pulled my body into a fetal position inside of a fire ring as if birthing myself ("One Black Hole/Two Black Holes"). Another started with my arms to my side (suggesting a powerlessness position); the arms came up; I gradually photographed my arms raising in the sequences as power was being gained. In that same series ("Pluto: Sticking My Tongue Out at the Patriarchy") a wagging tongue slowly emerges from the back of my body, which was painted to look like Walt Disney's Pluto, the dog. The name also referred to the patriarchal Pluto of the underworld in mythology.

GK: *What other kinds of rituals do you do?*

MBE: As purification rites the rituals erase negative energy and bring positive resonances into the body; they become a healing act.

I also teach my rituals to other women, as I did for the "Your 5,000 Years Are Up" exhibition in 1977. The ritual titled "Mourning Our Lost History" worked with mourning that turned into anger and ended with celebration. Eleven women sat in the center of an eleven-foot fire ring and chanted while seven other women, covered with an eight-foot-high cloaked sculpture moved ominously around the room echoing and extending the meaning of chants.

GK: *What does your concept of composing a "liturgy of the feminist movement" mean to you?*

MBE: It's basically a story of how we rallied together. We came out of isolation, learned to communicate with each other by trial and error, released our anger and rage to gain control of our lives, and began to define ourselves. We learned to comfort each other; we learned to feel good about each other. We unleashed our sensuality; released, unmuzzled, we began celebrating. The liturgy or ritual mirrors our evolving feminist process and ends with this celebration. The story of our new culture is the story of our liturgy: our sacred story.

In the ritual called "Memorial to Nine Million Women . . ." we chanted the actual names of women who were burned. We also chanted, "Have you asked yourself this question?," muffling the words by cupping our hands over our mouths. As the chant grew we articulated the words, representing our evolution in communication with each other and our awareness of our commonalities.

I also continue to do spontaneous rituals for friends: fertility rituals, healing, celebration, or commemorative, whatever is needed by an individual or a group.

GK: *Do you see any dangers emerging from practicing rituals?*

MBE: I feel that there is some danger of ritual becoming solidified and therefore, zapped of its energy—becoming repetitious rather than creative. Ritual should go beyond exercises. It should take us into another state, facilitate bringing about change and release. In fact ritual should be instrumental in releasing insights that push us out into futuristic, creative, energizing solutions to our problems in this world. When the ritual works, we emerge with enormous power: the power that comes from connecting with others, connecting with ourselves, and connecting with a power that we can recall after we leave the circle. Energy and power are the essence of creative ritual.

GK: *You tie together women's art and spirituality. How did you consciously get involved in the Women's Spirituality Movement? When did that begin for you?*

MBE: I was involved with Goddess a long time before the Women's Spirituality Movement. Many women like myself worked on our own, not having any idea that there were other women delving into the Goddess or women's spirituality. A conference called "Through the Looking Glass," held in Boston in 1975, allowed us to discover how many of us there were.

GK: *Did you begin with Jung and Neumann?*

Mary Beth Edelson
"Where Is Our Fire,"
Chico performance ritual
Spring 1979

Mary Beth Edelson
"See for Yourself,"
from Grapceva *series*
(pilgrimage to a neolithic cave,
Jelsa, Yugoslavia)
1977

MBE: What was available before the seventies was Jung, Bachofen,
and especially Erich Neumann's *The Great Mother*. That was
the eye-opener. Then *The First Sex*, by Elizabeth Gould
Davis, came along. But it was the feminist movement that put
us in contact with our womanness, our bodies, our sense of
self. This led us to an awareness that we needed to define
spirituality in our own terms. We are integrated thinkers, and
we soon noticed that our spirituality had been neglected or

defined for us by others—we needed to make our own searches.

GK: *How did the conference come into being?*

MBE: Five women from Boston called the "Pomegranate Productions" very bravely decided to chance sponsoring a conference with their own money and their own time, hoping to get a couple hundred women together. *Eighteen hundred* women showed up. It was an incredibly joyous moment for every woman the first time we got together and realized how many we were.

GK: *What other organization publications and periodicals do you see as part of the Women's Spirituality Movement?*

MBE: The journals *Womanspirit, Lady-Unique-Inclination-of-the-Night,* and the Goddess issue of *Heresies* represent the largest collection of articles on women's spirituality. Other conferences include one held on Staten Island immediately after the Boston conference; then in Santa Cruz, California, "The Great Goddess Re-emerging"; and your conference in Chico on "Feminist Visions of the Future." Books by Mary Daly, *Beyond God the Father,* and Merlin Stone's *When God Was a Woman* are important early contributions.[1]

GK: *When you look into the future of women's culture, what would you like to see occur as the patriarchy's five thousand years are up?*

MBE: Let me answer that in a more local sort of way. What I would really like to see women do is more collaborations, working together in small groups of no more than seven. Paying attention to our process and not just to the task or end product, creating a holistic life process. The "how and why" of the way we proceed is as critical as the finish. If the process has been lousy, then you're not building a brave new world or an enlightened community. We need to look to our own relationships. We also need to get out of our ghetto and into the world—we are strong enough now and need to be felt and seen everywhere.

I am hopelessly optimistic. I think that we'll be beautiful, strong, and powerful; that we will make it. Other people may eventually imitate our process, not only because it works but

Mary Beth Edelson
"Raising Firebird Energy"
(private performance ritual,
Port Clyde, Maine)
1978

because it is now so clear that this looted world must come around full circle to survive.

1. Since that time (1977) publications have proliferated. A selected listing:

   Daly, Mary. *Gyn/Ecology: The Metaethics of Radical Feminism.* Boston: Beacon, 1978.

Dinnerstein, Dorothy. *The Mermaid and the Minotaur.* New York: Harper Colophon, 1977.

Edelson, Mary Beth. *Seven Cycles: Public Rituals.* New York (110 Mercer St.): The author, 1980.

Griffin, Susan. *Woman and Nature.* New York: Harper and Row, 1979.

Halifax, Joan. *Shamanic Voices.* New York: Dutton Paperback, 1979.

Johnson, Buffie. *The Great Goddess and Her Sacred Animals.* New York: Thames and Hudson, 1981.

Pagels, Elaine, *The Gnostic Gospels.* New York: Random House, 1979.

Spretnak, Charlene. *The Politics of Women's Spirituality: Essays on the Rise of Spiritual Power Within the Feminist Movement.* New York: Doubleday, 1981.

Stone, Merlin. *Ancient Mirrors of Womanhood; Our Goddess and Heroine Heritage.* New York: New Sibylline, 1980.

ADDRESSES OF PERIODICALS AND SPECIAL ISSUES

Bread and Roses. Box 1230 Madison, WI 53701. Issue on women and spirituality (Vol. 2, No. 3). 1980.

Chrysalis. 635 South Westlake Avenue, Los Angeles, CA 90057. Issue No. 6 includes survey of women's spirituality and book reviews.

Heresies. Box 766, Canal Street Station, New York, NY 10013. "The Great Goddess Issue" (to be reissued). 1978

Lady-Unique-Inclination-of-the-Night. Box 803, New Brunswick, NJ 08903. All issues.

Womenspirit. Box 263, Wolf Creek, OR 97497. All issues.

WOMEN'S THEATRE:
CREATING THE DREAM NOW

Susan Suntree

In theatre the language and bodies of women are presented with few cloaks. Whatever effect a performer might want to create, the inner picture she has of herself will provide the boundaries of her performance. The playwright's or director's image of women shapes every decision about a woman character or performer. Rationally accepting fashionable ideas about women can only superficially shade the truth of an artist's convictions. Not only is it essential to uncover what our most basic images of women are, we must also discover the process of the creation of these original images so that, if we desire to, we might unravel that picture and begin another. Sorting the multifarious strands of our images allows us to weave again and again a more creative figure of ourselves.

The most direct and committed explorations of women's images in theatre have come from women themselves as women struggle to outgrow the psychic garb of patriarchal culture. Although such playwrights as Lillian Hellman and Clare Boothe Luce have provided traditionally structured plays that corroborate images of women as being male dominated and frustrated, these images are examined through emphasis on the experiences of the women characters. Recent work by women theatre artists has begun the difficult passage through negation and anger toward the creation of new images that challenge familiar assumptions.

Roots of this work can be seen in Gertrude Stein's experiments with form, especially language structures, as she sought to discover more than is already known about being alive.[1] Although her plays are often judged abstruse, her experiments provide a historical context for the work of such present-day playwrights as Megan Terry, Rochelle Owens, Alice Childress, Irene Fornas, and many others. Women continue to

Susan Suntree
in a moment from her ritual drama
Old Woman in the Snow
(photo by Heather Hafleigh)

write traditionally structured plays; however, much of today's women's writing is characterized by experimentation with form that yields new attitudes about the content of plays.

Many of Megan Terry's plays, for example *Viet Rock* and *Calm*

Down Mother, do not emphasize the development of characters. The action and impact of the content interest her most. Terry does not concentrate on how an individual states who she or he is, but on how circumstances and images stimulate personal responses and discoveries by actors and audiences.[2] This change in focus is related to work being done by experimental-theatre troupes in Europe and North America, where the concept of actor as artist rather than interpreter, and questions about an actor's relationship to an audience, are being confronted.

When there is a culturally accepted idea about women, it is easier for someone, traditionally a male, to feel confident, informed, and sensitive enough to create women characters, whose work on stage will reveal standard theories about men and women. Many theatre artists now realize that these images are the filtrate of a three-thousand–year history of misogyny. Consequently it is a serious challenge for anyone to create a woman character. Women theatre artists are especially sensitive to this issue. Many female characters created by the women playwrights of today are stylized, surreal, metaphorical, or totally autobiographical figures who yield to the unknown. These writers are too honest to settle for an illusion of reality when reality is in the process of being discovered. These creations of new images of women through new forms are some of the most important work being done in the theatre.

Throughout the country women are joining together to create women's theatre.[3] Although displaying a variety of styles, sizes, and professional intentions, the work of these groups has a significant commonality: they often derive their materials from the actual lives of women, including themselves. This intimate source of images has amazing power—and has created problems. As Joanne Temple has discussed, many women's theatre pieces have been unnecessarily homogeneous. Women forming theatre groups are often from similar socioeconomic backgrounds, which can challenge the players to find the dimensions of their experiences that are common to women from a variety of backgrounds.[4] After passing through vales of anger and negation to be rid of emotional connections to the old culture, women must be willing to enter the strata where the materials for theatre work include elemental experiences and primary concepts. Satires about birth control and mistreatment at work are genuine critiques. But work must continue toward the roots of our perceptions. By sharing the discovery of women's roots women's theatre can reveal a dimension of experience where the origins and spirit of sisterhood reside.

Contributing to this discovery of women's roots and expanding the definitions of modern theatre practice is the increasing use of ritual by women's groups. As Sherry Mestel, editor of Earth Rites Press, explains:

> Many of us as feminists have felt that we needed to develop an integration of our political analysis and our spiritual and psychic

awareness . . . at the present time wimmin are trying to recreate or reestablish rites and rituals to remember our old power, our collective unconscious which has been buried throughout recent history.[5]

A growing interest in Wicce[6] and in Native American women's rituals and point of view[7] has inspired the creation of dramatic forms expressing women's welling experience of inner strength and connection with nature, symbolized for many by various images of the Goddess. In my own work-in-progress the dynamics of women's theatre merge with my studies of folk dramas and rituals to create a cycle of four plays, *Old Woman in the Snow—Plays for the Seasons,* that are shaped like weavings from actor's experiences, primitive dramatic forms, and the immediacy of nature. Mary Beth Edelson, a New York performance artist, creates solo rituals that she documents as performance pieces, as well as choreographs group rituals. "What I am hoping for," she writes as introduction to a piece titled "Memorials to the 9,000,000 Women Burned as Witches in the Christian Era,"

> is that the performers and the audience will participate in connecting with each other as a single body during the brief life of the ritual. . . . In order for the audience to let go/release, trust needs to be established as well as the belief that this is an authentic experience.[8]

Experiments in form by women's theatre groups are often inspired by this felt need to be authentic, to show, through an embodiment in drama, real women's experiences. For example, The Wallflower Order, which began as a women's dance collective, now performs dance-theatre in response to the members' need to express more explicitly their experiences and politics.[9] Working with material drawn from actual women's lives, including the relationships among an ensemble itself, has demanded forms that traditional theatre has not developed. Women's theatre groups are notably collective in their approaches to shaping a piece. Experiment and improvisation are often mentioned as working methods, as opposed to the usual assumption that a director will define the performance—though a director, perhaps with newly defined status, is commonly included. Some groups choose a director for a particular piece, or members take turns directing. A few groups have writers as part of their ensembles and perform from scripts; others collaborate on a piece and write it as it develops. Terry Baum, cofounder of Lilith, a feminist theatre collective, speaking at the "Perspectives on Women in Theatre" series in San Francisco, described the evolution of Lilith's collective processes, which she sees as allowing more individual choices in the collective fabric.[10] Generally women's theatre groups use forms that are personal and fluid and reflect the genuine commitment the performers feel for their work.[11]

Because of the intimacy of the subjects explored in their plays some women's theatre groups perform only for women. Some have said that even when performed for mixed audiences their plays are created especially for women.[12] This intense connection between actor and audience carries remarkable energy, as well as a temptation to remain topically superficial or technically unevolved.

Women's theatre groups have an unusual opportunity. The intense personal interest women have in their images and history has created a kind of ancient original audience who believe that what is done on the stage may affect their lives in intimate, immediate ways. The personal commitment that women's theatre artists bring to their work is the most vital aspect of their relationship to their audiences. Both actor and audience join in an essential quest for themselves. The possibilities created by this kind of connection are boundless.

My encounter with the potential of women's theatre began during the winter of 1975–76, when I was involved in the Women's Ensemble of the Berkeley Stage Company, a theatre group in Berkeley, California. A meeting was called for people interested in forming a women's performing group using the Antigone myth as a focus. All the women who attended, including myself, formed the cast of nine players and a stage manager.[13] Few of us knew one another well or had previous experience in women's theatre. From the beginning we did not compete with one another, and this spirit informed the group's progress toward creating a cohesive ensemble. Our formal goal was to create collectively a theatre piece centered on our relationships to the Antigone myth, to be performed in about six weeks. After our first performances we revised our piece, *Antigone Prism*, during another six weeks of rehearsal. We were constantly altering and evolving our work since it arose from our self-perceptions, which were changing.

Our rehearsal methods involved exercise, discussion, improvisations derived from discussion and performers' suggestions . . . and discussion about how we discussed too much. We shared growing intimacy, fears, and amazement as our commitments to the work grew. Our initial recognitions about Antigone as myth yielded to the more difficult and rewarding task of finding ourselves in the myth and in creating a prismatic theatre piece with which to reveal our discoveries. We accepted the evolution of our work despite trepidations about the lack of a preconceived form. We began by sharing stories about our families and our ages, and through these stories we began to feel connected to one another and to our work. This led to further discussions about relationships, sexual politics, family, the search for new forms of expression, and feminism in the theatre. All of us had felt the constraints on women working in the theatre.

We came to see Antigone not as a person blinded by pride but as a woman accepting a restorative role in her culture. Most importantly, she chose herself by putting forth her belief in her own values and experiences. Her act of unrepentantly burying her brother in opposition to her uncle's decree was a positive step for women, despite the agonies she catalyzed. Her courage was reborn in us as we struggled to actualize our liberation. We became a nine-sided prism of Antigone. In Sophocles' *Antigone* the Chorus sings about how pride is the one real sin. Creon's rejection of his anima and of women revealed to us an essential aspect of pride: losing receptivity, closing oneself off. The hard historical fact of patriarchal pride is described by the Chorus as they admit to Antigone that she atones for an old sin. In the face of a grotesquely imbalanced society Antigone, risking death, chooses the unknown and thereby reveals her commitment to the creative powers that accept no less a risk.

How, then, did each of us experience Antigone's act? This would be the core of our performance. And of course we had to recognize how the plethora of trivia and the rigidities of institutions prevent us from experiencing the process of becoming ourselves. One of our improvisations at this juncture we called The Prism, in which each person performed a five-minute improvised solo based on a personal response to our work with the Antigone myth. The power and clarity that this exercise evoked directed us toward the final structuring of our piece.

As we worked our thoughts of the audiences we were to meet receded. Because we were audience to one another we grew accustomed to trying to speak with both honesty and tenderness. This atmosphere created the intimate tone of the piece we shaped and carried into performance. We never lost sight of our desire to communicate to an audience; the audience was always there.

The final shaping of our work created the most confusion and frustration. Our disagreements, voiced and implied, our tendencies to passivity and insecurity, were abundantly present. Unfortunately we did not adequately explore this material, but, pushed by performance dates, agreed on a rough format that finally evolved into a piece that was based on our prism exercise. We chose to open *Antigone Prism* by mixing with the entering audience, rather than separating ourselves behind a curtain. Our playing area was a long corridor with audience on three sides. Using lines from Sophocles' *Antigone*, which were echoed and moved from player to player, we began with the central problem presented by the myth: will you act to create yourself? Performers, who acted alone or used the ensemble to create images of their experiences, each responded to Antigone's question. After the last prism we formed an ensemble image chanting: "From my roots from my life I am born." Finally, still chanting, each performer left the circle and exited alone.

After each performance we offered wine and an invitation to talk with the actors, which gave us immediate feedback for our work. Generally people involved in theatre work felt that we had either created genuine drama or that our piece was not theatre at all because it lacked certain formal elements requisite of a play. A few people said they couldn't relate to the politics of our work, implying, it seemed, that it was not directly political enough or that we were not representative of the women's movement. Preconceived notions about women's experiences are in themselves a basis for women's oppression. Although all of us aspire to growth, making known our actual experiences is an essential politics. This introduces the question of theatre as therapy. At the center of the arts is the process of healing, through recognition in external images of our private experiences. When the internal and external worlds meet, though the image may be harsh, the resulting sense of truth and wholeness allows us the energy and affirmation to continue growing.

Mostly our audiences, who averaged about 70 percent women, were overwhelmingly supportive, many describing our work as the finest theatre experience they ever had. For us it was thrilling and bittersweet, since the group broke up thereafter. This was for many of us both the most popular and the most personally demanding show we had ever done.

The task of redefining women's images is being undertaken by women theatre artists working in a variety of groups and styles. Some women, who were formerly solely actors, are finding recognition as directors. Women theatre artists are introducing new concepts (such as child care) to the formats of their companies. The venerable image of women performers being young and childless is slowly changing, as JoAnne Akalaitis reports. Her troupe, Mabou Mines, absorbs the cost of child care for performers' children and has included obviously pregnant actors in their pieces. [14]

How we imagine ourselves to be is what we become. Experiencing the body creating new images of women and, inseparably, of men in performance is powerful input to expanding consciousness. With its emphasis on the use of actual experiences as source material and collective organization, women's theatre is a spirited member of the experimental-theatre community. Also women's theatre provides special leaven to modern theatre through the personal commitment of its performers, whose involvement is in contrast with the stereotypical actors' concerns with career and prestige. Personal commitment is a hallmark of women's theatre's relationship with its audiences, who often attend performances with a similar desire for crucial insights and affirmation. This engagement with social problems and personal experiences, presented to the audiences who live them and who attend a performance feeling that this theatre might really matter, underscores the power of theatre art to touch a core of reality and stimulate change.

It reveals an evolution of artistic consciousness moving closer to the mythic, that center where the unknown is courageously brought into relationship with the known, than to the distractions of criticism and ideological amusements that tend to absorb the avant garde. People are realizing that our bodies not only are vehicles of a historical culture but also of dreams that we can realize now.

Notes

1. Gertrude Stein. *Selected Operas and Plays of Gertrude Stein.* Edited and with an introduction by John Malcolm Brinnin. Pittsburgh: University of Pittsburgh Press, 1970, p.xiii.

2. Megan Terry. *Viet Rock and Other Plays.* With an introduction by Richard Scheckner. New York: Simon and Schuster, 1967, pp. 10–18.

3. Rosemary Curb, Phyllis Mael, and Beverly Byers Pevitts. "Catalogue of Feminist Theatre—Parts 1 & 2," *Chrysalis*, 10 (Spring 1980), 51–75.

4. Joanne Temple. "Women's Theatre Finds a Stage of Its Own," *Village Voice*, October 27, 1975, p.84.

5. Sherry Mestel, ed. *Earth Rites.* Vol. 2: *Rituals.* New York: Earth Rites, 1978, Introduction.

6. See Starhawk. *The Spiral Dance.* New York: Harper and Row, 1979.

7. See Carolyn Niethammer. *Daughters of the Earth.* New York: Collier, 1977.

8. Mary Beth Edelson. "Public Rituals," *Earth Rites.* Vol. 2: *Rituals.* New York: Earth Rites, 1978, p.47.

9. Krissy Keefer, member of The Wallflower Order. Interview, Nevada City, May 1980.

10. Terry Baum, speaking at the "Perspectives on Women in Theatre" series, Fort Mason, San Francisco, August 1979.

11. Lillian Perinciolo. "Feminist Theatre: They're Playing in Peoria," *Ms.* 4, 4 (October 1975), 101–104.

12. Charlotte Rea. "Women for Women," *Drama Review*, 18 (December 1974), 77 and 79.

13. The Women's Ensemble for *Antigone Prism* included Carole Goodrich, Kathryn Howell, Angela Paton, Elizabeth Ratcliff, Peggy Roggenbuck, Jean Schiffman, Danza Squire, Susan Suntree, Marianne Weiss. Greta Sholachman was the stage manager. Robert Slattery proposed the project.

14. Sally R. Sommer. "JoAnne Akalaitis of Mabou Mines," *Drama Review*, 20 (September 1976), 13–15.

Selected Bibliography

BOOKS

Brown, Janet. *Feminist Drama; Definition and Critical Analysis*. Metuchen, N.J.: Scarecrow, 1979.

France, Rachel, ed. *A Century of Plays by American Women*. New York: Richards Rosen, 1978.

Grimstad, Kristen, and Susan Rennie, eds. *The New Woman's Survival Sourcebook*. Chapter on "Theatre." New York: Knopf, 1975.

Heilbrun, Carolyn G. *Toward a Recognition of Androgyny*. New York: Harper Colophon, 1973.

Hoch-Smith, Judith, and Anita Spring, eds. *Women in Ritual and Symbolic Roles*. New York: Plenum, 1978.

La Tempa, Susan, ed. *New Plays By Women*. Berkeley, Calif.: Shameless Hussy, 1979.

Mestel, Sherry, ed. *Earth Rites*. Vol. 2: *Rituals*. New York: Earth Rites, 1978.

Moore, Honor, ed. *The New Women's Theatre: Ten Plays by Contemporary American Women*. New York: Vintage, 1977.

Niethammer, Carolyn. *Daughters of the Earth*. New York: Collier, 1977.

Sophocles. *Antigone*, in *Greek Tragedies*. Vol. 1. Edited by David Grene and Richmond Lattimore. Chicago: University of Chicago Press, 1960.

Starhawk. *The Spiral Dance*. New York: Harper and Row, 1979.

Stein, Gertrude. *Selected Operas and Plays of Gertrude Stein*. Edited and introduced by John Malcolm Brinnin. Pittsburgh: University of Pittsburgh Press, 1970.

Sullivan, Victoria, and James Hatch, eds. *Plays By and About Women*. New York: Random House, 1973.

Terry, Megan. *Viet Rock and Other Plays*. With an introduction by Richard Scheckner. New York: Simon and Schuster, 1967.

_____. *Approaching Simone*. With an introduction by Phyllis Jane Wagner. New York: Feminist Press, 1973.

JOURNALS AND MAGAZINES

Curb, Rosemary, Phyllis Mael, and Beverly Byers Pevitts. "Catalogue of Feminist Theatre—Parts 1 & 2," *Chrysalis*, 10 (Spring 1980), 51–75.

Drama Review, 18 (September 1974) 132–133. This issue contains a brief review of the New York Feminist Theatre Troupe.

Gillespie, Patti. "Feminist Theatres of the 1970's," *Theatre News*, (November 1977), 5*ff*.

Lamb, Margaret. "Feminist Criticism," *Drama Review*, 18 (September 1974), 46–50.

Moore, Honor. "Theatre Will Never Be the Same," *Ms*. 6, 6 (December 1977), 36–39, 74–75.

Pocock, Linda. "Interview: Andrea Ballis Inside Section Ten," *Majority Report*, (June 14, 1975).

Perinciolo, Lillian. "Feminist Theatre: They're Playing in Peoria," *Ms.*, 4, 4 (October 1975), 101–104.

Rea, Charlotte. "Women for Women," *Drama Review*, 18 (December 1974), 77–87.

_____. "Women's Theatre Groups," *Drama Review*, 16 (June 1972), 79–80.

Sommer, Sally R. "JoAnne Akalaitis of Mabou Mines." *Drama Review*, 20 (September 1976) 4–16. There are six interviews with women theatre artists in this issue.

Stone, Laurie. "Sister/Sister—Working It Out on Stage," *Ms.*, 7, 5 (November 1978), 40–45.

Wolff, Ruth. "The Aesthetics of Violence: Women Tackle the Rough Stuff," *Ms.*, 7, 8 (February 1979), 30–36.

NEWSPAPERS AND PLAY PROGRAMS

Lilith: A Women's Theatre Collective. Programs for *Good Food* (April–May 1975) and *Moonlighting: A Play About Women and Work* (April 1976). San Francisco.

Temple, Joanne. "Women's Theatre Finds a Stage of Its Own," *Village Voice*, October 27, 1975, p.84.

Susan Suntree *is a playwright, poet, and actor who lives in Grass Valley, California. Formerly she was a college English instructor, having an M.A. in English from the University of Kent, England. She is a researcher in folk drama and ritual.*

WOMEN'S IMAGES IN FILM

Barbara Hammer

Independent women filmmakers, women who make films for themselves and within the "art for art's sake" aesthetic, are most free to make
images that are particularly unique to them as women. There are image
clusters or methods of using imagery that are female; that is, we can find
similarities of image and image use in women's films. Whether these
women's images are "caused" or "come from" biological differences or
the differences in social training and acculturation I do not know.
Living as we do in this culture of rigid separation of conditioning for
women and men, we women are taking on the work of identifying
image difference for the growing understanding of women's culture. We
need to write and talk and discuss and argue and state as clearly as we
can what we feel to be our differences and hence our strengths.

I shall examine the images in films by myself, Maya Deren, and
Marie Menken; the methods of forms of film imagery in the films of
Joyce Wieland, Barbara Linkevitch, and Chick Strand; and the blend of
content and form in a film by Gunvor Nelson and Dorothy Wiley. In
talking about imagery I shall separate the personal imagery of interior
bodily states of feeling from the more universal ritualistic imagery of the
archetypes, although these are often one and the same. In discussing the
methods of how imagery is used I shall examine how the structure or
context determines the significance or meaning through creative editing, use of shots, manipulation of time, and change of focus.

The imagery that women use comes from states of feeling, in contrast
to cerebral, or abstract, imagery, which is not the idea or thing but
represents it. *Feeling images* are images that are the feeling, they make
the feeling. They do not have the secondary function of representation
but are the fact itself. The imagery is less likely to be separated from
what it is. When I begin to gather imagery for a film, I pay attention to
imagery that arises from meditation on body feelings, or I make note of

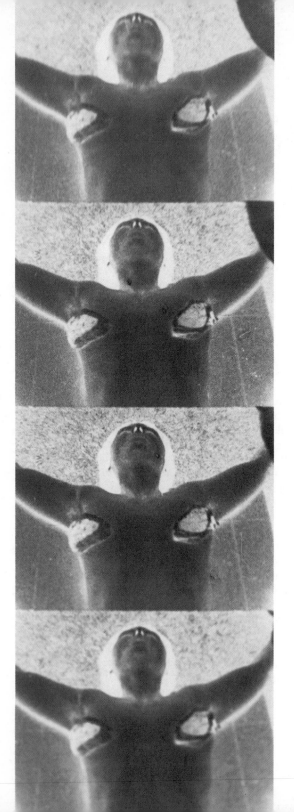

*Barbara Hammer
Frames from
"X"*

the visual scenes and significances I see in waking imagination and sleeping dreams.

Body images are prevalent in women's films. Women know the world through their internal organs, the muscular structure, the way the bones rest, the skin's sensitivity. This holistic epistemology, or method of relating to the world, means that many of the images in the films are directly from or of the body. In my film "X" I use imagery of disembowelment and meat slices or body carcasses. I had recently broken up with a lover; I felt used, I felt as though my guts were spilling out, I felt as though I was a carcass—and so that was the given imagery. How different might that imagery have been if I had been terribly cerebral and wrote a script about the dissolution of a relationship and then looked for images to fit the feeling, to stand in for the fact? What might I use with that method? Two cars bashed in and wrecked head-on? A house in flames? These images are not to be discarded, but it is clear that they are "out there," exterior, compared with the very interior image of body meat. The meat, the blood, the red, is the anger, the pain, the stripped-bare feeling.

In a positive and loving film of the female body, *Dyketactics*, I tried to postpone full-frame shots of two women in bed—shots that lose the intimacy and feeling quality of the closeup and so often miss the very essential of female love: the touch, the tenderness, the slow evolution through care, and the heightened sensitivity that characterize women's loving—until this softness, this touching quality is clear. The hundred and ten images in this four-minute film are edited to touch, or what I call "kinesthetics." The film moves from bare feet on dry grass to legs in water moving, to finger scooping a cantaloupe's milky seeds, to finger touching mouth, to water bathing, hair washing, tree touching, to digging in the earth, to reaching through air to the sky, to women hand-holding circle enfolding dance all one and together. No image unless touch. Once that sensuality of skin texture has been accumulated the film moves to the explicit shots of two women stroking and kissing and holding and making love.

Structural film is usually thought of as film that explores the nature of the medium, for example the zoom ratio of a lens, the sprocket holes of the film itself, the linear succession of static images that persistence of vision reads as movement. Conceptual or structural film can arise from a source other than the mind: the body. From scientific understanding and intuitive feelings I experience wisdom in muscles, internal organs, skin. Body intelligence is sister to the mind. Letting the body lead, letting the fluid imagery come from movement or kinesthetic sense, letting the concept, the structure, the order, be body determined is another way of making structural film.

In a recent film of mine, *Available Space*, my body gave me images

Barbara Hammer
Still from Dyketactics

and sensations of being tied to my camera, of being yoked into the rectangle of the frame, of being confined. The longest cable release I could find was still an umbilical cord. I wanted a private art again (I worked as a studio painter before becoming filmmaker) and would accept the limitations of a static camera, tripod, and cable release to gain this privacy of experience in shooting. At the same time I had an interior sense of the limitations of the film frame, which I experienced as a form of claustrophobia. I wanted to fill and define and push that rectangular frame as fully and from as many ways that I could. My body tells me to do this; from this sense of filling up the frame, pushing (literally with my hands and feet against the edges of the frame for the filmic image) against the walls of illusion, as determined by the arbitrary nature of the camera, projector, and film, I find, experientially, the next step, the next possibility, the next link. Film in this case is not a priori but is spontaneously considered, added, subtracted, linked, in an ongoing process of dialogue and exchange between the body and mind of the filmmaker. In *Available Space*, after I traced the permutations of filling and pushing the frame and the limitations, I began to rotate the projector with the finished film projection in all the available space in the theatre. Mounted on a 360-degree turning table, the total circle projection fulfills my physical need to use all the space available.

Maya Deren (1917–1961), the early filmmaker who helped establish independent cinema in the United States and who is lauded for the content and structure of her four completed films, wrote of her particular use of inner imagery. Deren's father was a psychiatrist who practiced Freudian symbolic interpretations of events and things. Deren reacted to this formalist tradition by creating her own concept that inanimate objects in her films did not represent more than themselves but held all the connotative significances within their form. The bread knife on the table in *Meshes in the Afternoon* (1943) does not represent a weapon or a penis; it is a cutting instrument and within its steel and sharpness gathers all its significance. Of course it has a different feeling-meaning depending on whether it is on the table between bread and coffee cup or in the hands of a woman stabbing. The way the objects are depicted is dependent on the inner state of the protagonist. In a letter she wrote: "*Meshes* is, one might say, almost expressionist; it externalizes an inner world to the point where it is confounded with the external one."[1] The knife, the key to the house, the figure in black with the mirror face, the dropping flower, the house in disarray, the spinning architectonic structure of hallways and stairway descents and window tubes—all these are feeling imagery that came from Deren's inner state of being as it moved from beginning flatness devoid of feeling in *Meshes* to heightened emotion.

> . . . it reproduces the way in which the sub-conscious of an individual will develop, interpret and elaborate an apparently simple and casual incident into a critical emotional experience.
> . . . Part of the achievement of this film consists in the manner in which cinematic techniques are employed to give a malevolent vitality to inanimate objects.[2]

Maya Deren was a leader in avant garde film in many ways besides this special use of inanimate objects. She was the forerunner of the structuralist filmmakers, describing in great detail the intricate formal concerns that accompany her contents from film to film. She was also an innovator of the ritual film, the film that extends beyond the subjective first person to the mythopoeic world of archetypal imagery. She described her intent in making *Ritual in Transfigured Time* (1946):

> In this sense, the pattern, created by the film instrument, transcends the intentions and movements of the individual performers, and for this reason I have called it *Ritual*. I base myself upon the fact that, anthropologically speaking, a ritual is a form which depersonalizes by use of masks, voluminous garments, group movements, etc. and, in so doing, fuses all individual elements into a transcendent tribal power towards the achievement of some extraordinary grace.[3]

Ritual in Transfigured Time is an exemplary film in its universal feminine imagery. The women dressed in black; the spinner, the holder of the thread, the three graces, the waiting figure in the doorway, the bride. The inanimate objects—wool, interior doorways, calla lilies, water, statues, shawls of textured cloth—all take on universal significance by a heightened sense of reality emphasized by editing and soundtrack even though they are the ordinary objects women use and are familiar with in their home world.

> *Ritual in Transfigured Time* develops even further the special emphasis upon form which governed, to an increasing extent, my previous films. . . . I would like to use the word "classicist" to describe *Ritual in Transfigured Time* precisely because it does not define according to the elements of the content—factual, fictional, abstract or psychological. It is a concept of method: a controlled manipulation of any or all elements into a form which will transcend and transfigure them.[4]

Deren repeats sections of the party sequence so that she can use the same scene more than once and so make universal movements that seem to have personal meaning. The repeated sequences have significance beyond the image of two people reaching for each other at a party and classically enlarges the scope of the film to ritual.

Marie Menken (d. 1971) was a visual poet of the stature of Maya Deren, but unfortunately she has not received the acclaim she deserves. Menken's imagery is that often found in women's films: moons, rain, paint, eggs, food, animals, minutiae like sidewalk cracks. Women look at small things, supposedly unimportant, that are found in or near their environment—which traditionally has been the home. Menken learned to pay attention to the small, and by doing so she enlarged a vision that otherwise might be confined. *Moonplay* is a living visual of the screen, in which the moon, shrouded in clouds, gives birth to herself in a tremendous animation of energy across and around, galloping in screen space. The camera vibrates in the filmmaker's hand, marking her breathing, and the moon lives for us a fantastic creature in eclipse and full splendor. When the moon begins to circle, the effect is breathtaking: a circle within a circle. Women know and feel the moon to be special to them as imagery for the early and still-active moon goddess spirituality of our heritage, matriarchy.

In the exquisite *Notebook* Menken records a visual diary, opening with a scene of near-white on white, of equivocal space undefined until two ducks enter screen right and the distinction between horizon and pond is clear. In this first section of *Notebook*, called "Raindrops," Menken is exceptionally subtle as she cuts from the active falling of the drops to the still circle of their fall. In this footage (which she saved for twenty years before editing into a final form) Menken shows us the sensitivity of her vision. In "Greek Epiphany" the highlights of candlelight of a Greek Orthodox procession and in "Night Writing," the neon moving lights of the street, define her as a lyrical painter of screen light.

Menken physically moves with her camera, carrying it close in her bag or slinging it on her shoulder. This is apparent in her films, which have the spontaneity of freedom with their unorthodox, unscripted, free-wheeling, painterly nature. When Menken moves into the exterior world of New York, she brings the feminine scrutiny of the parts within the whole. In *Excursion* she single-frames a boat ride around Manhattan Island, and the people on the boat move like the surge that the boat creates. We know the camera is in her hands by the intimate shake of the image. The shoreline moves: rocks and cars are the same in their animated units; a powerful revolution takes place as the passengers (a series of juxtaposed still shots, as movie film is) become moving hulks of mass. Menken performs the alchemical act of physics in the powerful revolution of mass to energy. In another film East River barges and boats are also shot in pixillation, or one frame every few seconds, so that large ships become toys moving atop the water in slides and glides, small and funny. In *Andy Warhol* she pokes fun at the world of industry and mass production. The animated painted Brillo boxes Warhol makes move in the same rhythm as the gallery viewers who have come to the opening of his Brillo show. In another scene Warhol is surrounded by his imagery of Jacqueline Kennedy and seemingly is bored with his repetitions; he sits in the middle of the redundant imagery reading, reading, never looking up or out, hiding behind inscrutable dark glasses.

This is our age, Menken seems to say, when the real workers who are loading the railroad trucks with the real Brillo boxes have become cultural workers like Warhol who imitate the real without the added value of use.

Besides her wonderful and luscious textural films of paint, *Dwigt-ana*, *Copycat*, and *Drips in Strips*, Menken made an amazing textural film in black-and-white of sidewalk cracks and cement flakes. The entire screen moves with the rhythm of her eye/lens and her walk; the sea of excess is crack upon line, the swimming accumulation of detail revolving in a morass of dizzy collecting. The screen space is lyrical, the subjective protagonist is the filmmaker, and the film we see is her perceptive and unique female vision.

Often the way in which imagery is used in independent women's films is as important as the imagery itself. In fact the successful film is one in which form grows from content so that image and use of image are inextricably interwoven like fine linen. Joyce Wieland and Barbara Linkevitch are two filmmakers whose films' structures grow from the contents of the imagery they use.

The Canadian Joyce Wieland's early film *Catfood* displays her fascination with animals, and in particular their eating habits. The minimal imagery is a cat devouring four or five fish on a white tablecloth. The structure or form is the simple but total eating of the fish. The camera is in several positions, yet the attention is on the cat devouring, rather savagely, the fish over and over again. The editing of repetitious consumption (that is, the form of the film) makes the content—the perception of the way a cat eats fish—a detail that a woman would perceive.

In Wieland's magnificent *Rat Life and Diet in America* the imagery is again small animals, this time gerbils, caged gerbils that represent the caged and frustrating life of Americans who live in a police state. The gerbils are seen within their cage; the soundtrack is an ominous buzz; the scope of a firing gun in red follows their movement; the lurking and immense head of a cat is outside the cage watching the charges, following every move closely. In this film Wieland combines animal imagery with political criticism: shots of Ché Guevara intercut with an escaped rat in the woods, plus the words "some of the bravest are lost forever," heighten the irony. I love the tongue-in-cheek (or, rather, "sticking-out-tongue") attitude as the gerbils run amok on a fancy dinner table, having finally escaped to the accompanying words, "they occupy a millionaire's house and get a bit to eat." Patriotic humor and the proverbial hostility toward Americans by Canadians is shown in the next scene, in which the rats escape to Canada and take up organic gardening, complete with a national song and the beautiful cherry festival. The propaganda says, "No DDT used here," and Wieland does not hesitate to

Barbara Linkevitch
Still from Chinamoon

tell us loud and clear at the end that "this is a corrective film," an early contribution to feminist ecology.

Barbara Linkevitch's films are examples of how creative manipulation of image and sound through editing heightens the sensual quality of her imagery. The films are intricately edited visual paintings of female sensuality: a closeup shot of a woman's hand sliding down her torso, the play of lip movements between two women face to face, low-angle shots accentuating a bustline, heavy makeup and curly hair filling or half-filling the frame. In *Traces* the camera is closeup to accentuate the textural sensuality of thickly applied lipstick and mascara. A cigarette is lit with a burst of flame, one nail-painted hand striking the match, and the image is body and paint and flame, and the overtones are seductive and diabolical. The freeze frame of the cigarette light stops time and motion, thus intensifying the compelling emotional quality of this film. Always the female body and the impending doom or threat of malevolence are in her films—the destructive side of Kali. One of the last images of *Traces* is a dinner scene in which a turkey is carved, a turkey as brown/red as the fingernails, the meat image again of the sexual body. Then the closeup of the fish hook leads to the pole, the fishing pole of power and tension, and then the mirror pond of the white reflecting face of death: female sexuality suffocated and destroyed.

In *Chinamoon* Linkevitch uses the blood red of roses and lipstick, wine and blood, in a bordello setting to make a tremendously sensual color film of closeups and focus change. The film moves from foreground image to obscurity to background image all in extreme close views of inanimate objects. Cloth textures of satin and silk, nylons, and patent leather shoes are intercut with the object imagery, now intensified by the closeups: Chinese statuary, wine glasses, shining daggers, cut and broken glass, tattoos, nails, mascaraed eyelids. It is a witch's cauldron, an evil witch. The pace of intrigue mounts to a degree unattainable with a medium shot or a long shot establishing environment. Instead Linkevitch creates an ominously beautiful surrounding of evil that is timeless and placeless but emotionally *there*.

Chick Strand is another filmmaker whose work is a wonderful personal combination of documentary and imaginative imagery. In *Guacamole* she shows us the details of life in a Mexican village. The details are lush and beautiful before her close telephoto photography, but the focus changes when the harsh reality of survival is recounted by a working man's monologue. Strand has an eye for detail and a quick-cutting hand that moves us intimately through the imagery of San Miguel de Allende as if a sorcerer had us under her wing showing us the little visions of the town. The screen is a huge mouth of a child on a trumpet, then it is a mouth of an old man playing, then it is fingers, then back to mouth. More intimate is her footage of a bullfight in a small ring with a zoom into the intense red blood pouring out of the bull's black back; it is both sensuous and horrible. We become as fascinated with the details as the filmmaker behind the camera.

An Indian dance is shot in closeup of feathers and beads and children's faces; animals closeup, a donkey's eye, a pig's snout, a baby donkey nursing. The voiceover soundtrack to these luscious images is a man who recounts the death he has known in his life: "She died in my arms talking about sister." The voice over the animals is: "Only time I ate meat was when we killed rats." A hoe is so close to the camera it is blurred in movement and frozen in a flash as it hits the ground, blurred when raised, still by the face, then down again with a blur. Enrapturing. The sound: "I went to the U.S. because there was not enough to eat here." The sad true talk continues through his drinking and finally to a return to Mexico and a new family life. "We are tired of machismo," the father says; his ethnic heritage has become a trap.

This same sensitivity to other people that Chick Strand shows in her Mexican films she applies to an autobiographical study of amnesia, euphoria, and ecstasy in her latest film, *Elasticity*. "I am looking for the face I had before the world was made," she said, describing the scrutiny she made in *Elasticity*.[5] It is a dream of meditation: the old woman looking for a stone, a glint of light filling the screen, the beauty of flypaper in a closeup, and an impressionistic series of old film reruns, on and on until the light of the projector hits the filmmaker in the face and the entire film is rerun backward, a single frame from each scene at a time until the first scene, of the old lady in the field looking for a stone, is reached. She tells us the secret of life: "A stone wants to be a cloud."

The content of a film can be expressly feminine, as in the most recent film of Gunvor Nelson and Dorothy Wiley. The feature-length *Before Need* is one of the most visually sensual and feminine films, featuring an extraordinary aging woman, Dorothy Wiley's mother-in-law, who recounts her life represented by a group of women and men of varying ages who emerge from the film little by little like fragments from a dream. This film is about feminine memory. It begins with the perceptual phenomenon of the baby, who learns to distinguish object from ground with the blankets, sheets, grapes, and marbles within view. As the baby's focus goes in and out from clarity so too does the old woman's in this brilliantly shot and edited poetic feature.

"It's like a memory or recitation of her different stages of life," recounted Gunvor Nelson at the premiere showing of the film. "It was like putting together a jigsaw puzzle without a picture," said Dorothy Wiley after commenting that it took a year to edit, "to search for a form in there."[6]

A striking feature of the film is the content editing, in which the image in one frame suggests the next cut (that is, the next image). For example, at one point the screen is filled with an extreme closeup of the bottom of an iron that has a scorched intricate lace design on its burned surface; the next image is a similar meticulous pattern of tattooed people. There is the contrast of the cut from the closeup of an iron on satin to a hot iron sitting on a steaming, melting, dripping block of ice.

Before Need is a well-constructed film about the process of women aging. Its form is integrally evolved from its content. The old woman finds that as she ages she gets "far enough away to see clearly"; she laments her earlier days, when she was "already too near to see it." The key statement emerging from the interwoven whispers, mutterings, and muted comments on the complex soundtrack—"We didn't know it then but this was our romance"—suggests that the richness of life passes all too quickly and without the appreciation it deserves.

We may not know it now, but this is our romance: we are immersed in a women's cultural revolution. I hope that the images and the screen are far enough away for me to see clearly as I try to distinguish the outstanding feminine characteristics of women filmmakers in their imagery and filmic constructive techniques. As feminism grows into the cultural warp of the societal framework, is integrated within the cultural norm, I hope that we do not become too familiar, too near, to see the natural, productive, and unique sources of imagery contributed by women filmmakers. I ask the readers as the viewing audience to recognize and appreciate the feminine imagery in film art. Although Maya Deren was speaking about the independent filmmaker in general, I ask you to read her words with women filmmakers and a feminine aesthetic in mind:

> It is not only the film artist who must struggle to discover the esthetic principles of the first new art form in centuries; it is the audience, too, which must develop a receptive attitude designed specifically for film and free of the critical criteria which have been evolved for all the older art forms. [7]

Notes

1. Maya Deren. "Letter to James Card," *Film Culture*, 39 (Winter 1965), 31.

2. _____. "Program Notes on Three Early Films," *Film Culture*, 39 (Winter 1965), 1.

3. _____. "Ritual in Transfigured Time," *Film Culture*, 39 (Winter 1965), 6.

4. *Ibid.*

5. Chick Strand. Discussion following her film show at Canyon Cinemateque, San Francisco Art Institute, January 29, 1976.

6. Gunvor Nelson and Dorothy Wiley. Discussion following the premiere of *Before Need* at Canyon Cinemateque, San Francisco Art Institute, September 27, 1979.

7. Maya Deren. "Movie Journal," *Film Culture*, 39 (Winter 1965), 31.

Selected Bibliography

Curtis, David. *Experimental Cinema*. New York: Universe, 1971.

Dawson, Bonnie. *Women's Films in Print*. San Francisco: Bootlegger, 1975.

Deren, Maya. *Film Culture*, 39 (Winter 1965).

Sitney, P. Adams. *Visionary Film*. New York: Oxford University Press, 1974.

Sullivan, Kaye. *Films For, By, and About Women*. Metuchen, N.J.: Scarecrow, 1980.

Barbara Hammer *is a filmmaker and video and performance artist, with M.A.s in film and literature from San Francisco State University. She has made over twenty-five 16mm films (available from Goddess Films, Box 2446, Berkeley, CA 94702).*

WOMEN AND FASHION

Barbara Kimball

Women have played an important part in the growth and advance of the fashion industry, most notably during the twentieth century. According to Marylou Luther, fashion editor of the *Los Angeles Times*, "This is the era of the woman designer; she is at her all time peak."[1]

This is also the era of fashion liberation, which has resulted from women's emerging freedom in lifestyles. Feminist Betty Friedan calls it a "sex-role revolution." It is only recently that women have freed themselves from the Parisian haute couture dictatorship, as exemplified by their rejection of the midiskirt in 1970. Women are becoming increasingly independent in their choice of clothing.

Where sex roles have been crystalized into male dominance and female submissiveness, as it has been for many centuries in many countries, apparel has often been designed to please the male. As "sex objects" women have submitted to miserable confinement and restriction, such as the tiny bound feet that crippled Chinese women, and, in the Western world, tortuously corseted bodies. As recently as the twentieth century women wore hobble skirts, which reduced walking to mincing little steps. Even little girls were corseted.

Fashion mirrors the times, reflecting social, political, spiritual, and economic factors. The fashion designer creates in response to these forces. Anatole France said, "Show me the fashion of a country, and I will write its history."

Pioneers

There have been pioneering women who have tried to help free women from restrictive role-confining fashions. One of them was Amelia Jenks Bloomer. She opened the Rational Dress Campaign in 1849 by wearing and promoting bloomers, which were a combination of long knicker-

Gabrielle "Coco" Chanel

bockers and cossacks plus a skirt worn over all. The outfit was not well received, and women were harassed when they wore the new style on the streets. Bloomer was a harbinger of the future popularity of pants for women, but she was a century too early.

Fashion authority Eleanor Lambert believes that "the women's movement brought a period of inhibition against the classic femininity in dress, but that has now balanced out. As women know who they are and their limitless potentials, they will no longer fear to express their sex through clothes."[2] Although various designers have laid claim to freeing women from the corset, the first woman designer to have great impact was Gabrielle "Coco" Chanel of Paris. She was a true pioneer in giving women good-looking clothes in which they could feel comfortable and be at ease, clothes that were more suitable to changing lifestyles. World War I brought women into new and more active roles outside the home. Chanel eliminated the pushed-out, exaggerated bosoms and derrières that were fashionable in 1914.

Diana Vreeland, former editor of *Vogue* and *Harper's Bazaar* and producer of the Metropolitan Museum of Art's highly successful fashion exhibitions, writes:

We all know that Chanel captured the true spirit of the twentieth century, and she remains the most important designer of the last sixty years. She had a complete view of a very modern woman. She turned out women who looked like Eton boys in cropped skirts, cashmere cardigans, and shirts. She realized that the times were changing and the long shadow of the Belle Epoque (1900–1910) had to be cut back. And in 1925 she came across with the sort of clothes we are still wearing today.[3]

In 1954 Chanel came out with the first tweed cardigan suit, with its short jacket, a classic style that is still popular and fashionable. Among other Chanel "firsts" are the first leather coat, the first pair of women's pants, the first jersey knits, and the first sleeveless dress.

Among Chanel's dicta:

It is not the dress that should wear the woman, but the woman who should wear the dress.

A dress that is not comfortable is a failure. To be elegant is to wear clothes that permit you to move easily, gracefully, comfortably.

Beauty is charm which has nothing to do with looks; and it is physical proportion—nothing too much, everything in balance.

In the difficult and wonderful battle of life, the simple woman emerges victorious, the sophisticated one, defeated.

Chanel biographer Marcel Haedrich feels that Chanel turned relations between men and women upside down: "Women pushed their way close to her in order to breathe the air of freedom. Coco was selling them a new art of living. Her own independent lifestyle and the new freedom of fashion which she introduced had a great influence internationally."[4]

In France, England, Italy

As the original hub of the fashion wheel and its founding "mother," Paris has been a magnet for creative talent. Rosette Hargrove of Newspaper Enterprises Association writes from Paris: "A resident buyer here sums it up this way: 'The reservoir of creators in France is bottomless.

There are more talented creators popping up every year. Not all are French. But all come to create because Paris offers a fashion atmosphere, a mentality that exists nowhere else in the world.'"

The Parisian haute couture was founded in 1856 by Charles Frederick Worth. Its impact is still powerful, but it has changed. Designers no longer attempt to revolutionize a line each year. In Paris now the *prêt-à-porter* (ready-to-wear) on the Left Bank coexists with the haute couture on the Right Bank. In addition to its custom fashions the haute couture has opened boutiques with ready-to-wear lines (plus parfumeries) in order to compete and survive. The wealthy and more conservative women support the haute couture; the designers of the Left Bank are frequently more innovative and daring.

Other outstanding French women designers who have earned special distinction for their contributions to fashion are Mme. Grès, Nina Ricci, Madeleine Vionnet, Elsa Schiaparelli, Mme. Joseph Paquin, Jeanne Lanvin, and Sonia Rykiel.

Mme. Grès, who has been turning out magnificant designs since 1936, is famed for her beautiful draped jersey dresses inspired by Greek costume. Her influence on fashion has also been important in the administrative arena. She served for many years as president of the elite Chambre Syndicale de la Couture Parisienne, a post most often held by men. She initially had wanted to be a sculptor. Dior said of her: "Every dress she creates is a masterpiece."

Madeleine Vionnet gained world recognition as the creator of the bias-cut, a classic dressmaking technique that is still used today.

Elsa Schiaparelli's force was that of a fresh, ebullient talent that alighted like a butterfly on the fashion scene, a talent that no doubt would have been equally successful in any other of the arts. "Shocking Pink" was her trademark—and shock the world she did. She was the first of the haute couture to experiment with synthetic fibers and was the first to use the zipper. She made a "glass dress" by mixing silk with fiberglass. In an attic workshop at the start of her career she parlayed the first dressy pullover top (silk with a white bowknot knitted into the front) into a highly successful fashion establishment.

Mme. Paquin helped to unite the leading French dressmakers into worldwide sales, a boon to the fashion world.

In England outstanding women designers are Jean Muir, Thea Porter, Zandra Rhodes, and Mary Quant.

Jean Muir is considered to be the genius of matte jersey. She helps women by designing "all-purpose" dresses, which can be worn in the daytime and on into the evening. She makes classic clothes with a long lifespan and is not concerned with trends. She designs for *Vogue Patterns*.

Muir admires women like Geraldine Stutz (president of Henri Bendel of New York) "who are marvellously strong and definite, but at the same time enormously feminine, people whose style of thinking comes through not only in dress but in everything they do."[5]

In Italy Mila Chon is considered by many to be the world's greatest tailor. Milan is her base, as it is for Rosita Missoni. Missoni and her husband, Tai, are famed for their beautiful knitwear, uniquely patterned and often feathery light in weight. For travelers these knit creations are ideal. Missoni, who handles the designing end (her husband does the fabrics) aims always for soft, free, comfortable clothes that can be worn any time of the day, summer or winter.

Fashion Freedom

The modern miracle of the availability of well-made clothes at modest cost owes much to the work of many dedicated American women in the ready-to-wear trade, a phenomenon of the twentieth century. Based in New York on Seventh Avenue, this industry has become a giant as a result of advanced factory methods, the development of miracle synthetic fibers, effective merchandising, the press, and creative design talent.

Some of the outstanding American designers who have helped to build this great industry are Bonnie Cashin, Pauline Trigère, Anne Klein, Betsey Johnson, Anne Fogarty, Adele Simpson, Claire McCardell, Mary McFadden, Molly Parnis, Vera Neumann, Hattie Carnegie, LaVetta, and Norma Kamali.

The rise of women to eminence in the fashion industry has not been without its struggles. Until the last part of the seventeenth century women's clothing was made entirely by men. There were fine women dressmakers (some better than the men), but theirs was a forbidden trade in France before 1695. For example, there was such opposition to women dressmakers by the men in the trade that they often broke into women's shops and destroyed all the garments. In 1675 the women petitioned Louis XIV for the right to make petticoats and other garments. They were finally granted the right to form their own corporation.[6]

More recent injustices to women workers resulted in the formation in 1900 of the International Ladies Garment Workers Union in the United States. Eleanor Lambert writes: "The Union first came to widespread public notice when a fire in the Triangle Shirtwaist Co. in 1911 killed 146 women in a crowded loft with too few fire escapes and bolted

Mary Quant,
creator of the miniskirt,
wearing one of her own dress designs

doors."[7] The ILGWU is now one of the most powerful and wealthy of all unions, and it has been a prime instrument in protecting the interests of women workers.

Designer Mary Quant (creator of the miniskirt) feels that fashion should be available cheaply to everyone. She believes that in the past some designers have helped to make women sex or prestige objects, saying: "I like to think this has changed and that it is fashionable to be a woman for one's own sake."[8]

Trousers have become a symbol of freedom for women. The unisex movement of the sixties opened the way for the popularity of the pants suit and the overall acceptance of pants by women. However, as always, fashion reflects the tempo of the times, preceded by evolutionary forces of many kinds. Chanel was one of these forces, and so was Marlene Dietrich, who startled the world when she first appeared in a man's full-dress "tail" suit.

Actually pants have been worn by Chinese women as far back as the Han Dynasty (206 BC to AD 220). Princess Tou Wan's burial suit had trousers constructed of pieces of jade.

Fashion writer Jane Dorner comments that "the history of trousers is in itself a comment on sexual attitudes, and one of the most significant developments of the twentieth century has been the movement towards Unisex garments, clothes that can be worn by both sexes"[9]—blue jeans and T-shirts, for example.

In addition to trousers and the comfort they provided has been the appearance of fashion coordinates, outfits that can be worn in different combinations. Designer Anne Klein was a pioneer in this area, and, according to Marylou Luther, she was a great editor and interpreter of fashion who clearly understood the mood of women and what they wanted in clothes.

Norma Kamali is another innovative designer. She helps women to think in terms of dressing as individuals rather than as sheep, followers of fashion dictators. Kamali has been known to cut evening clothes out of tablecloths, transform parachutes into jumpsuits, and make suits out of gold lamé curtains. She converted her canvas sleeping bag into a sleeping-bag coat, complete with flannel lining. She makes skin-tight bodysuits in Lycra or jersey with matching leggings, skirts, and chaps. Diana Vreeland says of her: "Norma Kamali is in everyone's view a remarkable designer with first rate ideas and a magnificent view of design."[10] Stanley Marcus of Neiman-Marcus considers Kamali to be one of the outstanding design talents in the country today.

Harriet Selwyn brings new concepts to fashion with her modular clothing units. She has six component parts that can be worn interchangeably throughout the year. Many of her designs are "one-size-fits-all." Selwyn claims she designs for the "homelies" of the world, and she feels that women have a right to wearable, comfortable, feminine fashions.

Natural Body Fashions

Since what women put on outside is in direct relationship to what is going on inside, the present-day freedom of women that is developing in

Betsey Johnson

all areas of their lives is manifesting in more natural body clothes. Women want to be free from constricting, confining garments.

Outstanding in her contributions to this freedom is Betsey Johnson of New York. She was the first to change her patterns to suit women's changing figure with lower bosoms and thicker midsections, and, according to Marylou Luther, this has had a significant influence on the industry at large. For Johnson her work is all really a good time. She is more proud of her low-priced T-shirts, pants, and drawstring skirts than of her own more expensive line. She designs patterns for Butterick for women and children, including maternity clothes. Johnson explains: "I approach my work thinking... would I want to wear it?"[11]

The natural body-sweater is the forte of Sonia Rykiel of Paris's Left Bank. She uses herself as a model for her creations. It bothered her that most clothes were wide at the top and narrow at the hips when most women are narrow at the top and broader around the hips. She claims that her designs all evolve from the same basic body-sweater. Actress Jeanne Moreau says of Rykiel's clothes: "Enfin, a woman can feel her body, move with entire freedom, and be herself completely."[12]

Holly Harp of Los Angeles creates clothes that make women aware of their bodies, and her designs reflect her own awareness of natural body rhythm and movement. There is a flow and gracefulness to her clothes. Harp believes that the most important thing about a person is attitude, level of consciousness. She feels that the key to freedom is self-acceptance. This inner awareness translates into an outer awareness of the body and how it can best be clothed. Harp believes that it is almost impossible in life to be free if you are denying certain aspects of yourself, including your sexuality. Her philosophy: "We need to relax and accept ourselves."[13] Harp is best known for her after-five clothes. She believes there is a place for fantasy in fashion.

Pauline Trigère made the first bodysuit, like an exercise suit to wear under pants or skirt. It has been widely copied. Trigère was trained early on in her mother's sewing shop. She works directly with fabric to achieve the elegant, flowing line for which she is famous. Trigère has won every major American fashion award. She gives credit to Vionnet for the concept of the flowing line, but the beautiful gowns she consistently turns out are uniquely her own creations.

Claire McCardell, twenty years ahead of her time, based her dress designs on the principle that form follows function, with comfort and utility being the prime requisites. Although she was influenced by Paris, she evolved her own special American style, and along with Anne Klein she was among the first to bring out interchangeable coordinates. And she also launched the American version of the dirndl and her wraparound "popover."

Today's "miracle" synthetic fabrics requiring no ironing have been a great boon to modern women as a time saver. These fabrics come in numerous forms and combinations of acetates, nylons, polyesters, stretch fabrics, and acrylics blended with many of the natural fabrics of cotton, wool, and silk. In 1978 the industry advanced by producing shirts that combined all-cotton fabric with permanent-press properties. Flame-resistant polyester has also been developed. Many women have made their contribution to the development of these fabrics.

Fashion doyenne Diana Vreeland has helped to inform the public about these new fabrics (while still emphasizing the desirability of the natural fabrics). Many consider her to be the first lady of fashion, so widespread is her influence. She has been a powerful force in promoting greater fashion freedom for women. As an influential taste-maker Vreeland is a catalyst. She has helped promote pants for women, as well as separates, boots, tights, bikinis, and boutiques. She is an educator and a woman of great taste in whatever she undertakes.

Movie and retail designer Bonnie Cashin feels that clothes are only successful when they really work well for the activities of our modern lives in today's cities and for our ways of travel. She writes, "Maybe what I feel about naturalness and simplicity and the pleasure of texture and color comes through."[14] In the opinion of Marylou Luther, Cashin has pioneered a true American sportswear ethnic style. She is famous for her leather line, including coats, bags, and boots. She was a pioneer in the "layering" concept, derived from the Chinese and based on the principle of insulation. Clothes were put on one over the other like a nest of Chinese boxes with pockets of air trapped in between. Pieces were added or subtracted according to temperature. Cashin believes that women are now bypassing artificially created obsolescence, where clothes become obsolete because of yearly fashion dictates. Cashin's clothes are classics with enduring quality.

Cashin is on the Design Arts panel of the National Endowment for Arts assessing applications for grants. Her newest project is the Innovative Design Fund, a public foundation just starting. She hopes to encourage the interaction between the science/technology and the art/design disciplines to develop new ideas and directions in what we wear and how we live to meet the changing patterns of living.

Mary McFadden would like to be known as the designer who has developed an art form into a commercial enterprise. She reinterprets modern and primitive art as a wearable commodity. McFadden established a workshop to develop tribal sculpture in Inyanga Province in Rhodesia. She believes that fabrics should be used as an art form.

Bonnie Cashin

Many women are grateful to Vera Neumann for her comfortable, easy-care slacks and blouses at low cost. Neumann in 1979 did a hundred million dollars of business in retail sales, part of which was in fashion and part in other design enterprises. Inspired by nature, she creates designs in vivid colors, which are translated to fabric by her special silk-screen printing process.

Lilly Pulitzer of Florida made her mark by building a very successful business around one item—the comfortable little cotton shift dress. She makes it up in seven hundred ways, generally in colorful, splashy prints, long and short, but it is basically just one simple garment.

Anne Fogarty has gained recognition particularly for her designs for the junior figure. She promoted the jumpsuit and the bikini. After adapting men's coveralls into black corduroy for a *Life* magazine story she has made coveralls in all fabrics a part of her fashion line in every season. Fogarty believes that discipline results in a clearcut picture of one's own identity as a person and that it is easier to clothe a clearcut image than a hazy "mirage."

Miniskirt creator Mary Quant had always wanted the young to have fashions of their own, twentieth-century fashions. Quant explains, "I didn't think of myself as a designer. I just knew that I wanted to concentrate on finding the right clothes to wear and the right accessories to go with them."[15] Quant feels that no one designer is responsible for a fashion revolution, that all a designer can do is to anticipate a need before people realize that they are bored with what they already have.

In designing her clothes Adele Simpson feels strongly that they must be comfortable and practical. Since the body is fluid, she believes that clothes must always move easily—they must never be contrived. Simpson won her first job on Seventh Avenue in 1926 as a result of a "flapper" dress she designed. In her long and successful career she has won many coveted fashion awards. She and her husband, Wesley, traveled widely and collected art treasures over many years. Simpson has given this collection to the Fashion Institute of Technology in New York, and it will be a rich source of inspiration for designers.

California's Women Cinema Designers

New York's Seventh Avenue is the hub of the fashion industry in the United States, but undeniably the influence of California's cinema designers and the stars who wear their clothes has been a strong force. Marlene Dietrich's first appearance in a man's full-dress "tail" suit plus top hat was in her first made-in-America film, *Morocco*, in 1930—and she "wowed" them! She later wore tails and a silver top hat in *Blonde Venus* in 1940 and a full man's Navy uniform in *Seven Sinners*. Because of this Dietrich influence (plus that of Chanel and other social forces) women gradually accepted trousers in their wardrobes.

In 1932 Alice Marble shocked Wimbledon by appearing in tennis shorts. And in 1930 the first backless bathing suit had made its appearance. According to cinema fashion historian Satch La Valley, it was Irene, the film designer, who actually helped to change swimwear styling because of her swimsuit designs for star Esther Williams. Her designs were not only handsome but were built for comfort and *swim-*

ming. The retail manufacturers began to make suits along these lines, and women loved them. Thus a new trend was born.

Irene (Gibbons) was a Hollywood designer of great importance during the Hollywood glamour period from the 1930s to the 1950s. Her designs were dramatic but elegant and wearable. Irene followed Adrian at MGM as designer and became a fashion luminary. She also succeeded in the ready-to-wear fashion business, and in the fifties it was the "in" thing to have an Adrian or Irene tailored suit.

La Valley credits Renie Conley (Oscar winner for *Cleopatra*) with almost singlehandedly creating a better fashion look for the secretary, the white-collar worker. Designer Conley gave Ginger Rogers, in *Kitty Foyle*, a neat and tailored look for her role, with white collar and cuffs. Secretaries followed suit and took on a smarter look as a result of this picture. The impact was strong.

Eight-time Oscar winner for costume design, Edith Head has had an impact on fashion in the five decades that she has worked in the film industry. To help the low-budget woman she designs for *Vogue Patterns*.

In her autobiography, *The Dress Doctor*, Head writes:

> From the first day at the studio, I was fascinated, enthusiastic, and willing, but I hadn't the least notion I'd ever survive. To this moment I wonder why I did. Perhaps it was because I worked hard and was willing to tackle anything—paint polka dots on china silk butterfly wings for Peter Pan, paint shoes with printed patterns to match the printed gowns to be worn by a Gloria Swanson or a Jetta Goudal.

She found a magic power in clothes, and "I decided to stick with them."

Head won her first Academy Award for Best Costuming for *The Heiress* in 1949, and seven more Oscars were awarded to her in ensuing years. In *The Jungle Princess* (1936), starring Dorothy Lamour, Head introduced the sarong, and audiences were delighted. The influence was felt in the fashion industry.

Contributions to Fashion by Outstanding Black Women

The Black Fashion Museum in the heart of Harlem is the dream-come-true of its founder, Lois K. Alexander. As a black woman she sustained throughout her adult years the idea of a school where black youths could learn the modus operandi of the garment trade. More recently she conceived the idea of a museum to honor the contributions of blacks to the evolution of fashion. She has brought both of these plans to fruition.

Edith Head

Alexander opened her Harlem Institute of Fashion in 1966, starting with small quarters and three ancient sewing machines. A woman who had the courage to bring reality to her dreams, she had the joy of attending the opening of her Black Fashion Museum in October of 1979. The museum is adjacent to the Institute at 155 West 126 Street in Harlem and displays garments that are the work of blacks, from the 1800s to the present. For example, there is a copy of Mary Todd Lincoln's inaugural gown; the original was made by ex-slave Elizabeth Keckley.

Aided by a $20,000 grant from the National Endowment for the Arts, Alexander toured the country searching for authentic black designs. She states that in former times black designers were labeled seamstresses even when they were designers. Alexander's many outstanding achievements set a fine example for other women.

Another black woman of notable accomplishments is fashion designer LaVetta of Los Angeles. LaVetta designs for the high-fashion trade, custom and wholesale, and is the only black person in the country designing and marketing her own line. She sells to exclusive stores (such as Neiman-Marcus) and to an impressive number of celebrities.

LaVetta says, "Nothing gets me to the point where I feel that I'm inadequate. I just don't believe that there is a dress designer in the world who can make prettier clothes than I can."[16] This confident spirit grew out of years of preparation. LaVetta was taught to sew by her seamstress-designer aunt, and as a young woman of fifteen she left home to make it on her own. And make it she did. LaVetta has a flare for showmanship and believes that the politics of being a designer are more important than knowing how to sew. She attends major Los Angeles events in a chauffeured Rolls Royce limousine wearing one of her own creations.

This multitalented woman is prominent on prestigious art councils. She is the only black woman on the Board of the UCLA Arts Council and is the only black woman on the Board of the Los Angeles County Museum of Art's Fashion Council. LaVetta succeeded in a move to include blacks as museum docents. The achievements and courage of LaVetta are an inspiration to women everywhere.

Fashion Futures

As women designers of the past and present have created fashions that reflect the many-faceted influences of the times they live in, so also will the designers of the future be influenced. Mary Quant believes that "the way fashion changes radically will depend upon political changes in Europe and the West."

We have the example of the political revolution in China and its impact on the clothing of the people. The "uniform" look of jacket and pants (with variations) tends to deemphasize sex differences, and the young people find sexual attractiveness more in the political ideologies of the individual rather than in the clothing they wear.

Edith Head believes that "in the future we will have a simplification of design and fabric and the whole fashion picture will, I hope, return to sanity."[17]

There will continue to be scientific advances in the world of fabrics and production methods. Former *Vogue* editor Jessica Daves predicts that possible thermostatic waves will be incorporated into fiber from which the cloth is woven, in such ways as to make the material change with the weather. Also in the experimental stage is an ultrasonic cleaning closet that can automatically clean the clothes each night.[18]

Daves also considers the possibility of being clothed in light, the newest favorite child of science. She suggests that each of us may have a small permanent battery that will be able to change our light-made garments from red to black or white or blue and alter the planes and length of the skirt and the shape of the body by its refractions.

If women have more leisure, it is possible that there will be a renaissance of fine stitchery, such as embroidery and appliqué.

Women designers of the future will design more and more clothing for men. Indeed, the trend has already begun.

Blue jeans have become ubiquitous on young people of both sexes, and unisex fashions will no doubt be on the increase. As men and women team up more and more in egalitarian relationships, this will show up in clothing.

The popularity of work clothes, such as coveralls, painter's pants, French jeweler's smocks, and lumberjack shirts, will continue to rise due to their practicality, comfort, and price. Now that the women of the Western world have discovered the advantages of pants they are not likely to give them up.

We are in debt to all of the dedicated women over the years who have made contributions to fashion for the benefit of women. From the factory workers who labor long at their sewing machines to the top-flight designers, fabric makers, buyers, salespeople, women of the press—all play a vital part in the fashion picture. Opportunities for careers in this field are without limit, and the future will certainly find increasing numbers of women making their contributions to the art of fashion.

Women of today are pushing back their horizons. They are not allowing themselves to be poured into a mold of conformity and crystalized patterns of the past. This is an open-ended era of splendid opportunity for women in all aspects of their lives. Fashion is one means of creative expression, and each woman is best served by expressing her own unique individuality in her clothing. She should dare to be herself, and in so doing she will find the joy of the true Renaissance Woman.

Notes

1. Marylou Luther (fashion editor of the *Los Angeles Times*). Telephone interview, Los Angeles, January 1976.

2. Eleanor Lambert. Interview by mail, December 1979.

3. Diana Vreeland. Interview by mail, Metropolitan Museum of Art, New York, January 1980.

4. Marcel Haedrich. *Coco Chanel*. Boston and Toronto: Little, Brown, 1971 and 1972, p.93.

5. Bettijane Levine, in the *Los Angeles Times*, June 12, 1977.

6. Anny Latour. *Kings of Fashion*. London: Weidenfeld & Nicolson, 1958; New York: Coward-McCann, 1958, p.6.

7. Eleanor Lambert. *World of Fashion*. New York: Bowker, 1976, p.281.

8. Mary Quant. Interview by mail, London, England, February 1976.

9. Jane Dorner. *Fashion, the Changing Shape of Fashion Throughout the Years*. London: Octopus, 1974; New York: Crescent, 1974, p.81.

10. Vreeland, interview.

11. Caterine Milinaire and Carol Troy. *Cheap Chic*. New York: Harmony, 1975, p.185.

12. Pamela Andriotakis. "In Style," *People Magazine*, April 5, 1976, p. 28.

13. Holly Harp. Telephone interview, Los Angeles, January 1976.

14. Stanley Rosner and Lawrence E. Abt. *The Creative Experience*. New York: Grossman, 1970, p.245.

15. Mary Quant. *Quant on Quant*. New York: Putnam, 1966; London: Cassell, 1966, p.43.

16. Louie Robinson. "A Designing Woman," *Ebony*, December 1979, p.100.

17. Edith Head. Interview by mail, Universal Studios, Universal City, California, December 4, 1975.

18. Jessica Daves. *Ready Made Miracle*. New York: Putnam, 1967, p.236.

Barbara Kimball *is a freelance writer with a background in art and fashion. She received her B.E. degree from UCLA in Interior Design and Fashion. She worked in the costume department of Paramount Pictures and was a fashion publicist for Maison de Couture Rosevienne in Paris. She raised two children; one is the editor of this book.*

III. MUSIC

WOMEN'S MUSIC

Ruth Scovill

There is no simple definition of Women's Music, and to create unnecessary boundaries by defining it would only restrict its natural
growth. At one end of the spectrum Women's Music might include all
music written or sung by a woman. On the other end it might be music
written by, for, about, and only to women. One extreme would say that
the presence of a man in the audience changes the experience of the
music and women's absolute ownership of that space and time. The
other extreme would argue that even songs that stereotype women's lives
are still about the experiences of women and therefore are women's
music. The most common usage—and that accepted for the purposes of
this article—lies somewhere in the middle.

The creation and presentation of Women's Music reflects a consciousness of *women–identification*. Written by and for women, it speaks
to their real lives, providing role models and choices that popular music
has rarely offered to them. In contrast to popular music's prevalent
degradation of women, Women's Music holds the feminist and
humanist ideals of self-affirmation and mutual support.

This chapter will discuss the three main components of Women's
Music: lyrics, production (which includes light, sound, and performance), and musical structure.

That women around the country began to experiment with performance, lyrics, and musical form at what appeared to be the same time,
1972, was not by accident. Among other things a structure was needed
with a woman-identified consciousness to support this music, both
spiritually and financially. The women's movement of the late sixties
created a ready-made audience for Women's Music.

The first visible stage was the all-women bands, such as the Chicago
and New Haven Women's Liberation Rock Bands, which played
mainly at women-only events. Previously the traditional gathering
places for women had been limited. All-women feminist events offered

an opportunity for women to get together on a larger and more supportive scale. This space was important for women and the movement
because it allowed women to interact and grow with each other, without
outside and misdirected criticism. Sophie Drinker had written in 1948:

> If women would sing first for themselves, sincerely and enthusias-
> tically, ignoring critics with preconceived notions about either
> women or music, their song would eventually burst out of the
> bounds of home, sickroom, or club and would flow into that
> stream of rhythm, melody, [and] harmony which is forming
> the music of tomorrow.[1]

The early women's rock bands usually played existing rock music
with the lyrics rewritten from a feminist viewpoint. The belief was that
one way to reach young women with the message of feminism was
through the popular rock-music format of the time.[2] Eventually it became evident that women needed to say more, both with lyrics and
musical form, than was possible within the rock format.[3] It was at this
time, 1973, that the second stage, the development of the entity known
as Women's Music, began to emerge.

The first heralding of this second state was the release of the album
Lavender Jane Loves Women,[4] which was closely followed by the First
National Women's Music Festival in Urbana-Champaign, Illinois, in
1974.[5] From that point Women's Music grew at a phenomenal rate, as
women realized not only the uniqueness but also the commonality of
their music.

Part of this new music included the development of a special performance, production, and technical process. Women realized that they
would have to learn and develop every aspect of presenting their new
music in production. Performers who wanted to maintain artistic control of their music and the environment in which the music was presented could not do so under existing publishing and recording contracts. Women who had rarely been allowed entrance in the technical
or business aspects of the music industry needed to learn these skills
through their own woman-identified interpretations. Hence a new
production process developed.

Lyrics

Lyrics are the easiest and most tangible means of documenting how
Women's Music differs from popular music. Compared with other
lyrical forms, the new images of Women's Music exhibit a healthier
expression and a more realistic approach to personal interaction.

Lyrics have in the past portrayed women in a limited way. Some popular-music lyrics have been extremely subtle, others incredibly blatant, in their sexism, but all show little understanding of a woman's life. This includes many songs sung by women. Two successful exceptions to this in rock music during the 1960s were Leslie Gore's "You Don't Own Me" (she also recorded "It's Judy's Turn to Cry") and Gale Garnett's "We'll Sing in the Sunshine" (her only hit record). Two songs from a decade of protest were not very many; the great majority of lyrics defended male superiority and female subservience.

Rock music of the fifties was based on a relatively naïve sexism of follow-the-status-quo-and-you-will-live-happily-ever-after. Songs did not realistically express the experiences of being a woman or present choices or strong role models for women. The choices that did exist were based on the double standard that bound women for ages: angel/devil, virgin/whore, sweetheart/bitch, mother/castrater, girl next door/"easy lay." As the decade progressed women fell into the role of "groovy chick."[6]

Most popular songs have been written by men, and so portray a male viewpoint. The majority of performers are men, and most concerts are produced by men, with male sound and lighting technicians. In reality popular music is not for women, because, from the record companies to the radio stations, men own the music industry. As Bob Bohle states:

> When you turn up your car radio and punch those buttons from station to station, what do you hear? Male deejays. Disc jockeys determine what records will be played over the air. When you go to a concert and see your favorite groups on stage, do you know who put them there? Concert promoters and managers almost exclusively determine who will perform what concerts at what venues. And they are almost all men. Even roadies [crew members] are usually male. The same goes with linernotes [album copy] writers.
>
> A few calls to record companies in Hollywood revealed that the promotion departments (whose job is to sell records) are mostly composed of men, except for the women who answer the phones. Curiously, the bulk of publicity department personnel at record companies are women. Publicity handles print media and miscellaneous duties like getting reviewers to concerts. However, publicists have almost no power to formulate policy, unlike promotion.[7]

As the rock counterculture became more complex, volatile, and "honest" in the sixties, so did rock music. In the context of rock honest meant that the lyrics about women seemed more openly contemptuous.

This attitude, which seems to have existed all along, was finally sanctioned and given voice. Classic examples of stereotyped images of women can be found in almost all the lyrics of the Rolling Stones. One popular example is:

> Under my thumb her eyes are just
>   kept to herself
> Under my thumb well I can't still
>   look at someone else
> It's down to me, the way she
>   talks when she's spoken to
> Down to me, the change has
>   come, she's under my thumb.[8]

The best way to show the differences in the lyric content of Women's Music is to compare it with the traditional images of women in rock music. The music lyrics presented here have been chosen from two generations of rock music, the mainstay of the popular-music industry for the last twenty years and conveyer of some of the most extreme examples of stereotyping and antiwomen bias in songwriting.

These examples were chosen with awareness that they come from varied stages of each music's history and from a variety of songwriters. It is important to show that sexism in popular music has been a constant and continuous thread throughout its history, much as healthy and realistic images have been a constant through the history of Women's Music. The following are examples of a similar subject expressed in two different ways.

Competition with other women

Popular Music:

> Now it's Judy turn to cry
> Judy's turn to cry
> Cus Johnny's come back to me.[9]

Women's Music:

> I only knew him briefly, not
>   enough to call it deeply
> We knew each other briefly,
>   but not as long as you and me
> So if he's the man that
>   you're after

We'll that I can understand
It's more important to me
      that we don't fight
      because of a man.[10]

Dependency

Popular Music:

I worship your opinions
I imitate your ways
I try to make you grace me
With a word of praise.[11]

Women's Music:

Threw the bone out the window
      and Charlie out the door.
Though the load ain't any
      lighter I ain't slavin' any more
Since Charlie ain't around
Tellin' me what to do
Well I got some time to think
I got my own point of view.[12]

Sexuality

Popular Music:

You're alright, you put up such
      a good clean fight
I'm afraid that you lose
      tonight
S-L-U-T
She may be a slut but she
      looks good to me.[13]

Women's Music:

I love to see you in the low-
      light, love.
And touch your secret weakness
      with my fire.
Let's burn together all through
      the night
I'm just a dream child of desire.[14]

Relationships

Popular Music:

> Ain't gonna waste any time with you
> Have it ready cause I'm comin'
>   on thru
> Just shut your mouth and turn
>   off the light
> Waited long and I been blue,
>   come on baby, wanna rock
>   with you
> Makin' a mess all over the floor
> Keep it going till I get more.[15]

Women's Music:

> Well it seemed like so little was
>   spoken
> 'Bout ending the games
> We just kept waking up still
>   together
> And feeling the change
> And I loved you for facing my
>   crazy eyes
> And using your strengths to
>   build mine
> And learning compassion, and
>   growing more mellow and kind.
> I'd waited so long I'd forgotten
> What I had waited for
> Now in our balance I've learned
>   to uncover
> All I'd wanted and more.[16]

Self-image in relation to social place

Popular Music:

> Well I was born a woman, I didn't
>   have no say
> And when my man finally
>   comes home,
> He makes me glad it happened
>   that way
> Because to be his woman
> No price is too great to pay.[17]

> I will not live a life
> Forever on my knees
> You tell me: why not change
> To make you more at ease
> To please at ease ... at ease to
>   please
> The waves of hate crash over me
> And wash me clean of fear
> The ocean of my anger swells
> To cover all who hear.[18]

Women's Music has created a fuller image of women, which in turn has opened up the possibilities of how a woman can relate to the world. It is woman-identified because it speaks of self-affirmation and independence; of women working together in new ways; of women caring for, sharing with, and loving each other; and of women getting in touch with their power by getting in touch with themselves.

Women's Music does not denigrate or stereotype women. Because women belong to all classes, races, ethnic backgrounds, shapes, and sizes the lyrics cannot be discriminatory. Women's Music is a humanist lyrical form. In talking about strong women no one is idolized at the expense of someone else. By being pro-woman the music becomes pro-people.[19]

Women's Music offers women unlimited choices. In this way a young woman is helped in choosing her own lifestyle as she grows. However, because this new music challenged the norm and met resistance from society it was necessary for women to develop their music among themselves, and so without outside influences a different process was able to develop.[20]

Production

It was clear from the beginning of Women's Music that there would be no point in presenting nonoppressive lyrics in an oppressive atmosphere. The performers wanted to play their music in a new, more supportive way, and this manifested itself in how they presented themselves and their music on stage.

Performance, however, is more than the performer on stage. It is the whole event, from the producer's first conceptualization of the event to the workshops following the concert. As with lyrics, women have lent their experiences as women to the production process. Hence the performers, technicians, and producers have combined to create a nonoppressive and enriching environment in which to present and develop women's culture. The audience in return has created an enthusiastic environment in which Women's Music can grow.

Women have consciously altered the concert environment the better to suit the music that is being performed, and ultimately their own needs. In a Women's Music production all the women—producers, technicians, performers, and audience—are constantly interacting with each other. Their efforts combine to alter the concert as a whole.

The differences of Women's Music from popular music in the performer/audience relationship can best be seen in the three areas of accessibility, vulnerability, and responsibility. Responsibility to the audience means not abusing the power given them by being public figures and instead building a trust that creates a balance of power. Some other ways that responsibility manifests itself are: offering several ticket prices (for women who are unable to pay the higher price), holding workshops after the concert (to demystify the performer's work), and writing lyrics that speak to the real lives of women.

Accessibility includes meeting the members of the audience after the performance in the lobby and in workshops to give the performer a personal contact with the women who support her. The audience sees that the performer has human limitations and is a real person. The performer becomes a woman who is doing her work, the same as a teacher, homemaker, or doctor.

The performer of Women's Music does not pretend to be the model of the perfect woman. She is growing, as we all are. On stage she incorporates the vulnerability of growing and struggling into the role of a strong woman. In a male-defined culture that places so much emphasis on power this type of vulnerability, considered a weakness, would not be tolerated. In Woman's Music power has been redefined, and the honesty in admitting one's humanness has become part of the foundation for the strength of Women's Music.

Because the performer remains responsible, accessible, and vulnerable she avoids the "star tripping" that is prevalent in popular music. Its absence brings down the unnecessary walls placed between the audience and performer. A more equal situation exists, creating a healthier way of presenting a music and a message, thereby making that message more powerful because it is presented honestly.

The three elements of responsibility, accessibility, and vulnerability do not end with the audience-performer relationship. The collaborative arts of sound, lighting, and concert production also reflect this balance by working together to facilitate communication between audience and performer and by being accountable to the women's community.

Lights and sound are major contributors to a production. Used correctly they help present the music in the most powerful, nonassaultive way possible. The best sound and lights do not direct attention to themselves.

> At the center of the rock universe is the star—flooded in light . . . and the source of incredible volumes of sound. The audience remains totally in darkness: the Stones kept thousands waiting several hours, till nightfall, before they would come on stage at Altamont. . . . And watching a group like the Mothers of Invention perform is a lesson in totalitarianism—seeing Frank Zappa define sound and silence with a mere gesture of his hand. There is no psychic or visual or auditory space for anyone but the performer.[21]

Lighting and amplified sound were seldom a part of early Women's Music, which began in places like small coffeehouses, where they were not usually needed; there was also little money to pay technicians, and few qualified technicians were available.

As the concerts grew more sophisticated, sound and lights became necessary, and as women began to perfect their technical art, they were able to meet the needs of larger concerts. The improved lights and sound, which audiences expect at a professional event, helped to legitimatize the events.

How women technicians interpret their art creates differences from the sound and lighting of rock concerts. In Women's Music a conscious effort is made to find the most effective way to present the music. Their choice of color and timing are ways that women can differ from male technicians in interpreting their art.

> There should be women technicians because there's a movement of women who want to work together, and have all-women-produced events, because of wanting to develop some kind of new creative energy or some kind of rapport within the women who are doing it. If you don't have women technicians, then you're not going to develop things from a woman's point of view.[22]

Once women gained these skills they helped train other women so that the technical network continued to grow. The Women's Music concert has been one of the few places that women can acquire these skills. The mastering of the technical art has grown side-by-side with the other facets of Women's Music.

The producer is the nucleus of a Women's Music production. She is responsible for every detail and is the connecting link among all the facets that combine to create a concert. She is accountable to the performers, technicians, and the women's community, pulling together all the parts into a feminist whole.

The Women's Music producer's goal is to create a professional event. She plays a major part in the interpretation of the music by linking the collaborative efforts during the production. The producer also participates in postconcert workshops. Here she is able to demystify her work by giving a step-by-step account of how a production is put together. She too brings a woman-identification to her work.

The performer, technician, and producer combine with the Women's Music audience to create a truly equal and healthy event. Each adds her own woman-identified parts to create the whole. Each brings with her a consciousness to be responsible to the women's community and hence the ability to alter completely the concert process as we have come to know it.

Musical Structure

> In the interval, women's music as a musical genre has also evolved steadily from its unpretentious beginnings when feminist content was simply infused into conventional popular music forms. While such lyrical innovations continue to inspire, delight and raise consciousness, feminist musicians have begun the profound and far-reaching search for [the kind of] breakthroughs [in this music] that are occurring daily in women's lives.[23]

In musical structure, as well as lyrics, Women's Music can express all the feelings that have characterized the other facets of this music. *Some* composers believe that there is a *possibility* of a unique musical form that is emerging from a sort of "collective musical unconsciousness."[24] This possible new form would be born of biological and social experiences common to all women. Society obscures female differences by equating "different" with "inferior." The refusal to make that equation permits the existence of a different musical form.

Form is more difficult to analyze than lyrics, especially in Women's Music, because relatively few composers have ventured beyond the traditional forms. There are, however, a few Women's Music composers who have extensive musical training and who have not only gone beyond the existing musical limitations but have been able to put their thoughts about what they are trying to do into words.

The following excerpts are from a letter written by Kay Gardner in February 1977 that specifically addressed the issue of musical form in Women's Music. (See, too, the interview with Gardner in the next chapter.)

... I've found innate to the women musicians performing today ... writing in a similar form. I searched formal analysis literature and found that this form was not explored. Upon identifying
the form as circular, I began then to utilize it in my own compositions.

Circular form is related to three already defined forms as I see it:
1) the round, a very ancient primitive form, 2) song and trio
(ABCABCAB) and 3) rondo (ABACADAE). One difference in
circular form is that the climax or moment of most tension is in
the middle! Therefore the formal outline ABACADAEADACABA
or ABCDEDCBA (not just melodic content but harmonic interest,
rhythm and/or instrumental color adapt to this form). ... Another
difference is that the structure following the climax is the same as
that leading up to the climax, only backwards. This is a way of
relieving the tensions slowly and makes for a flow of movement. ...

... My formal theory is directly related to the biological difference in sexual expression between men and women. The orgasmic climax in men is a release at the *end* of a buildup of
tensions and energy. On the other hand, the orgasmic climax for
women is in the middle of her sexual expression with the afterplay
being as important as the foreplay, and with the potential of beginning the cycle again immediately, thus creating the circular form.
Women are naturally cyclical beings, operating on a lunar cycle
regarding both menses and parturition. It is not unusual that we
think and create in an organic form.[25]

Women are biologically different from men, and an open mind will
allow the possibility that these differences might also manifest themselves in how and what women create. There are other possible differences in the form of Women's Music, some of which are discussed by
Margie Adam in the following excerpts from an interview conducted in
June 1977.

Part of what women's music is about is pursuing the possibility
that there are theoretical concepts which are uniquely woman-
identified. ... That is not to say that the principles that have been
developed to this point in Western music are incorrect or poorly
thought out. On the contrary, I think they are fine as far as they
go. I would like to suggest that there is at least the possibility that a
set of woman-identified theoretical musical principles
exists ... which have only recently begun to be consciously explored as such.

... One of the things that makes it so difficult to explore alternatives is that the established musical theory is everywhere around
us: on TV, the radio, in elevators, at school, in the supermarket,
not to mention schools of formal music training.

... What is most important is that there is created a cultural environment where as many women composers as possible can present their music. *Then* we can start to extrapolate and define. . . .

One of the things I notice about some contemporary women writers is that they share an interest in rhythmic complexity—and willingness to risk stepping out of the standard "set-a-beat-and-stick-to-it-no-matter-what" mode into nonrepeating rhythmic patterns. This through-composed rhythmic structure also compliments a lyric and melodic style which has the potential to communicate a much broader range of feeling. . . .

The relationship of melody to chord and vice versa can be as complex or simple as the composer chooses. I think in women's music, one of the things that affects this relationship the most is the use of space. The concept of space in music has something to do with how you use the space between the notes, horizontally and linearly, and how that effects the rhythm; how much space you allow physically in dealing with a possibility which is, at present, totally without perimeters.

I have this sense that there is this pool of common experience which we all have in common as women—I would call it a kind of collective woman's unconscious, not unlike the Jungian theory of dreams. His study showed that everyone, regardless of race, sex, geography, etc., experienced the same archetypal dreams of falling, running away from some pursuing evil and so on. . . . I have this theory that womankind has her own set of archetypes, experiences that all women share, whether or not they are aware of them. . . . Since we are dealing with a *possibility* that such a unique thing as women's music may exist, let's continue the idea. . . .

There is no question in my mind that the power of music is in its subtlety. The subtlety of its shapes, of the space beside it and around and inside it, of the relationships of rhythm, melody, and lyrics: all of these have a significant effect on the listener whether or not he or she is aware of it. . . .

When we talk about musical form, we are examining, among other things, rhythmic patterns, melody, chord progressions, and tonality. While we work to develop new approaches to these formal characteristics, my sense is that women composers and songwriters are already right in the middle of shaping new relationships between these elements. Space in music is about what you put in, and what you leave out. In women's music, there seems to be more use of open chords, fourths and fifths, instead of cluster chords. Within arrangements, there is more "room" between the various instrumental lines. There seems, again, to be more willingness to risk in the kind of melodic leaps or chordal progressions used. These "felt" characteristics come at me as stark contrast to much of the conventional music around us, where everything is filled up. The production of the music, as well as its arrangement, does not allow any space to explore the song. It is not by accident that this highly produced... music exhibits a general lack of lyrical or melodic interest.

A few other thoughts: I have observed that in women's music, one is likely to find an abundant use of the pedal tone. One note in the bass (which is often the tonic of the key) stays the same, and the melody and chords move through several other progressions. Right at the juncture of moving from that pedal tone to a more active bass line is an incredible release of tension/energy. This same tension-release aspect appears over and over again in women's music in the shape of musical suspensions. Simply, a suspension is a rhythmically strong dissonant note played in place of a harmonic note and then resolved to the harmonic note. The effect of the suspension is musically literal: it subtly "suspends" emotion and then gives a feeling of release as its resolution.

In many ways, it is easier to talk about the connection of form with lyric content. The challenge in women's music is to speak to the most confrontive issues and ideas while still maintaining the poetic and musical integrity of the art. Quite possibly, a most likely and effective way to communicate new and/or controversial ideas is to seek out a most musically interesting yet accessible structure. In terms of lyrics, I think the closer one stays to poetic and emotion-based expression rather than prose-like intellectual concretes, the more space the listener has to become involved with the song.

There are those of us who want to explore women's possibilities in everything. It is a very conscious thing—in a sense it intellectualizes the most important nonintellectual beginnings of the development of a possibility like women's music. However, it also seems like it is necessary for that development to consciously *not* do what we have been conditioned to do, to consciously *not* repeat musical conventions in a derivative manner.[26]

There will come a time when enough Women's Music has been composed so that we shall be able to analyze the form to know whether a unique women's form does in fact exist. For now, however, it is enough to say that there are many women who are pushing the limits of traditional music in order to try to find a form that best expresses their woman-self. As Sophie Drinker predicted in 1948, women have had to "sing first for themselves" to create and present their music. The result is an art that validates women's lives and helps strengthen their identity as women. Performance, production, and sound and lighting combine to present the music and the message in the most powerful way possible, producing an on-stage illustration of the feminist content of the lyrics. Many composers of Women's Music believe that because of sociological and biological differences, women may be able to create a different musical form, a sound that speaks to their souls because it expresses lyrically and melodically the events and rhythms of their lives.

As male-defined rock music was born from rhythm and blues, which was born from classic blues, which was born from ballads, and so on, so will Women's Music grow and develop through generations of women freeing themselves from their restrictive socialization and a male-bound definition of culture.

Notes

1. Sophie Drinker. *Music and Women: The Story of Women in Their Relation to Music.* New York: Coward-McCann, 1948, p.293.

2. Susan Abod. Interview, Champaign, Illinois, June 1976.

3. Margie Adam. Interview, Davis, California, April 1976.

4. Kirsten Grimsted [sic]. Liner notes to *Mooncircles*, by Kay Gardner. New York: Urana Records, 1975.

5. Margie Adam, interview.

6. Marion Meade. "Does Rock Degrade Women?" *New York Times*, March 14, 1971.

7. Bob Bohle. "Women in Rock: Where Are They," *Musicians News*, March 1977, p.16.

8. Mick Jagger and Keith Richards. "Under My Thumb," on Rolling Stones, *Hot Rocks 1964–1971*, London Records, 2ps 606/7. © 1966 Abkco Music, Inc. All rights reserved. Reprinted by permission.

9. Lewis and B. Ross. "Judy's Turn to Cry," on Leslie Gore, Mercury Records, 72143 (a 45 RPM). © Glamorous Music.

10. Holly Near. "It's More Important to Me," on Holly Near, *Hang In There*, Redwood Records. © Holly Near.

11. Carly Simon. "Slave," on Carly Simon, *Playing Possum*, Electra 7E 1033. © 1975 C'est Music and Jacob Brackman (Maya Productions). Used by permission. All rights reserved.

12. Beverly Grant. "Janie's Janie," on The Human Condition, *Working People*

Gonna Rise, Paredon Records, p-1024. Permission granted by Great Gramaphone [*sic*] Music Inc. per Fairyland Music Corp. (A.S.C.A.P.) for special usage of lyrics as quoted from "Janie's Janie," Copyright © 1977.

13. Todd Rundgren. "Slut," on Todd Rundgren, *Something/Anything*, Warner Brothers, 2BX 2066. © 1972 Earmark Music, Inc. Screen Gems Columbia Music, Inc. Copyright Registration #EU 317720.

14. Cris Williamson. "Dream Child," on Cris Williamson, *The Changer and the Changed*, Olivia Records. © Bird Ankles Music 1975. All rights reserved. Used by permission.

15. Justman and Wolf. "Back to Get Ya," on J. Geils, *Bloodshot*, Atlantic Records, SD 7260.

16. Meg Christian. "Valentine Song," on *Meg Christian: I Know You Know*, Olivia Records LF 902. © 1974 Thumbelina Music. All rights reserved. Used by permission.

17. Martha Sharp. "Born a Woman," on Sandy Posey, MGM Records, K13501 (45 RPM). Used by Permission. © Painted Desert Music Corp.

18. Margie Adam. "I've Got a Fury," on Margie Adam, *Songwriter*, Pleiades Records, HB 2747. © Labyris Music Co. Used by permission.

19. Adam, interview.

20. As observed by the author during firsthand participation in concert production.

21. Susan Hewitt. "Cock Rock," in *Twenty Minute Fandangoes and Forever Changes*, Jonathan Eisen, ed. New York: Vintage, 1971, p.145.

22. Leni Schwendinger. Interview, Oakland, California, June 1977.

23. Grimsted, liner notes.

24. Margie Adam. Interview, San Francisco, California, 1977.

25. Kay Gardner. Letter to R. Scovill, February 1977.

26. Adam, 1977 interview. Adam revised the material in February 1978.

Ruth Scovill *is a television production manager in New York City. In the past she has helped to produce several Women's Music productions, and her M.A. thesis is about feminist music. This chapter was edited from that thesis.*

FEMALE COMPOSITION
Interview with Kay Gardner

*K*ay Gardner—*composer, conductor, and flutist—is music director and principal conductor of the New England Women's Symphony in Boston. She holds a Master of Music degree from the State University of New York at Stony Brook and has studied conducting privately with Antonia Brico and at the University of Michigan with Elizabeth Green. A self-taught composer, Gardner has had her works performed internationally and on recordings:* Mooncircles *(WWE ST-80) and* Emerging *(WWE ST-81), issued by Urana Records, and* A Rainbow Path *(EKR ST-101), issued by Even Keel Records.*

GK: *Please describe the background of women's music.*

KG: Women have been making music for centuries. We haven't heard a whole lot about it because women haven't been running things for centuries. We started off with lullabies; we started off with chants to Mother Nature for rain. We started off in primitive cultures as women who had a knowledge of the earth, knew how to raise the energy for certain things, knew the vibrations of the earth, knew circlings, because we ourselves are cyclical beings. Being on a lunar cycle, we recognized the moon as our mother; we recognized it as a feminine symbol. Our music was often made to the moon. We often made music to celebrate the birth of children and made sympathetic music while that child was being born. The child was born into music. We made music into death because we celebrated rebirth at the same time as death. We often wailed, and that sent the dead one into afterlife. We wailed; we chanted; we cried; we wrote and sang lullabies.

The saga was a women's form of music and was originated in Russia when women rowed people across great lakes. They would make up songs and stories as they went. We are an ancient music maker, we as Woman.

I've done a fair amount of research on women in music because I began to discover that there is indeed a woman's form in music. I believe I identified that form. I believe that women write innately and naturally in circular form, and that the form parallels our own cycles. Just as the moon grows full, just as we grow full with blood each month, so our music grows full. Our climax in our lovemaking happens not at the end of our lovemaking, but somewhere in the middle. That is how our natural, innate music is shaped.

When I first identified this form, I was very excited. I heard a woman sing in New York City, Jeriann Hilderley, who now has an album of her own—brilliant musician, brilliant artist—a total artist who lives her art; who *is* her art. She came out on stage with a multicolored marimba (one of those mallet instruments with long pipes). She had painted each pipe a rainbow color. All the lights were lowered. There were candles, suspended cymbals, and brass bells on the marimba. She started playing rolling chords and chanting with them. In the middle somewhere she began yelling out with an almost orgasmic sound, which embarrassed many of us in the audience because we were not prepared for it; then the work tapered off into a chant again. I thought, "This is really unique; it's very weird." I loved it because I love weird things.

Two weeks later I traveled to Boston, where I heard a singer, Lou Crimmins, sing her process piece "Woman-She." It was called a "process piece" because she was constantly working on it. It was, "Woman she, woman she, woman she, I am a woman," and it went on and on and it built and built until it became an Amazon war cry *in the middle*; and then tapered off again. This came two weeks apart from two different women who did not know each other, two women whom I will call primitive musicians; not that they are primitive women, but in that they did not have the academic background that I have.

I identified the form of their pieces as *circular form*. It's related to the round, which is, I think, probably a woman's form. (In summer camp, that's the biggest thing—singing rounds together around the fire.) The rondo form is music that has a section A, then a section B, which contrasts to A, then goes back to A. Then it may have a section C, which contrasts to both of those, and back to A and then perhaps D and then to A again (ABACADA). But it goes in a linear way; it goes in a straight line. The circular form which I identified goes: ABACADACABA. So it can start

Kay Gardner

over and over again, just as we do in our cycles, just as the moon does in her cycle, just as lovemaking happens for women as we can make love over and over again.

So, I've been writing music in this form. I find it very comfortable. I don't know if I will limit myself to writing in it all my life;

but it is a very good basic form in which to write and feels very, very natural to me.

I think that cyclical nature relates to all humans because we are made up of cyclical molecules and atoms. The world is cyclical; the universe is cyclical. All reality is related to cycles. So, we're all cyclical beings. But we women can identify our cycles more easily because we menstruate according to a lunar cycle, every twenty-eight days or so.

From conception to parturition is a ten–lunar-month period. This is our natural cycle, and very obvious. Males, I would expect, have cyclical natures too. If we think of the moon as being a very strong force, we know that energy is highest at the full moon and that the bodily fluids, like the tides of the earth, are at their fullest at that time. Men are also cyclical: it is not as obvious because they don't bleed monthly as we do.

I identified the women's form as related to orgasm. One could also identify male musical form the same way because the climax usually happens at the end. That may be kind of far out, but why not? It makes sense to me. It's a biological difference; we *are* different biologically, and we have to recognize that and go with it.

The problem for women composers is that we haven't had female role models. Male music has been the only teacher for us for a long time. The theoreticians are males, and they are teaching in their forms. We, as women, are only beginning to identify our own forms.

Plutarch said that Sappho invented the mixolydian mode, so I began to write in that mode because it was invented by a woman. Plutarch said it was a mode which befits passion and women as passionate beings. It's been a really interesting mode to write in. I've been rediscovering old modes and using them as bases, but trying to move on, trying to look forward. I've done a great deal of research in this.

Now I'm reading a lot of science fiction. I've gone back and now I want to go forward. In order to do that I must center myself, try to free myself of all the patriarchal influences, become totally womanly and discover that the ideal, the goal, is eventually to unite the masculine and feminine and become whole. But we as women have had to identify so much with men that we haven't figured out who we are, what *our* identity is. So for a long time I've been searching for that—what my woman-music is. In fact I isolated myself for five years and listened to no music *except* women's music. There wasn't a whole lot to listen to. Little by little I was able to find out who I was musically as a woman.

GK: *How do you begin your own composition?*

KG: Sometimes I start harmonically and the melody comes above it, as in "Touching Souls" on my *Mooncircles* album. In "Lunamuse" I used the harmony of a drone and an ostinato, or something that repeats over and over again. And the melody defined the form. But it could be harmonically defined; it could be rhythmically defined.

GK: *What are other differences in women's music besides the compositional form?*

KG: Obviously the words in feminist music are different. There are those who are writing lyrics from the most radical standpoint: Alix Dobkin, Sirani Avedis, Teresa Trull, and Meg Christian. They're writing strongly lesbian-identified lyrics, woman-identified lyrics, rhetoric in some cases. That's a big difference right there; that's obvious. There are some pieces that Meg Christian has written that are in that circular form. The song "Scars" is in circular form, and she didn't even know she was doing it. Both Margie Adam, another strong feminist songwriter, and Meg Christian have used this form unconsciously. Meg hasn't acknowledged that she's often writing in the circular form, but she is. A lot of the traditional music just started off just using the traditional folk (verse, chorus, verse, chorus) form. I'm seeing that change: it's exciting. It would be really great if our words and our forms were totally woman identified.

GK: *Do you find differences in classical women composers' form as well?*

KG: Most classical women composers' teachers were men. So they write in the same forms that the men wrote in. There are very few published female composers. Right now we're literally and figuratively digging them up and finding pieces by them. There are really not that many so far. It's very hard to tell at this point whether there was a specific form that wasn't dictated to them by their male teachers.

GK: *Who are your favorites?*

KG: I love Lili Boulanger, who was Nadia Boulanger's younger sister. Nadia Boulanger was probably the greatest composition teacher in the world (she died in October 1979). Copland, Walter

Piston—many famous composers studied with her. It's ironic that she would be the great teacher of all these male composers. Lili Boulanger wrote very lovely, very French music. I really like the lightness of her music.

I also like Ursula Mamlock, who does very intense things in twelve-tone series. You can almost count on your fingers the number of women composers whose music is being played today. It's really a shame, but we're trying to do something different about that.

[THE REST OF THE INTERVIEW OCCURRED THREE YEARS LATER.]

GK: *As you're exposed to more and more women's work, do you find verification of the circular theory of women's compositions, or what are you finding in terms of patterns of women's music?*

KG: I'm finding it more in content and orchestration. My theory may just be totally wrong. I don't know. Unless you find a composer who is extremely original, it's hard to tell. In some of the works, yes, I have found that circular form with the climactic tension in the middle, but in the more academic works I find it still at the end in the old, patriarchal way.

Thea Musgrave's work "Night Music" had its tension in the middle. She's extremely original. She's alive, conducting her own works, and lives between Virginia Beach and Santa Barbara. She's excellent, and internationally probably the best-known female composer right now.

Another characteristic of women's compositions is that the works have nature as inspiration. It's very unusual to see a piece like Pauline Oliveros's "To Valerie Solanos and Marilyn Monroe in Recognition of Their Desperation." It's one of the only bitter pieces that I've seen. "The Long Look Home," by Ruth Shaw Wiley of Estes Park, Colorado, is based on five ecological poems. The last movement is called "Nuclear Energy" and it's extremely powerful. That's the only violent thing that I've seen a woman write about so far. Of course she's not writing about nuclear energy as a way out, she's writing about its horror. Otherwise most pieces are nature oriented: "Night Music," "Deep Forest," "Wandering Breezes," my own "Rain Forest."

Another thing I've wondered about is that perhaps women have chosen different instrumentation than men have in their compositions. Perhaps they lean toward the treble instruments because that's their hearing range. This hasn't been proved wrong. But I've been seeing more and more women's works with trombones and tubas, so that theory is in dispute.

GK: *Women hear higher frequencies?*

KG: I think that's probably true. It seems to be one of the differences. None of the music I've heard so far is insipid, which is often a critique of women's compositions. There is some extremely strong orchestral music written by women.

GK: *Is it passionate?*

KG: With passion and intensity of expression. "A Short Piece for Orchestra," by Julia Perry, a black composer from Akron, Ohio, has some really incredibly painful places in it, sighing and moaning. It all resolves at the end, but there is that kind of intensity in the middle getting the emotion across.

GK: *What about your work with the conductor Antonia Brico in Denver? How did that serve as a bridge to what you're doing in Boston with the New England Women's Symphony?*

KG: Brico was the inspiration for the New England Women's Symphony; during the 1930s she founded the New York Women's Orchestra. The point she needed to prove was that women can play any orchestral instrument. That point was made. We didn't need to make that point; everyone knows that now. What we needed to prove was that women can conduct and that there are fine women composers. So the founding of New England Women's Symphony was inspired by her story, I think, more than any of her actions.

GK: *How long did you study with her?*

KG: I really studied with her for a period of two months. When she's on the East Coast, I go to where she's conducting and apprentice on that level.

GK: *That's a wonderful kind of connection.*

KG: It really is. I wish I could go to Denver; she's going to conduct the Denver symphony for the first time in many years, although she's lived there for forty years. This is the first time she's been asked to conduct their big orchestra, and she is really ecstatic, but it's such a bitter ecstasy in a way. But she's not thinking of the bitterness side now, she's just preparing for the time and conducting. (Her specialty is Sibelius.)

GK: *The New England Symphony . . . how is that going; how did you get it started?*

KG: Basically it was my brainchild. It's evolved from the work of three composers, Nancy Barrett-Thomas, Leslie Judd, and myself. We're looking for a full-time professional manager. We hope to begin a program where we will take a nucleus of about thirty musicians from the orchestra to various smaller colleges throughout New England in order to implement their own school orchestras and to get women's music heard. So we'll become more of a touring orchestra rather than just a home-based-in-Boston orchestra. That seems to be a very good step. Now we're busy having fund-raising events in order to cover the deficits from this season's concerts, but it seems to be going ahead despite financial struggles.

GK: *When did you perform your first symphony concert?*

KG: The first concert we gave was on December 3, 1978, so this is only our second season. We gave two more in Boston, and we were very lucky to have extremely good PR and a full house, plus the fact that we're doing something totally unique. But last year was pretty much an amateur effort. This year we're totally professional, and it's making a difference. It makes our budget bigger.

GK: *Do you mean that people are now being paid?*

KG: Now the orchestra members are being paid. Last year it was pretty much a volunteer effort. But this year it's definitely a paid orchestra, so the quality of the musicianship is better. If we're going to present women's music, we want to present it as best we can.

GK: *What percentage of the performers are women?*

KG: I would say 90 percent are women.

GK: *And this is from auditioning behind . . .*

KG: Behind a screen. We sit behind the screen and the musician comes in, performs, and is scored. Those with the highest scores

170   *Music*

get in. This year we've had quite a few more men auditioning. One is in a principal position. They're dedicated musicians and are grateful for the opportunity to play music that is unfamiliar to them.

GK: *Are you conducting?*

KG: I'm principal conductor and music director at the moment, which means that I choose the program and I'm the continuing link from program to program. We also bring in one established conductor and one relatively new conductor for each program, so it isn't just a one-person thing. The run-out concerts to colleges will work on a rotating basis with four or five conductors so that others will have the opportunity to present major portions of the concerts by themselves and get podium experience.

GK: *What about the research finding women composers? Are you doing that too?*

KG: I'm not personally doing that. We have several people on our staff who are at the library all the time. Nan Washburn utilizes the New England Conservatory library and the Boston Public Library. We have a woman in Philadelphia who goes to the Fleischer Library to look up things for us. Then there are quite a few women doing their graduate work in women's music literature. Pamela Susskind did her dissertation on the works of Clara Schumann. So various women are putting energy into their masters and doctorates by researching these women composers.

There are two professional associations of women composers in the country. One's the International League of Women Composers, of which I'm a member, and the other's the American Women Composers. These organizations have lists of over a hundred composers each. Some very well-known female composers aren't even affiliated with these groups.

GK: *How many women are working with you in organizing the orchestra?*

KG: Of the major workers there are five of us and then another five to ten when it comes close to a concert time. All of us have other things. The freelance musicians are excellent. Most of them have master's degrees, and most of them are from the New England Conservatory at this point. But we've had musicians traveling all the way from St. Louis to play with us.

GK: *It is very important. It's a pioneering effort, and it must be a rallying point for women composers to know that there's a place . . .*

KG: They don't quite trust us yet, but I think they will. I think they will as we get better and better with getting our publicity out and getting better exposure. I think a lot of them are afraid that it's going to be a special-interest thing and that only a certain few will have their works performed. The women who really push us the hardest are the ones who get their works done. Women have to know that they have to hustle to get their works performed anywhere, but we will listen to them before anyone else.

GK: *So a composer could send you a tape?*

KG: Yes, a tape and a score and a list of works they've done and their background too.

GK: *It's amazing to think of how much energy it takes to get the orchestra off the ground and that you did it.*

KG: I can't believe it either. It seems like last year was almost a time warp. We worked so hard to get this off the ground and put so many thousands of our own money into getting it off the ground—and it's going to continue. That's what's exciting about it. We've had to go through changes because of moving from volunteer status to professional status. It's hard, and you can't fire a volunteer if she doesn't do a good job. We had a volunteer on our publicity last time, and that's why we went in the hole because we didn't fill the hall. Last year we filled the hall every concert, so we now only hire professionals.

It saves money plus it doesn't take the personality out of it all. Last year the spirit of the orchestra was a bit more than it is this year because for many who were in the orchestra there was strong feminist commitment. They needed to do it and they were fighters, so the spirit was there. This year it isn't so much spirit but beautiful musical competency.

GK: *What about the impact of the New England Women's Symphony on your own work?*

KG: What's really exciting about working with an orchestra is learning about the instruments firsthand. Even though I was an orchestral musician for ten years, being in an orchestra and learning the scores to conduct an orchestra are two different things. In learning the scores I'm learning composition from many different composers. With my "Winter Night, Gibbous Moon: Saga for Eleven Flutes" I feel I've come into my own as far as style. For the five years that I've been composing in earnest, I've been teaching myself by writing in many different styles. I think I've finally hit upon the style that feels the best to me. It is a combination of very lyrical, melodic lines with more avant garde techniques used as mood provokers or accompaniment. For example, I have the whole flute section blowing lightly into their flutes to create the song of wind, and the piccolo plays a hornpipe over that. I'm not threatening the listeners with avant garde techniques without giving them something that's familiar too—melody.

This season the New England Women's Symphony did a piece by Barbara Kolb, "Crosswinds." She had just a simple direction at one point. She wanted the loudness to be "imperceptible." I used that term in my own piece. Little things like that from many, many of the composers are valuable techniques. I feel very fortunate to be able to learn from women in this way, without taking formal lessons, by learning from how they write. Musgrave's "Night Music" also was very instructive to me because she has an improvisational section in it. She has a real sense of theatre in her music. I think women artists are leading a movement for integration of total art.

GK: *I think that's true for women in lots of areas.*

KG: Women are leaders in the holistic health movement and in other fields too.

GK: *Yes, maybe because there's not the same attachments to old form.*

KG: It's hard to get away from old forms because they're so accepted. In the women's movement or in any other field we must let go of conditioning, especially that based on expectations of society or family.

GK: *Or your academic training?*

KG: Yes. There's a composer-conductor up here in Maine who writes melodic music just as I do. He said that seven years ago, if anyone wrote anything tonal they would have been laughed out of academia because nothing was supposed to have a melody. But now melody is returning. I think many composers are writing melodic music because we feel that the lack of melodic music is an indication of the dis-ease of society. In her book *The Haunted Pool* George Sand talks about that in painting—about the obligation of the art world to present things of beauty: "Art is not a study of positive reality, it is the seeking for ideal truth."

GK: *What about albums; you have two?*

KG: I have two on the Wise Woman/Urana label. I am doing another album, *A Rainbow Path*, on my own label, Even Keel Records. I like having the control.

GK: *It seems that a lot of women do that—have their own companies.*

KG: I think it's easier that way to keep track of everything. When you get a record company that has more than one artist, then they have a hard time keeping up with the finances. Right now it's really hard in the record business for several reasons, one of which is that vinyl is an oil-based product, so it's very, very difficult to get quality recordings.

GK: *Are you still combining music and spirituality?*

KG: I've been doing the Music and Healing Workshops for about two years now at various colleges all over the United States. We practice looking at auras, seeing what colors they are, healing each other's auras, singing specific tones to see if they affect specific parts of the body and what colors come to mind. I think consciously about color when I'm writing. In "Winter Night, Gibbous Moon" I chose a dark key because it's about the night. As it gets closer to sunrise the tonal centers rise also. I am using color as a conscious part of my art, and I'm talking to people about that potential in their own works, whether or not they choose to use it. Different colors and tones are related to the different chakras, or energy centers of the body. Taking a listener from the very dark aural and visual tones to the very light ones is giving them a more total experience.

GK: *So the musical tone itself then has power to affect one's aura?*

KG: Music's tonal vibrations and color radiations are two elements that travel along parallel wavelengths. Particular vibrations and radiations touch specific parts of the body—the seven tones (middle C through B-flat), seven colors of the spectrum (in the order of red through purple), and the seven chakras (base of the spine to the crown of the head) are related.

GK: *How did you get from your academic musical background to the awareness of spirituality and connecting the two in music?*

KG: I really don't know, but I was never academically trained in composition. I've had theory, like everybody, but I never took a composition course and I'm glad. It's awfully hard to be original when you have everybody else's ideas in your head. You have to separate them all. I just jumped into composition and taught myself. I guess any spiritual connections come from childhood. I think musicians and artists feel very close to their own spirituality and tend not to lose that perspective.

GK: *You can see auras then?*

KG: I'm learning. I'm very new at it. There are many in my workshops who are much, much better at it than I am.

GK: *That's intriguing to think   that it's something that can be learned.*

KG: Ninety percent of the people who participate in workshops who have never seen them before, see them. We're told that only schizophrenics see them, but we all, except for those who are really not very open-minded, can see auras. Anyone can do it. All you do is dim the lights slightly and just look past somebody—don't focus on them. Look next to them and you'll see the same kind of image that you see as a ghost on your television screen. You have to be in a very dim light. You'll be able to see the aura on anyone if you remember not to focus your eyes. If you wear glasses, you take them off. It works. What we're trying to discover in these workshops is, do certain tones affect the color of the aura? You have to get pretty good at seeing an aura, so that's going to take a little while to figure out, many workshops. Another question is, do the colors of the aura around certain parts of the body change? It's fascinating.

GK: *What are your goals? Is it to free yourself a bit from the symphony to do more composing?*

KG: I will never give up composing. I am now writing a short opera based on a Gertrude Stein libretto, "Ladies' Voices." It's a two-page opera of nonsense sentences, a real challenge to figure out how it can be treated operatically. It will be performed by the Down East Chamber Opera Company here in Maine and the Southwest Chamber Opera Company in Sante Fe in 1981.

And I've also got applications in several orchestras for guest-conducting positions. I'll continue working with the New England Symphony. I'll also be going out doing lectures, concerts, and workshops more and more at colleges and universities. I'll still be doing conducting, performing, composing, and lecturing.

IV. LITERATURE
AND DREAMS

MADONNA OR WITCH: WOMEN'S MUSE IN CONTEMPORARY AMERICAN POETRY

Debora Ashworth

The American woman poet has, in the past, earned her place alongside male contemporaries by conforming to the tastes of a strong male tradition in poetry. Rarely did a woman express the theme of her feelings as a woman artist in a circle dominated by men. Female themes, when women's poetry was mentioned at all, were considered neither interesting nor suitable material for "serious" poetry.

What makes poetry possible, according to critics, is the poet's ability to universalize personal experience—though for centuries a woman's experience was thought to be anything but universal. It is disturbing to observe the insecurities that have often caused the woman poet to destroy herself and her art. Alive, she tends to reaffirm the male theory that the only source of creativity available to her is her own self-destructive energy. The male poet leans toward madness graciously; he is in fact romanticized for his madness. The woman artist, on the other hand, sticks her head in an oven to ensure her fame. Despite the process of meeting male standards, women poets have consistently struggled to explore their own voices.

Women poets form a distinctive group in contemporary literature. As Florence Howe, coeditor of the women's poetry anthology *No More Masks!*, suggests:

> They write about themselves as artists, their (female) muse, their lust for fame. They write sometimes about fathers, and occasionally their mothers; occasionally, too, their children. . . . They create and re-create themselves, their feelings, in thought or in action.[1]

The woman poet is exploring her art through religious and myth images. A key to understanding this new phenomenon is the transformative effects it seems to have in the poetry itself, for the poet can project onto it her strengths and vulnerabilities, awareness, and fears. By reexamining those religious symbols and myths that haunt and oppress her daily life she can transform them into a positive source of energy and discover, perhaps, her own muse—the source of her creativity.

God the Father?

"How I would like to believe in tenderness," wrote Sylvia Plath in "The Moon and the Yew Tree." But perhaps the poet must transform this "tenderness" so that, losing its male definition, it can no longer threaten her. Denise Levertov explores this theme in "The Fountain":

> The woman of that place, shading her eyes,
> frowned as she watched—but not because
> she grudged the water,
>
> only because she was waiting
> to see we drank our fill and were
> refreshed.
>
> Don't say, don't say there is no water.
> That fountain is there among its scalloped
> green and gray stones,
>
> it is still there and always there
> with its quiet song and strange power
> to spring in us,
> up and out through the rock.

Denise Levertov, *The Jacob's Ladder*. Copyright © 1961 by Denise Levertov Goodman. Reprinted by permission of New Directions.

The imagery in this poem is predominantly feminine: the fountain and its Madonnalike custodian represent the energy of the poet. That "quiet song and strange power" serves as both a redeeming and creative source for the artist.

Religion, as Louise Bernikow notes in *The World Split Open*, has always been an appealing theme for women artists:

> Religion . . . is an acceptable subject because it focuses on the men who are God the Father and the Son and suits patriarchal taste. . . . The religious experience, a receiving experience, however intense, is never considered unfeminine.[2]

More and more women have utilized this acceptability to deal with their oppression and anger. The male image of God the Father provides a focus for the poet, for she wants both to understand his place in her life and to destroy him.

A recurring tactic in women's poetry has been to approach this male god through a Madonna image. The Virgin Mary as symbol of femininity is an acceptable vehicle by which to address the male god. The interesting emphasis in present-day poetry, however, is Mary as woman. Her human characteristics are examined. She becomes more than the Mother of Christ and symbol of chastity.

Anne Halley explores this new motif in her poem "Housewife's Letter: To Mary." Here, the biblical meeting of Mary and Elisabeth (mother of John the Baptist) symbolizes the spiritual meeting of all women:

> That Mother's meeting, visit, when
> Elisabeth first felt her son
> leap into life: Mother of God
> and Prophet's Mother, forward bowed
> embracing secrets, each in each
> they celebrate each other's fruit. . . .

Reprinted from *Between Wars and Other Poems*, by Anne Halley, Copyright © 1965 by the University of Massachusetts Press.

Anne Sexton, too, deals with this ambiguous image of the Madonna as woman and god. In "Mary's Song" she explores Mary's strength and power:

> Out of Egypt
> With its pearls and honey,
> Out of Abraham, Isaac, Jacob,
> Out of the God I Am,
> Out of the diseased snakes,
> Out of the droppings of flies,
> Out of the sand dry as paper,
> Out of the deaf blackness,
> I come here to give birth.

From *The Death Notebooks*, by Anne Sexton, published by Houghton Mifflin Company. Copyright © 1974 by Anne Sexton. Reprinted by permission.

Indeed Sexton offers interesting alternatives to traditional religious themes, as illustrated in an earlier poem, "Consorting with Angels," in which she proclaims, "I am no more a woman/than Christ was a man."

Mary, however, is still seen primarily as an image of love—a spiritual source of energy. Her function is still to nurture the Christs of the world. But the other side of this image of nurturing woman is the destructive force that many poets have explored. There exists the need to conquer god, as in Sylvia Plath's "Lady Lazarus" or Marge Piercy's "Noon of the sunbather." This confrontation with God the Father is achieved when the poet assumes a godlike persona, when she gathers her strength and goes like David before Goliath (for want of a feminine analogy), with words to be slung like pellets into the face of patriarchal oppression.

That the poet will no longer remain silent is evident in the poetry dealing with power and its attainment. Marge Piercy exclaims in "A Just Anger": "I am a burning bush," that is, an upsurge of power. Again, this theme is represented in Diane Di Prima's "Canticle of St. Joan":

> Blessed be the holy saints, now and forever.
> Blessed be Margaret & Bridget
> Blessed be spruce & fir.
> The sacred waterfall, Diana's bath, the wind
> which brings iron clouds.
> They fly out of the sea to the north, they recommend
> that I wear woman's dress, they do not see
> that I am Luci-fer, Light bearer, lead & I follow
> Mother, Sara-la-kali, sacred Diana. . . .

Later in the poem, when she is being burned at the stake, Joan exclaims:

> My hair is burning and the mist is blue
> which cracks my brain, I am not in the flame, I am the flame
> The sun pours down, the Voice is a mighty roar
> O little children's bones: the sword & cup
> are shivered into stars.

Copyright © 1971, 1974, 1979 by Diane Di Prima.

She is not merely in the flame, but is the flame; and, like the Salamander invoked earlier in the poem, the source and exponent of her own creative instincts.

This power is not necessarily destructive so long as the poet defines it for herself. Denise Levertov's "Earth Psalm" suggests in this vein, "I could replace/God for awhile, that old ring of candles." The poet must acknowledge this creative source and deal with other forms of oppression, such as the devastating myth of the virgin.

The Myth Explodes

> *No matter what life you lead*
> *The virgin is a lovely number.*
> —Anne Sexton, "Snow White and The Seven Dwarfs"

Myths frequently revolve around woman as either virgin or witch. If she is not one, she is the other. But the present-day woman poet, in examining the effect of these myths on her life, is finding that she can be both. Lyn Lifshin's "But Instead Has Gone into Woods," offers a possibility:

> A girl goes into the woods
> and for what reason
> disappears behind branches
> and is never heard from again.
> We don't really know why.
> She could have gone shopping
> or had lunch with her mother
> but instead has gone into
> woods, alone, without the lover
> and not for leaves or flowers.

Reprinted with the permission of Crossing Press, from *Black Apples*, 1975.

This wilderness represents the poet's source of creative energy; exploring it enables her to experience and utilize the animal instinct that has been denied expression by the patriarchal culture it threatens. The century-old "girl do not go to the forest, there is danger there" is more accurately interpreted as "girl do not go to the forest, I can't watch you there." Consequently the lure of the wilderness is the lure of freedom. Once outside the realm of social convention the poet may experience all aspects of her personality, not just the nurturing virgin or the seductive whore (an image often interchanged with that of the crone.)

In questioning her position in the world and its relation to her growing awareness the poet is dealing with her fear of otherness, the repressed aspect of her personality that only surfaces as either virgin or witch. Anne Sexton examines this theme of otherness in her transformative account of the fairy tale "Rapunzel":

> A woman
> who loves a woman
> is forever young.
> The mentor
> and the student
> feed off each other.
> Many a girl
> had an old aunt
> who locked her in the study
> to keep the boys away.
> They would play rummy
> or lie on the couch
> and touch and touch
> old breast against young breast

. . . .
We are two clouds
glistening in the bottle glass.
We are two birds
washing in the same mirror.
We were fair game
but we kept out of the cesspool.
We are strong.
We are the good ones.
Do not discover us
for we lie together all in green
like pond weeds.
Hold me, my young dear, hold me. . . .

From *Transformations*, by Anne Sexton, published by Houghton Mifflin Company.
Copyright © 1971 by Anne Sexton. Reprinted by permission.

This awareness derives from a woman's ability to dive deep into her own past, "to see the damage that was done/and the treasures that prevail," as Adrienne Rich suggests in "Diving into the Wreck." It is the process itself, the wading through the countless mythologies of one's own life, that the poet must come to.

The poet overcomes her initial fear through action, locating and confronting these destructive forces that have been associated with her. In Sexton's "Hansel and Gretel," for example, Gretel pushes the witch into the oven not to save Hansel and more than just to save her own life; she is trying to conquer her own oppression. Gretel sees her moment and acts on it, pushing the oppressive image of crone into the oven. Thus the poet transforms the fearful image of witch into a positive creative source and in so doing learns that the mysterious powers associated with women through this image are as positive and nurturing as the image of Mary. Alice Walker's "Medicine" illustrates this constructive power:

The
medicine
is all
in
her long
un -
braided
hair.

Reprinted with the permission of the author and publisher, Harcourt Brace Jovanovich, Inc., from *Once*, 1968.

Here the medicine, the power, are as natural as her body, and the image of it, as Jean Tepperman shows in "Witch," evokes enthusiasm:

I have been invisible
weird and supernatural.
I want my black dress.
I want my hair
curling wild around me.
I want my broomstick
from the closet where I hid it.
Tonight I meet my sisters
in the graveyard.
Around midnight
if you stop at a red light
in the wet city traffic,
watch for us against the moon.
We are screaming,
we are flying,
laughing, and won't stop.

The poet no longer needs to fear the myth itself, acknowledging first the oppressive impact on her life and second its inauthentic source of power—the self-reinforcing influence of a male-defined culture.

Conclusion

The woman poet of today is drawn back again and again to the source of her creativity. For her it is not so much a question of inspiration as it is one of inevitable self-confrontation, the consequence of which leaves women, as Carolyn Kizer has termed, "narcissists by necessity." It is this same confrontation, however, that makes the woman artist an iconoclast by necessity as well.

For the poet her position between narcissism and iconoclasm is precarious at best and destructive at worst. The question now becomes one of self-preservation in the face of transforming and assimilating the countless images imposed on that self through centuries of patriarchal definition. As mortal she is fascinated by the spiritual elevation of her role as goddess and fearful of, yet intrigued by, the power associated with the destructive image of witch, or what is known in archetypal terminology as the Terrible Mother.

Some poets approach this question as a means of self-affirmation, as in the "Kali" poems of Lucille Clifton; for others it is a key to the transformative directions of our lives, as in Olga Broumas's *Beginning with O*; still for others it is a source of spirited playfulness, as seen in

Susan Griffin's "The Great Mother." And perhaps behind this question of otherness lies woman's muse.

The image of muse for the poet is still both spiritual and mythic in origin but also deeply rooted in that creative wilderness she has only recently begun to explore. Moving outside the social norm, wandering through a forest, and possibly losing one's way make this wilderness dangerous country to be sure, but for the poet it is an unavoidable challenge that is self-affirming in its explication. It is interesting to note that in recent years the muse has manifested itself as animal with greater frequency, an animal of vision and intellect. The image of animal, as opposed to the conventional image of muse in its all-too-human form, is the more agile creature in this world of contour and anomaly, a world as lush and mysterious as woman's past. And though the poet's experience as woman is certainly reflected in the experience of her subject, the experience, as one viewed outside the perimeters of human interaction, is transformed into a more far-reaching response—the poet begins to perceive the world through her own developed senses. Still, the image itself, whether it appears as the wolf at the door or in the room in poems by Maxine Kumin, the lioness in Adrienne Rich's most recent poetry, or the monkey in poems by Audre Lorde and Irena Klipfiz, is still an image of vision, of creativity, of consciousness.

Notes

1. Florence Howe. Foreword to *No More Masks! An Anthology of Poems by Women*, Florence Howe and Ellen Bass, eds. Garden City, N.Y.: Anchor/ Doubleday, 1973, p.xxviii.
2. Louise Bernikow. Foreword to *The World Split Open: Four Centuries of Women Poets in England and America 1522-1950*, Louise Bernikow, ed. New York: Vintage, 1974, p.7.

Selected Bibliography

Di Prima, Diane. *Revolutionary Letters*. San Francisco: City Lights, 1971.

Levertov, Denise. *The Jacob's Ladder*. New York: New Directions, 1961.

_____. *O Taste and See*. New York: New Directions, 1964.

Lifshin, Lyn. *Black Apples*. Crossing Press, 1975.

Plath, Sylvia. *Ariel*. New York: Harper and Row, 1961.

Rich, Adrienne. *Diving into the Wreck*. New York: Norton, 1973.

Sexton, Anne. *The Death Notebooks*. Boston: Houghton Mifflin, 1974.

————. *Transformations*. Boston: Houghton Mifflin, 1971.

Debora Ashworth *is a resident of Oregon. She received her B.A. in English from Skidmore College in New York.*

MIRROR IMAGES

Marge Piercy

I do writing of several kinds, and each feels quite distinct to me. I write essays, reviews, and articles (like this one) in a spirit that reminds me of writing papers for school: almost always at the last minute to a deadline. There is usually a clear purpose to it, for instance, giving a push to some book I think important, such as Alice Walker's *Meridian*, Audre Lorde's poetry, or Bell Chevigny's *The Woman and the Myth: Margaret Fuller's Life and Writings*. My aim is to be as clear as possible. The purpose overrides aesthetics. I usually try to make a few important points.

I try to be open about the fact that it is my opinion I am putting forth and about the political stance that informs that opinion. I regard writing these pieces as a duty that I carry with other women who have some access to print media. Writing reviews feels more like sharing the life-support jobs in a household than like creativity to me, although I know there are people who find the essay an exciting form.

My lack of commitment to reviews or essays does not mean that I do not get excited about ideas but that not enough of the rest of my psyche is involved for the act to feel to me as I am accustomed to feeling during writing. I do not respond the same way toward other prose nonfiction: for instance, Adrienne Rich's *Of Woman Born* moved and excited me and served me as much as any of her absolutely first-rate poems. I think of my nonfiction as impersonal, duty-oriented, like tithing: something you must put back in the movement, something you must do for other women's work, mostly.

Collaborating on Plays . . .

My only play I wrote in collaboration with Ira Wood. I worked with other people frequently in the past writing articles or pamphlets, usually in the course of political work. In the North American Congress on Latin America, in Students for a Democratic Society, and in the women's movement I wrote with six or seven collaborators. Until I worked on *The Last White Class*, however, I had never collaborated on something that I viewed as art rather than as direct and immediate agit-prop or how-to information.

Collaborating is interesting—which is like saying that marriage is interesting—and you wonder how other people manage it without murdering each other. It was hard in different ways than it is to work alone. It required a discipline of openness to ideas not originating with me and a stubbornness in defending my better ideas. I think that it is good to have a relationship in which collaborators can scream at each other and to have some way to make up. We certainly screamed a lot. We wrote the whole play together line by line. In each draft we took different scenes to rough out, but then week by week we got together and did the actual writing. I think that in collaboration the ultimate advantage goes to the one at the typewriter because that person determines what finally gets typed. (We figured this out early and took turns.)

As for writing for the theater, it is still exotic to me and problematical. I remain unconvinced a year after the first production that plays are an effective way of reaching anybody. For a writer it feels very complicated and round-about. I am familiar with the orneriness of characters in novels who won't lie down and die when you tell them to, but the orneriness of actors was new to me. I can imagine that the chills and fevers of opening night could be addictive, but probably more so if I were only a novelist and not also a poet who gets to have my own opening night every time I give a reading.

. . . and Saying Poems . . .

My poetry appears to me at once more personal and more universal than my fiction. My poetry is of a continuity with itself and with the work of other women. No one who reads a lot in women's anthologies can avoid being struck by how we are all opening new ground for each other, how we create new kinds of poems, call attention to old daily experiences never named, and thus never recognized, how we help each other along the way.

I speak mostly in my own persona or in a voice that is a public form of it—the spokesperson role. Some poems come out of my own experiences and some poems come from the energy of others' experiences coming through me, but they are all fused in the layers of my mind to my voice. I stand up in public and say them to audiences. That makes me directly and immediately accountable for what the poems mean, how they move you. I can see what is working and what is not, I can hear where I have failed to hew my rhythms, to set just the right word in. I can hear my failures of nerve. I can hear where I relied upon rhetoric that came to me used rather than making it clear out of our daily language. I can hear muddiness that is laziness: not working through until the simplicity emerges from the noise.

I am constantly reworking the poems I read until they are published in book form. I consider magazine publication some halfway point. When I am putting a book together, I rewrite 40 percent or so of the poems. I don't always read a poem the same way. I may put in or leave out. It is a performance, after all, and the form on the page is notation. Even when I am performing a poem from one of my books, I may alter it. I have had members of the audience who have been following in a book tell me I had made a mistake, which makes me smile. There are mistakes, certainly, when I miss a line or inadvertently transpose lines. But I also alter the poems experimentally or in response to something in the evening or the audience. This is a minor point anyhow. The vast majority of the time once the poems have appeared in book form they are as I want them, and I leave them and perform them as written.

I want my readings to be an emotional experience, an affirming experience—one in which we together experience what we hope for and what we fear, what makes us weaker and what makes us stronger, where we have been and where we are trying to go. I try to have some notion of who is in the audience, in order to create a program and an order that can work. There is a considerable pool of poems I am drawing from at any time, up to three hundred or so poems I regularly read.

Since I am still standing up and saying some poems I wrote fifteen years ago as well as some I wrote last week, I sense a continuity with my poetry inside my own career as well as across the boundaries of lives. Some poems I cannot any longer feel close to, can't feel good about saying, but others remain utterances I still want to say. I associate the strenth of poetry with a sense of telling the truth: the truth of a moment, perhaps, the truth of the way the winter light falls on the path or the truth of a painful encounter or the truth of mass murder. I think of poetry as utterance that heals on two levels.

The first level of healing is that of the psyche. Poetry is a saying that uses verbal signs and images, sound and rhythm, memory and dream images. Poetry blends all kinds of knowing, the analytical and the synthetic, the rational and the prerational and the gestalt grasping of the new or ancient configuration, the separate and fused hungers and satisfaction and complaints and input of the senses, the knotted fibrous mass of pleasure and pain, the ability to learn and to forget, the mammalian knowing (the communication you share with your dog), the old reptilian wisdom about place and intent. Poetry has a healing power because it can fuse for the moment all the kinds of knowing in its saying.

Poetry can also heal as a communal activity. It can make us share briefly the community of feeling and hoping that we want to be. It can create a rite in which we experience each other with respect and draw energy.

Fiction is as old a habit of our species as poetry. It goes back to *tale*, the first perceptions of pattern, and fiction is still about pattern in human life. At core, it answers the question, what then? And then and then and then.

Poetry is an art of time, as music is. Rhythms are measured against time: they are measures of time. A poem goes forward a beat at a time as a dance does, step by step, phrase by phrase. Fiction is *about* time. First this, then that. Or this—then before it was that. Therefore this. From the perception of the seasons, of winter, spring, summer, fall, of the seasons of our lives, of the things that return and the things that do not return, of the drama of the search and finding of the fruit, the seed, the root that sustains life, the looking and the hunting and the kill, the arc of the sex act, the climax of giving birth: these are the sources of the fictional intelligence. If you make such a choice (being kind to an old woman on the road, running down an old man, marrying Bluebeard against all advice, apprenticing yourself to a witch), what follows?

. . . and Selling Stories . . .

I do not write much short fiction. I used to, but I could not get it published. In the sixties there was no place open to me to publish most of my fiction, no place to publish serious short stories about the lives of women from a viewpoint anything like mine. The only stories of mine published then were a few with a man as protagonist and a couple about childhood. With the founding of women's periodicals many of my short stories could find a home. It made me feel very good to see them in print at last, as if the dead had finally risen, but the habit of writing short fiction has almost failed in me. Of course I have not been paid for them. The only short fiction I ever made any money on at all was a piece about a religious fanatic who became a rock singer, which was published in the *Paris Review* and then anthologized several times.

I have written a couple of stories in recent years, but only a couple, less than one every three years. Basically the decision is economic, and then habitual. I am accustomed to thinking of poem ideas, novel ideas, but no longer invent short story ideas.

. . . and Living Inside Novels

My novels feel very different to me, each a small world. A novel is something I inhabit for two or three years, like a marriage or a house. It owns me. I live inside it. Then it is done and I pick up and go to find a new home, often with a feeling of terrible desolation and loss and depression. What will become of me? What will I do now? How will I live? What will I think about? While I am writing a novel, it occupies me and stains my life.

When I am writing first draft, it drains my dreams wan. I have simple anxiety dreams, simple sexual dreams, blatant wish fulfillment or terror. In later drafts my dreams flesh out again, rich and various. The first draft is scary to me. I can't risk interrupting it for long as the flow may be broken. The momentum is important, pushing off into space. I think of it as building a bridge in midair, from one side of a river. I am always terrified that the whole thing is unsound. Sometimes my identification becomes dangerous. I lose a sense of myself in my characters until I have trouble functioning in my own life. I can't sleep, I can't get out of the character or the novel. Those are the dangers of first draft.

I like revisions. It's work that has more play in it, less spinning from the gut. I know I can get through it; the problems are large, perhaps, but smaller than the horizon. I can get my mind around them. Between the second and third drafts I have the habit of circulating my manuscript to friends. I show it to seven to ten people, some writers and some not. I ask for criticism. That is the time I care most what people say about my work. I can put criticism to work then. I can accept or reject bit by bit, but I need that kind of feedback, what works and what doesn't, what others are seeing when they look at the work.

As a political writer I frequently have a fair amount of research to do on a novel. For *Going Down Fast* I had to understand the uses of urban renewal to the conglomeration of real estate and corporate powers that control cities, and I had to understand Chicago history and politics. For *Woman on the Edge of Time* I had a lot of studying to do about the brain and psychosurgery, about how it feels to be in a mental institution, and a lot of research to do preliminary to thinking about a good future society.

I have a very nice memory annex that I use for just about everything, from what I do instead of a diary (notes from time to time) to ways of keeping and organizing and accessing research data to notes on plot and character and future novels. The system uses edge-punched, or edge-notched, cards and a series of randomly generated codes that use one-, two-, three-, or four-hole codes according to the predicted frequency of use—according to my project, my habits of mind, what I think I'll be doing and caring about. I once wrote a book about this system of information storing and retrieval called *The General Practitioner*, but nobody wanted to publish it.

Anyhow, that saves me a lot of time in getting at the large amounts of information I use up and the large amounts of notes I take. Otherwise I think I would drown in notes. I clip periodicals heavily and keep files on things I think possibly useful. Novelists are always hungry for information. I am always way behind clipping things, let alone reading them. My house is full of glaciers of yellowing newsprint creeping through the rooms.

I wrote six novels before the first one that was published, *Going Down Fast*. That has the least women's consciousness of any of my novels, but then it was written from 1965 to 1967, when I had the least of any time in my life. One of the earlier books that could not be printed was close to a feminist novel, *Maud Awake*, and that was one of the things about it besides its great length that made it impossible to publish in the mid-sixties. *Going Down Fast* marked the first time I had written with a male protagonist, in part. The novel is told from two major viewpoints and a number of minor ones and is a fairly classy example of what you can do with multiple viewpoints in showing political process and the exercise of powers and powerlessness. I find it a little "literary" and overwritten now, but only a little. It was my love-hate musing on Chicago, where I lived for four years, the hardest of my life. So far, that is.

Dance the Eagle to Sleep I still like a lot. Nothing else like it came out of the sixties, and I think that it stands up very well. I doubt that it would find a publisher today: the politics are too harsh and direct. It had enough trouble finding a publisher in 1969. It was turned down by twenty houses before Doubleday took a tiny chance on it with a minuscule advance and a two-book contract that tied me up till 1975. It has more in it to me of what the heart of the New Left felt like than anything else I've read, and I think that a lot of people who were passionately involved felt or feel that way about the novel. I did not try to write a realistic novel about the SDS but produced a dream-nightmare version of what was going on in our psyches at the same time that I recreated a lot of the kinds of jargon, interactions, relationships, and political concerns that characterized that world. I think that choice was a wise one, and it certainly was a shrewd one in terms of being able to write about the New Left without describing events that might have proved useful to the government and its unceasingly multimillion-dollar surveillance of all of us active then and now. You pay for that and so do I. I don't think you get your money's worth. Wouldn't you rather spend it on a vacation or meals cut?

Small Changes was an attempt to produce in fiction the equivalent of a full experience in a consciousness-raising group for many women who would never go through that experience. It was conceived from the beginning as a very full novel that would be long, almost Victorian in its scope and detail. I wanted, I needed, that level of detail in the lives of my two women protagonists. The novel is as much about who is doing the housework at any given point as it is about who is sleeping with whom.

Woman on the Edge of Time is my favorite of my novels. I simply think that it's the best I've done so far. My first intent was to create an image of a good society, one that was *not* sexist, racist, or imperialist: one that *was* cooperative, respectful of all living beings, gentle, responsible, loving, and playful. The result of a full feminist revolution. To try to imagine people of such a society was my hardest task. I think that Consuelo Ramos is the best character I ever created, the fullest and deepest.

The High Cost of Living is about the price of moving from the working class to the college-educated working class. It also explores the limitations of cultural feminism and separatism; why I do not believe that feminism without an economic and class analysis works. But it's also about loneliness and the rigidity that prevents us from being able to love each other. It's about labeling and about lying.

Vida has as protagonist a political fugitive, a woman who has been living underground since 1970. On one level it is about the sixties and the seventies. On another level it is about two sisters, both politically committed, and some of the inner and outer forces that make one woman a feminist and another more oriented toward the male Left. On another level it is a love story about two people trying to build love and truth on the margin of danger and desperation. On another it is a study of the destructive effects of male sexual jealousy.

I think of each of my novels as being a different world, almost. I think that each is written fairly differently, and I think that for each novel, just as there is an appropriate length given in the basic idea (that *Small Changes* would be five hundred-plus pages long and *The High Cost of Living*, less than three hundred), so there is an appropriate language for the character and the action. When I do what is popularly called fine writing, I do my best to strike it out. That wasn't true in *Going Down Fast*, but I think I have been more disciplined since then. However, I can imagine a novel in which such literary language might be appropriate. I think that the novel I am beginning now will necessarily be more complex in its structure and language because it concerns the nature of creativity as a central focus.

Another strong difference between fiction and poetry is that poetry is really almost independent of reviews for getting out to people. Poetry readings are more important, as is inclusion in anthologies. There are many alternate sources of information about poetry, and many shades of opinion are represented in writing about it. There is no single source or single few sources of rating, as there is with novels. With novels the reviews in a few New York–based publications can make or break a novel in hardcover and determine whether you will ever hear of it: whether it will be advertised, reviewed elsewhere, ordered by bookstores, or even printed a year to a year and a half later in mass-market paperback.

Reviewers do not perceive books as having a political dimension when the ideas expressed in the novels—the attitudes toward toward wealth and poverty, social class, capitalism, sex roles, what masculine and feminine are, what's normal—are congruent with their own attitudes or those they are used to hearing discussed over supper. When reviewers read novels whose attitudes offend them or clash with their own ideas, they perceive those novels as political and polemical, and they attack them.

This gives a few periodicals whose interests represent the interests of a few people who tend to be doing right fine under the present system a great deal of power to determine what fiction the rest of us are apt to be reading next year. Naturally I object to this system of screening books, since my novels always have something to offend everybody, but especially tend to offend the reviewers of those powerful periodicals. I'm feminist, I'm of the Left, and I like to write about working-class people. When I don't offend, I am simply writing about people they don't tend to give a shit about. That's all right; I find suburban novels about adultery boring myself.

I find much more poetry that I can enjoy than fiction. Among the fiction writers whose work I read with pleasure are Alice Walker, Toni Morrison, Alice Munro, Margaret Atwood, Joan Haggerty, Toni Cade Bambera, Stanislaw Lem, Gabriel García Márquez, Thomas Pynchon, Doris Lessing, E. M. Broner, Rhoda Lerman, Joanna Russ, Suzy McKee Charnas, Vonda McIntyre, Samuel R. Delany, Fanny Howe, Tillie Olsen, and Grace Paley. There are so many poets I like that I couldn't even make a short list. Adrienne Rich, Denise Levertov, Audre Lorde, and Diane Di Prima mean a lot to me. I probably read more poetry than I do fiction. I also read a great deal of nonfiction on a variety of subjects, from natural history to economics to biography.

Still, at the moment, there is more poetry that speaks to me as a woman, a feminist, a political person, someone hungry for ideas, information, confirmation of my experiences, knowledge of other people's, than there is in any other form of writing. I think that many women share that perception, which is one of the reasons we fill poetry readings where women we respect say their poems to us.

Marge Piercy is a poet and novelist who identifies herself as a "political writer" concerned with issues of sexism, racism, and classism. She has a history of political activity in Left organizations and later in feminist ones. She lives in Massachusetts. Among her books are Small Changes, Vida, The Moon Is Always Female, To Be of Use, and Living in the Open.

THE USE OF STORY IN WOMEN'S NOVELS OF THE SEVENTIES

Carol Burr Megibow

Carol Christ in *Diving Deep and Surfacing,* a study of Doris Lessing and Margaret Atwood, defines "story" as "all articulations of experience that have a narrative element. . . ."[1] She goes on to argue that

> women's stories have not been told. And without stories there is no
> articulation of experience. Without stories a woman is lost when
> she comes to make the important decisions of her life. She does
> not learn to value her struggles, to celebrate her strengths, to
> comprehend her pain. Without stories she cannot understand her-
> self. Without stories she is alienated from the deeper experiences
> of self and world that have been called spiritual or religious. She is
> closed in silence. The expression of women's spiritual quest is
> integrally related to the telling of women's stories. If women's
> stories are not told, the depth of women's souls will not be known
> [p. 1].

In women's contemporary fiction this lack of stories that express the female experience is a problem, faced in different ways. Because the man's view of the world has been articulated so many times his stories have become archetypal, having the power of myth in their culture. Now that women have ended their long silence they must decide whether to make their world view part of the culture by subverting and adapting the traditional stories or by rejecting them through a radical demythologizing process. Both the form and content of women's fiction are deeply affected by the writer's attitude toward the mythic tales of the patriarchy. Clearly these tales are dangerous tools; in the hands of woman, who has been the created rather than the creator, they may continue the lie, pull her back into her gilded cage through assumptions she cannot fully understand. On the other hand, if the woman writer rejects these patriarchal stories, she feels the frustration and anger of exclusion from their archetypal power.

In the eight American novels to be discussed, four demythologize, tearing away at the stories that have made woman a slave in her culture. These four—Joyce Carol Oates's *Them*, Rita Mae Brown's *Rubyfruit Jungle*, Marge Piercy's *Small Changes*, and Marilyn French's *The Women's Room*—see traditional stories as male and strike out at them in various voices, denying their validity for the female experience. The other four—Margaret Atwood's *Surfacing*, Maxine Hong Kingston's *The Woman Warrior*, Leslie Silko's *Ceremony*, and Toni Morrison's *Song of Solomon*—subvert and adapt traditional stories to their experience as women and to their perception of the world. These novels (I am considering *The Woman Warrior* as fiction because of its use of novelistic devices) will be discussed in chronological order to suggest the solidifying of attitudes for or against story.

I claim a bias: the novels that harness the mythic materials are more powerful, more vivid expressions of a female world view than are those that reject the past. Women are masters of subversion, having learned the art as a tool for survival in the patriarchy; now that they are able to articulate their perceptions, a revolution is afoot.

Them (1969), by Joyce Carol Oates, is a coldly angry treatment of one version of the patriarchal tale—the American Dream—as it looks from the position of poverty and ignorance. Oates focuses on a poor Detroit family to make her point. Maureen, the female protagonist, has nothing but the romantic stories of falling in love and living happily ever after to pit against the ugly violence of her experience. In a letter to "Dear Miss Oates" Maureen accuses her of teaching "mainly lies" about the nature of life:

> While I was asleep everything had kept on!—no end to it, a jumble of people and things—photographs of tanks and soldiers, people lying in the street-everything keeps going. The books you taught us didn't explain this. The jumble was hidden somehow. The books you taught us are mainly lies I can tell you.[2]

The stories here are the enemy, the liars, deceiving the hearer about the world, leaving her unprepared for survival. Maureen does not survive; instead of passing beyond the patriarchal myth of romance she shuts out what her experience shows her and chooses the security of a loveless marriage. There is no real consolation for her suffering, only the numbing of it in the prescribed mode. Although Oates seems to provide an alternative to the traditional story in Maureen's brother, Jules, his flight to California fails to transcend the romantic abyss that ties him to a woman who has unsuccessfully attempted to kill him. Thus, while the novel effectively demythologies the traditional stories connected with the American Dream, it fails to subvert or adapt them to contemporary realities.

The next novel, Margaret Atwood's *Surfacing* (1972), proves the standard by which the uses of story in the other novels can be measured. Here a white middle-class woman is able to transcend the lies Oates described through the Canadian Indian rituals of her childhood. When the novel begins, the nameless narrator is among the living dead, denying her past and therefore herself by lying about her art and her relationships. Setting out as a young woman to be an artist, she has become instead an illustrator, drawing distorted images of bowdlerized fairy tales:

> The stories aren't what I expected; they're like German fairy tales, except for the absence of red-hot iron slippers and nail-studded casks. I wonder if this mercy descends from the original tellers, from the translator or from the publisher; probably it's Mr. Persival from the publisher, he's a cautious man, he shies away from anything he calls "disturbing." We had an argument about that: he said one of my drawings was too frightening and I said children like being frightened. "It isn't the children who buy the books," he said, "it's their parents." So I compromised; now I compromise before I take the work in, it saves time. I've learned the sort of thing he wants: elegant and stylized, decoratively colored, like patisserie cakes. I can do that, I can imitate anything: fake Walt Disney, Victorian etchings in sepia, Bavarian cookies, ersatz Eskimo for the home market.[3]

Her relationships with people, like her art, are decorative lies that require endless compromise of her vision and her experience.

This imitation of the patriarchal story cannot, however, survive the emotional intensity of the narrator's return to her literal and spiritual home, the isolated Canadian island on which she was reared. Away from the plastic world of the "Americans" she begins first to lose the false sanity of her self-deceptive story and then to create her own story through adapting native rituals. Her mangled princesses are fed to the fire; indeed all that constitutes her false history is systematically destroyed:

> When nothing is left intact and the fire is only smoldering I leave, carrying one of the wounded blankets with me, I will need it until the fur grows. . . .
>
> I untie my feet from the shoes and walk down to the shore; the earth is damp, cold, pockmarked with raindrops. I pile the blanket on the rock and step into the water and lie down. When every part

of me is wet I take off my clothes, peeling them away from my flesh like wallpaper. They sway beside me, inflated, the sleeves bladders of air.

My back is on the sand, my head rests against the rock, innocent as plankton; my hair spreads out, moving and fluid in the water. The earth rotates, holding my body down to it as it holds the moon; the sun pounds in the sky, red flames and rays pulsing from it, searing away the wrong form that encases me, dry rain soaking through me, warming the blood egg I carry. . . .

When I am clean I come out of the lake, leaving my false body floated on the surface, a cloth decoy; it jiggles in the waves I make, nudges gently against the dock [p. 208].

Her body and spirit are purified in a ritual that asserts the relationship between self and nature against the dehumanizing logic of "civilization."

The narrator goes even farther, rejecting the gods she has used to free her as offering only one kind of truth, a past truth that alone cannot save her. She must invent her own tale:

This above all, to refuse to be a victim. Unless I can do that I can do nothing. I have to recant, give up the old belief that I am powerless and because of it nothing I can do will ever hurt anyone. A lie which was always more disastrous than the truth would have been. The word games, the winning and losing games are finished; at the moment there are no others but they will have to be invented, withdrawing is no longer possible and the alternative is death [p. 223].

Here is the power of story to heal, to tell the truth, to make the pain meaningful. The old stories tell women that they can only be victims, passively accepting powerlessness as the natural condition. Atwood refuses, claiming the power and right to tell her own tale. What this tale will be is only hinted at, but one suspects that it will be like the novel itself in its adaptation of mythic tools to a woman's life.

Atwood articulates woman's need to have power over her own life, her own stories, in *Survival: A Thematic Guide to Canadian Literature.* Here she outlines the steps necessary to move from victimhood to freedom: (1) Deny that you're a victim. Direct anger against your fellow victims; (2) Acknowledge victimhood but explain it as God's will, history, fate: you may play it out as resigned or rebellious, but of course you will lose. The explanation displaces the cause of oppression to something too vast to change; (3) Acknowledge victimization but don't accept it as inevitable. This dynamic position can slide back to (2) or attempt to progress to (4). Here you can make real decisions about what can be changed and what can't. Anger can be directed against what is oppressing you; and (4). Be a creative nonvictim. Atwood describes this as almost impossible in an oppressive socity, but glimpsed in moments of insight that can be brought back to the daily existence of struggle described in (3).[4] Clearly, as the narrator of *Surfacing* moves through the lies that have denied her a true past, she moves from (1) a denial of her victimhood to (2) an acknowledgment of her situation that can see no hope of change to (3) a rejection—perhaps temporary—of her victimhood and a glimpse of what her life might be like without it. There is a vision of a story in which woman and nature control the world through an archetypal union. Although the narrator must return to "America," the place in the mind and in the world that oppresses the female self, she will carry back a boon, a true story.

Atwood's vision, with its realistic appraisal of the state of women's stories and its tentative provision of tools for the invention of such stories through the adaptation of prehistoric materials, is a standard bearer of the new women's culture. Her radical reworking of male myth shows what can be reclaimed from the past to mold the future. In this light the story elements of *Rubyfruit Jungle* (1973), by Rita Mae Brown, prove to be almost pure demythologizing, but unlike the situation in *Them* the process is carried out by a woman who cannot be destroyed by the loss of myth. Molly Bolt comes to the ugly world portrayed in the novel with a completely realized story. Molly brings wisdom without guilt—a vision complete and ready for heroic acting out in victorious opposition to the traditional tale that brought psychic death to Maureen and temporary madness to the protagonist of *Surfacing*. It is wonderful contemporary wish fulfillment, replacing the death of marriage in earlier romantic stories with a career and financial independence.

As a child Molly is told all the appropriate socialization stories, intended to humiliate and frighten her into submission; when she is playing with her friends, she rejects the role of nurse because it is expected:

> One time Cheryl decided to play nurse and we put napkins on our heads. Leroy was the patient and we painted him with iodine so he'd look wounded. A nurse, I wasn't gonna be no nurse. If I was gonna be something I was gonna be the doctor and give orders. I tore off my napkin, and told Cheryl I was the new doctor in town. Her face corroded. "You can't be a doctor. Only boys can be doctors. Leroy's got to be the doctor."
> "You're full of shit, Spiegelglass, Leroy's dumber than I am. I got to be the doctor because I'm the smart one and being a girl doesn't matter."[5]

There are many such exchanges in the novel, each adding to one's sense of the world's ugliness and Molly's beauty, a witty reworking of Cinderella with the stepmother routed not by a prince but by the spunky autonomy of a lone woman. By the end of the novel she has undone the traditional tale by producing a film of its effects on her stepmother, Carrie. Through this act Molly shows not only her mastery of filmmaking but also her clear understanding of who the oppressors are. Carrie, who cruelly reminds Molly of her bastard origins, is not the enemy but the victim who denies she is one and directs her anger at fellow victims. Because Molly has reached the point of making real decisions about what can be changed she is able to help Carrie tell her story and by so doing heal the split created by a false fairy tale. Thus the novel ends as it began, with the heroine in control of her story and therefore safe from destruction:

> What the hell. I wished I could be that frog back at Ep's old pond. I wished I could get up in the morning and look at the day the way I used to when I was a child. . . . Damn, I wished the world would let me be myself. But I knew better on all counts. I wish I could make my films. That wish I can work for. One way or another I'll make those movies and I don't feel like having to fight until I'm fifty. But if it does take that long then watch out world because I'm going to be the hottest fifty-year-old this side of the Mississippi [p. 246].

The romantic story has been turned upside down to show its absurdity; the heroine stands free and independent of its programmed victimhood. But Brown does not explain how Molly, and by extension all women, makes her self; that self appears ready-made from the beginning and therefore can only show what the new woman might look like in the woman's myth that has not been realized. It is a stirring image without the guidelines to replicate it.

Marge Piercy's *Small Changes* (1974) brings one quickly back to reality by working out what its title suggests: women are fortunate to make even slight changes in the standard male myth. By detailing the lives of two very different women—Beth and Miriam—Piercy like Oates forces us to look at the world that traditional stories never prepare us for. The process begins abruptly with a black-comedy vision of Beth's wedding, a tale told by idiots in expensively ugly clothes and no identities other than the commercial ones that have been sold to them. Beth, who really wants to go to college, ends up instead in a grotesque marriage to a papier-mâché villain who tries to force her to become pregnant. Soon she flees to Boston, beginning a slow journey to self-knowledge and political rebellion. Each vignette is another stab at women's place in the patriarchal story; chapter titles provide the ironic thesis for the next episode—"The Happiest Day of a Woman's Life," "Love Is a Woman's

Whole Existence," and "Motherhood Is a Woman's Creativity" are vivid enough to make a poem of the novel's progress from false myth to painful truth.

Miriam's story makes up the heart of the novel, presenting in its protagonist the woman who seems to be making great changes, only to fall victim, in the final section, to the frightening power of the status quo. Miriam is an intellectual, free-thinking and independent, an Amazon in the Molly Bolt mold. But she is also inescapably female—large, full-breasted, sensual—an anatomy that Freud said was destiny. She looks, according to an idolized mentor, like a courtesan instead of a computer expert:

> ". . . you have an unusual intuitive mind—the best thing one can say about any scientist. But you're an attractive, a very attractive woman. So you'll do nothing. Why should you?"
>
> "You're an attractive man. Why do you bother if all that matters is sex appeal?"
>
> "Ah, that is not the same and you know it. Only homely women survive to accomplish in their field. Or perhaps a woman who has the luck to become widowed. Who would ever have heard of Madame, if Monsieur Curie had survived. The husband stands in the light, the wife in the shadows." . . .
>
> "You would go much farther, my dear, as a grand courtesan—such as the hetaeras of ancient Greece, cultivated, highly-regarded, a class of women apart—than as a systems analyst. . . ."[6]

Thus the ancient patriarchal myths rise up and terrify the sensitive Miriam, driving her into marriage for protection against a brutal world—a choice reminiscent of Maureen's.

The traditional stories are clearly the enemy in *Small Changes*, driving Beth out of her marriage and eventually into hiding and Miriam out of a budding career and into a numbingly traditional marriage. Perhaps Beth will be able to subvert these stories from the underground; perhaps Miriam will break free of the institutions that require prostitution, but women have little choice: they have no stories of their own and can only slightly change the stories written for them by the patriarchy. Beth seems closer to articulating her own experience than does Miriam, but the novel rejects resolution in favor of an angry attack on the myths that block that articulation.

Only *Surfacing* prepares the reader for the effective blending of myth and reality found in contemporary ethnic fiction. Of the four white, middle-class women writers discussed thus far, only Atwood passes through the false story to a healing ritual story. Thus, opening the pages of Maxine Hong Kingston's *The Woman Warrior* (1975), Leslie Silko's *Ceremony* (1977), and Toni Morrison's *The Song of Solomon* (1977) brings a shock of pleasure, as the dangerous tools of the traditional stories are harnessed to express the woman's experience.

It can be argued that *The Woman Warrior* has no place in a study of fiction; it is after all a memoir, not a novel. But the issue of story is in part the issue of ordering external reality as life does not; its truth is imposed on the experience, thus creating as well as reflecting the life it portrays. In Kingston's work the ordering is as fierce as that of poetry, giving metaphor its own ghostly reality in a world ruled by ghosts. For example, the opening section of the memoir, "No Name Woman," is both history and metaphor, a family disgrace that becomes in Kingston's hands an archetypal tale of woman's place in Chinese culture. This "story to grow up on," as her mother calls it, involves an aunt who becomes pregnant outside of marriage: ostracized by villagers and relatives, she drowns herself and her baby in the family well. Haunted by the ghost of her aunt, Kingston dedicates her spiritual quest for self to this nameless woman:

> My aunt haunts me—her ghost drawn to me because now, after fifty years of neglect, I alone devote pages of paper to her, though not organized into houses and clothes. I do not think she means me well. I am telling on her, and she was a spite suicide, drowning herself in the drinking water. The Chinese are always very frightened of the drowned one, whose weeping ghost, wet hair hanging and skin bloated, waits silently by the water to pull down a substitute. [7]

Here is a dangerous tale, potent with the traditional devaluing of woman, threatening to drag the author into its watery death. But Kingston faces this danger, defuses it with words, the weapons of the swordswoman whose story constitutes the second section of the memoirs:

> The swordswoman and I are not so dissimilar. May my people understand the resemblance soon so that I can return to them. What we have in common are the words at our backs. The ideographs for *revenge* are "report a crime" and "report to five families." The reporting is the vengeance—not the beheading, not the gutting, but the words. And I have so many words—"chink" words and "gook" words too—that they do not fit on my skin [p. 53].

The myth of the swordswoman is the antidote to the history of No Name Woman, the alternative to death and the revenge against the cultural norms that see woman as only wife or slave. In this myth a young Chinese girl is educated to take control of her destiny and bring that boon to the aid of her people. It is a risky way of life that involves carrying the grievances of her family on her back and disguising herself as a warrior to avenge those grievances; neither marriage nor pregnancy deter her.

Kingston, a first-generation Chinese-American, is caught between these twin heritages, struggling against a culturally based fear of becoming No Name Woman and toward her rarely achieved opposite, the Woman Warrior. "Nobody supports me," she says, so "I mustn't feel bad that I haven't done as well as the swordswoman did; after all, no birds called me, no wise old people tutored me. I have no magic beads, no water gourd sight, no rabbit that will jump in the fire when I'm hungry" (p.49). But she does have the words at her back, driving her to avenge the cultural split she feels within her and thus to master her fate.

The split is further articulated in the third section, "Shaman," which tells the half-mythic, half-historical story of Kingston's mother. In China, Brave Orchid is a medicine woman, capable of influencing the good and evil spirits in her role as midwife. But in America, Brave Orchid becomes as dangerous as No Name Woman, carrying her ancient secrets like ghosts to punish the American-born Maxine: "She pries open my head and my fists and crams into them responsibility for time, responsibility for intervening oceans" (p.108). Because this woman represents both the greatness and the horror of Kingston's cultural heritage she must be both incorporated and exorcized, an exceedingly painful and complex task that must be mastered so that Maxine can translate the Chinese stories into the American setting.

To emphasize this complexity Kingston introduces Brave Orchid's sister, Moon Orchid, to the American scene. Moon Orchid, unlike her sibling, is totally without the qualities of a swordswoman. Although Brave Orchid pushes her to assert her Chinese rights as wife of a thoroughly Americanized Oriental husband, the effect is only to drive the displaced flower to madness and death. It is a frightening tale that, like its Chinese counterpart, No Name Woman, threatens Kingston with its ghost of failed womanhood.

The beautifully poetic resolution of the split is found in the final section, "A Song for a Barbarian Reed Pipe." After brutally confronting an avatar of No Name Woman in the form of a silent Chinese schoolmate and venting her long pent-up anger at her mother's apparent will to make Maxine a wife or a slave—"'Not everybody thinks I'm nothing. I am not going to be a slave or a wife'" (p.200)—Kingston learns to face what terrifies her and defeat it with words, like the song the legendary Ts'ai Yen created to tell her story of the barbarians (Americans for Kingston) to her own people. She introduces the story as a successful adaptation of a traditional tale to *her* experience: "Here is a story my mother told me, not when I was young, but recently, when I told her I also am a story-talker. The beginning is hers, the ending, mine" (p. 206). Ts'ai Yen, a poet born in AD 175, is captured by a barbarian chieftain, becomes a warrior, bears two children, and learns to appreciate and then master the barbarians' art:

> Then, out of Ts'ai Yen's tent, which was apart from the others, the barbarians heard a woman's voice singing, as if to her babies, a song so high and clear, it matched the flutes. Ts'ai Yen sang about China and her family there. Her words seemed to be Chinese, but the barbarians understood their sadness and anger. Sometimes they thought they could catch barbarian phrases about forever wandering [p. 209].

Kingston has sung just such a story in her memoirs, and it translates well, showing the incredible power of story to subvert and adapt the traditional tales that have caged women's souls and bound their feet into tales of sadness and anger.

With the Woman Warrior's words at our backs we are prepared for the combination of mythic and realistic materials that make up Leslie Silko's *Ceremony*. The author sets the stage for her tale with three renderings of Laguna Indian legends. The first compares the author's tale to the creation of the world by Thought-Woman, who "is sitting in her room/and whatever she thinks about/appears"; what appears is the story Silko tells; "I'm telling you the story/she is thinking."[8] This role as transmitter (and interpreter) of traditional materials is similar to Kingston's role in her memoirs and thus shares its archetypal power.

The next legend is the very heart of both the technical and thematic significance of story, not only in *Ceremony*, but also in the works of some contemporary women novelists as they attempt to harness the tale:

> I will tell you something about stories,
> [he said]
> They aren't just entertainment.
> Don't be fooled.
> They are all we have, you see,
> all we have to fight off
> illness and death.
>
> You don't have anything
> if you don't have the stories.
>
> Their evil is mighty
> but it can't stand up to our stories.
> So they try to destroy the stories
> let the stories be confused or forgotten.
> They would like that

They would be happy
Because we would be defenseless then.

He rubbed his belly.
I keep them here
[he said]
Here, put your hand on it
See, it is moving.
There is life here
for the people.

And in the belly of this story
the rituals and the ceremony
are still growing [p.2].

The stories become confused, forgotten, but they are powerful life forces in the hands of true warriors of the word. This is the essential conflict of *Ceremony*, the protagonist's effort to reclaim his story from the witchery of the dominant culture. Like the Americans in *Surfacing* and the ghosts in *The Woman Warrior*, the white society almost destroys Tayo, a young Laguna man, by forcing him to live contrary to his values. Naïvely enlisting with his brother, Rocky, to fight in World War II, Tayo experiences the horror of Rocky's death and the keen sense that the so-called enemy are his brothers also. He returns a broken man who tries unsuccessfully to vomit up the ugliness of the lie. He is told that he should think only of himself in order to get well, but he can only cry "for all of them, and for what he had done" (p.14). The medicine he is given drains his memory and with it the stories that can heal him.

Tayo slowly agonizingly relearns these stories through a series of guides, predominantly female, who restore him to his body and his people through their collective wisdom. The first of these guides is his grandmother, who calls in a medicine man: "'I've been thinking,' she said, 'all this time, while I was sitting in my chair. Those white doctors haven't helped you at all. Maybe we had better send for someone else'" (p.34). Night Swan, an ageless avatar of Mother Earth, reminds Tayo of his manhood and the rightness of his quest: "'You don't have to understand what is happening. But remember this day. You will recognize it later. You are part of it now'" (p.105).

Perhaps the most significant of the female guides is Ts'eh, a mythic and human woman reminiscent of the swordswoman. Appearing to him as he begins the final phase of his quest for identity, she makes him feel joy to be alive: "Being alive was all right then: he had not breathed like that for a long time" (p.189). The effect of this new life is immediately demonstrated in Tayo's ability to sing his people's song to the rising sun:

He stood up. He knew the people had a song for the sunrise.

> Sunrise!
> We come at sunrise
>   to greet you.
> We call you
>   at sunrise.
> Father of the clouds
> You are beautiful
>   at sunrise.
>   Sunrise!

He repeated the words as he remembered them, not sure if they were the right ones, but feeling they were right, feeling the instant of the dawn was an event which in a single moment gathered all things together—... [pp. 189–190].

Until this moment Tayo was unable to remember the song, too sick with the false tale to reclaim himself or his communal relationship with "the people."

With his newfound strength Tayo is able to continue his journey, unafraid: "The woman had filled the hollow spaces with new dreams" (p. 229). Ts'eh teaches him a true story: "... he could see the story taking form in bone and muscle" (p. 236). But this new ceremony must face several trials before completion: the temptation to violence as he watches his friends destroy each other with hatred, the pressure to reject the Indian way of life because unvalued by the dominant culture, and finally the human tendency to keep his story to himself instead of sharing his boon with the people. Again, the woman—Thought-Woman and all her human representatives—saves him: "The transition was completed.... The ear for the story and the eye for the pattern were theirs; the feeling was theirs; we came out of this land and we are hers." And Tayo thinks of her (Grandma, Night Swan, Ts'eh, Nature) then: she had always loved him, she had never left him; she had always been there" (p. 267).

Thus, although Silko employs a male protagonist in her novel, the spirit that created it and the guides who lead us through it are female. The story is ancient but changed to meet the author's perception of the world and her need to make a healing ceremony for all oppressed people in an inimical culture. Perhaps by becoming the carrier of Thought-Woman's story Silko also heals the breach between men and women who falsely direct their anger toward each other instead of toward the lie that divides them.

If the healing effect of *Ceremony* is achieved in part by the bringing together of female nature and male humanity, the same can also be said of Toni Morrison's *Song of Solomon*. Here the black male protagonist, Milkman Dead, must be led to his people, his heritage, through the guidance of his half-mythic, half-human aunt, Pilate. As in *Ceremony*, story is seen as the thread of continuity, all-important to an oppressed group that has been exiled from its homeland. The central tale that restores Milkman to his personal and communal past is the legend of the flying Africans. Morrison adapts the story of African-born slaves who fly away from their plantation to show the power of a cultural past to free the individual from an alienated, earthbound existence. She also places the women at the center of the family, giving them the role of culture carriers in a strange land.

The novel begins with the failed flight of Robert Smith, a black insurance salesman who, we learn later, cannot fly because he has adopted the hate-filled ways of the white, patriarchal Americans. In this scene all the clues to the direction and resolution of the novel are provided and then, gradually as in a mystery, worked out. For example, Milkman's mother, pregnant with him, begins her labor at the sight of Smith departing from the cupola, and Pilate, Milkman's aunt and spiritual guide, sings the story of the flying Africans:

> O Sugarman done fly away
> Sugarman done gone
> Sugarman cut across the sky
> Sugarman gone home. . . .[9]

Milkman comes close to duplicating Smith's failure; his alienated life makes it difficult for Milkman to discover the source of his emptiness. But through Pilate and the legend of the flying Africans he learns to love himself and his people, becoming a true culture carrier.

Although the mythic elements of Milkman's birth are known to Pilate, he himself has no idea of his place in the story; as the narrator tells it:

> The next day a colored baby was born inside Mercy for the first time. Mr. Smith's blue silk wings must have left their mark, because when the little boy discovered, at age four, the same thing Mr. Smith had learned earlier—that only birds and airplanes could fly—he lost all interest in himself. To have to live without that single gift saddened him and left his imagination so bereft that he appeared dull even to the women who did not hate his mother [p.9].

Milkman's last name—Dead—seems appropriate to the protagonist for the first half of the novel. His mother's nine years of breast-feeding her son have earned him an insulting nickname; his aunt has the name of

Christ's betrayer; his father, Macon, is hated by the blacks because he makes his money at their expense; and Milkman cannot feel for anyone, not even himself. But against this earthbound alienation stands Pilate, and although it takes most of the novel for Milkman to understand her importance in his life, he is instinctively drawn to her; when he first meets her, he "knew that with the earring, the orange, and the angled black cloth, nothing—not the wisdom of his father nor the caution of the world—could keep him from her" (p. 36).

His father's wisdom is to "own things" (p. 55); the world's caution is not to care. Thus Milkman lives for thirty years, driving Pilate's daughter, Hagar, to madness through his selfish indifference and driving his frightened, lonely sister, Lena, to cry: "You are to blame. You are a sad, pitiful, stupid, selfish, hateful man. I hope your little hog's gut stands you in good stead, and that you take care of it, because you don't have anything else" (p. 218). But a quest has begun through the magic of Pilate that turns Milkman into someone who can fly. At what he thinks is his father's bidding, Milkman goes in search of gold, supposedly hidden where Macon and Pilate grew up. It is his first solo flight from his deadly family and his deadly relationships: ". . . Milkman wanted to do this by himself, with no input from anybody. This time he wanted to go solo. In the air, away from real life, he felt free, but on the ground . . . the wings of all those other people's nightmares flapped in his face and constrained him . . ." (p. 222). The first thing he finds on his journey is the pleasure of kinship:

> All his life he'd heard the tremor in the word: "I live here, but my *people* . . ." or: "She acts like she ain't got no *people*," or: "Do any of your *people* live there?" But he hadn't known what it meant: links [p. 231].

He hears the story of his grandfather's murder by whites; of Pilate's earring, in which she carries her name and a link with the past. Milkman begins to miss something in his life, the stories of his people. But he still thinks that the gold will salve his loneliness, so he goes on, finding along the way a heritage far more precious than things. He finds Circe, an ageless crone reminiscent of Night Swan, who raises dogs in the plantation home of the whites who had killed Milkman's grandfather. She provides clues that Milkman understands only later and draws him to her as Pilate had before.

Milkman, unable to find the gold and knowing how to relate to people only through money, stumbles on his quest. He ends up in Shalimar, Virginia, his family's first American home. Here he listens to the children sing of Solomon's son, who whirls about and touches the sun, reminding Milkman of his childish disappointment at not being able to fly (p.267). Because of his cultural alienation he insults the villagers and is almost killed; once again he feels the death of his name, the hordes of people trying to take his life:

> His own father had tried while he was still in his mother's stomach. But he'd lived. And he had lived the last year dodging a woman who came every month to kill him and he had lain just like this, with his arm over his eyes, wide open to whatever she had in her hand. He'd lived through that too. Then a witch had stepped out of his childhood nightmares to grab him, and he'd lived through that. . . . Now he walked into a store and asked if somebody could fix his car and a nigger pulls a knife on him. And still he wasn't dead. . . . Fuck 'em. My name's Macon; I'm already dead. He had thought this place, this Shalimar, was going to be home. His original home. His people came from here, his grandfather and his grandmother. . . . But here, in his "home," he was unknown, unloved, and damn near killed [p.273].

But Milkman has yet to come alive; his refusal to take responsibility for the pain of others makes him deader than his name. It is when he comes closest to death, at the hands of his closest friend, Guitar (who thinks Milkman has the coveted gold), that Milkman is born to himself and his heritage. Suddenly all the clues that Pilate and Circe have provided fall into place; he is able to establish a relationship with the blacks of Shalimar, and he is able to feel love for a woman, appropriately named Sweet, since Milkman is on his way to becoming Sugarman of African legend. Like Tayo, who after his union with Ts'eh is able to dream new dreams, Milkman spends a truly peaceful night in Sweet's arms:

> It was a warm dreamy sleep about flying, about sailing high over the earth. But not with arms stretched out like airplane wings, nor shot forward like Superman in a horizontal dive, but floating, cruising, in the relaxed position of a man lying on a couch reading a newspaper. Part of this flight was over the dark sea, but it didn't frighten him because he knew he could not fall. He was alone in the sky but someone was applauding him, watching him and applauding [p.302].

Now, when he hears the children's song of Solomon, he knows what it means; it becomes his story. Piece after piece falls into place until he rushes eagerly home to share with Pilate the gift she has given him, the gift of life: "With two exceptions, everybody he was close to seemed to prefer him out of this life. And the two exceptions were both women, both black, both old. From the beginning, his mother and Pilate had fought for his life, and he had never so much as made either of them a cup of tea" (p.335).

Pilate breaks one of her wine bottles over his head, for while he has been flying Hagar has died of unrequited love for him. But Milkman has a real gift for her, the knowledge that the sack she thought carried a white man's bones and that Macon had thought carried gold was filled instead with the bones of Pilate's murdered father. So together they travel back to Shalimar to bury him on Solomon's Leap. Pilate places her earring in her father's grave, and stands up just in time to catch the bullet Guitar has aimed at Milkman. With the life ebbing from her body she asks him to sing something for her. What Milkman sings is the story of the flying Africans with one important change: Sugarman has become Sugargirl, an adaptation of the original tale that shows Milkman's incorporation of Pilate's spirit. Thus, although Pilate dies, she has taught him the meaning of flight—loving and taking responsibility for those you love.

The novel ends with Milkman's flight: "Without wiping away the tears, taking a deep breath, or even bending his knees—he leaped. As fleet and bright as a lodestar he wheeled toward Guitar and it did not matter which one of them would give up his ghost in the killing arms of his brother. For now he knew what Shalimar knew: If you surrendered to the air, you could *ride* it" [p.341]. The story is complete because Milkman has learned and adapted the story of his people. He has become through the spiritual guidance of Pilate a fully human being and a culture hero. Morrison thus masters the dangerous material of black slavery, personal alienation, and political violence as the three other novels that harness story were able to do. With *Surfacing*, *The Woman Warrior*, and *Ceremony*, *Song of Solomon* bends the mythic to a woman's perception of the world, making archetypal truths accessible to contemporary female experience.

The final novel shows the solidifying of a literary trend that is probably dominant in women's fiction of the seventies, that of angry demythologizing. Marilyn French's *The Women's Room*, like Joan Didion's *Play It As It Lays*, Judith Rossner's *Looking for Mr. Goodbar*, and many other works by white middle-class American women, strips away everything in its attack on the patriarchal story. Mira, whose childhood reading is an escape from the ugliness of her family, could easily be Maureen or Beth. All feel the hostility of external reality, and their feeling is corroborated again and again by their experiences. The traditional stories are insidious tools of the patriarchy, demanding total capitulation or perpetual revolt. Mira, whose name is probably a pun on mirror, ("Mira lived by her mirror as much as the Queen in *Snow White*") functions in the first third of the novel as a victimized reflector of cultural norms, even to marrying a man named Norm.[10] The narrator, who proves in the end to be a demythologized Mira, views the fairy tale Mira tried to live from the barren truth of the Maine coast:

> When I was a child, fairyland as it appeared in the books was the place I wanted to live, and I judged my surroundings according to how well they matched it: beauty was fairyland, not truth. I would gladly have deserted the real world to go there, willingly abandoned my parents. Perhaps you call that incipient schizophrenia, but it seems to me that that's what I did in the end, lived in the fairyland where there are only five basic colors, clear lines, and no beer cans cluttering up the grass.
>
> One reason I like the Maine coast so much is that it allows so little room for such fantasies [p.12].

The narrator seems to find Mira ridiculous for her belief in good fairies, for her refusal to accept the ugly truth, but she is more angry for Mira, more self-pitying finally, than she is critical: "When I think of her, my belly twists a little with contempt. But how do I dare to feel that for her, for that woman so much like, so much like my mother?" (p.16).

Mira's childhood is an outline of oppression; bright and misunderstood, she retreats into books, especially fairy tales and myths. She recognizes her victimhood but can see no way to escape it, thus falling easily into a loveless marriage and a nightmarish life in suburbia. There is no guide, mythic or earthbound, to help Mira understand her situation or make changes. Her fellow housewives are in the same cage and, although sympathetic, can provide no real help because they, like Mira, are only mirrors of the prevailing story. It takes Norm's abandonment of the marriage to force real action—return to college. With each step that Mira takes in her fairytale life the narrator interjects highly ironic exegesis, stripping away comforting images to show their patriarchal underbelly: "But the truth is I am sick unto death of four thousand years of males telling me how rotten my sex is"; "It is too late for me to care. Once upon a time I could have cared. But fairyland is back behind the door" (p.290).

As Mira's friends fall into one or another version of the abyss, Mira discovers that there is no justice and goes on with her life, a survivor, hovering between the second and third positions on Atwood's scale of victimhood. More and more stories fall by the wayside as she experiences academia at Harvard; indeed, in a chapter where the narrator and Mira seem one, the story is analyzed and rejected for good because people would rather kill than change one word of the story:

> I guess the stories are all we have, all that makes us different from lion, ox, or those snails on the rock. I'm not sure I want to be

> different from those snails. The essential human act is the lie, the
> creation or invention of a fiction. For instance, here in my corner
> of the world, a major story is that it is possible to live without pain.
> They are removing hooks from noses and psyches, gray from hair,
> gaps from teeth, organs from bodies. They are trying to remove
> hunger and ignorance, or so they say. They are working on a
> pitless peach, a thornless rose [p. 387].

How far from the song for a barbarian reed pipe, the ceremonial paean
to story in *Ceremony*, the tale of the flying Africans. Patriarchal culture is
a lie, an effort to live without pain.[11]

The male myths are dissected, analyzed, and rejected in an increasingly pointed way as the novel progresses. The most violent version of
the woman-hating tale is the rape of Chris, daughter of Mira's friend
Val, a tale that ends with Val's being blown apart by police bullets.
French never stops her attack because, "you see, the story has no ending" (p. 683). But Mira has stopped reflecting the patriarchy and refuses
to forget what her experience has shown her. As she says: "Forget: lethe:
the opposite of truth" (p. 687).

This analysis also has no ending because the issue of story is central to
the creative process. The stories are all we have, the way we make
meaning of our pilgrimage, the way we make our identities as human
beings. But there are clearly contradictory attitudes toward the role of
story in America. In the novels discussed in this study, the white
middle-class women writers seem to see story as the patriarchy's weapon
against the female of the species. They either describe it with detach-
ment, as in Joyce Carol Oates's *Them*, or create a Superwoman to fight
it, as in Rita Mae Brown's *Rubyfruit Jungle*, or rail against it in the
words of the women's movement, as in Marge Piercy's *Small Changes*,
or cry out in pain at its devastation of a life, as in Marilyn French's *The
Women's Room*. Because story is the culture's way of devaluing the
female experience it and the culture it supports with its archetypes must
be rejected. The rejection in every case means loneliness, a radical
separation of the self from family, social institution, and romantic love.
The consolation is in its most negative form the dulling of pain and in
its most positive form angry autonomy, but in no place along the con-
tinuum is there community.

The other, strikingly different, use of story approaches the traditional
cultural myths as weapons that can be harnessed to express the female
experience and view of the world. In *Surfacing* Margaret Atwood seems
to share the view of the other white, middle-class women—that story is
the lie invented by the patriarchy. But as the novel progresses the
protagonist reasserts her connection with the land, the animals, and the
rituals of nature once experienced by the Indians. That connection with
the ancient stories gives her new power, a power that culminates in the

protagonist's refusal to be a victim. Maxine Hong Kingston also moves from the patriarchal story that destroyed No Name Woman and threatens her own life to an artistic adaptation that controls the story by telling it in a new way. She is a stranger in a strange land, but she finds a language of sadness and anger that both the barbarians and her people can understand. In *Ceremony* the patriarchy is defeated through the agency of story, first the traditional one and then the personalized version that Tayo is able to articulate to his people at the end of the novel. Leslie Silko emphasizes the matriarchal elements in Indian legend and culture to counteract the poison of the dominant society. Thus Tayo's healing is a ceremony of story, created and carried through the generations by women. The same female vision and female guidance direct Toni Morrison's protagonist in *Song of Solomon*. Milkman moves from his father's learned ethic of owning things to Pilate's natural instinct for openhanded love. Using the story of the flying Africans, Morrison gives archetypal power to one individual's quest for identity, showing in Milkman's final flight her female sense of what a human being can be.

Critics have argued that the use of patriarchal stories is a denial of women's real situation in history. But in fact myth determines the shape of human life, so only by harnessing it to express the female perception of experience can women strike at this mythic core. The journey back is thus an act of subversion that marks a step forward for women's stories and the world view behind them.

Notes

1. Carol Christ. *Diving Deep and Surfacing.* Boston: Beacon, 1980, p.1.

2. Joyce Carol Oates. *Them.* Greenwich, Conn.: Fawcett, 1969, p.309.

3. Margaret Atwood. *Surfacing.* New York: Popular Library, 1972, p.61.

4. Marge Piercy. "Margaret Atwood: Beyond Victimhood," *American Poetry Review* (November–December 1973), p.41.

5. Rita Mae Brown. *Rubyfruit Jungle.* New York: Bantam, 1973, p.31.

6. Marge Piercy. *Small Changes.* Greenwich, Conn.: Fawcett, 1974, p.371.

7. Maxine Hong Kingston. *The Woman Warrior.* New York: Knopf, 1976, p.16.

8. Leslie Silko. *Ceremony.* New York: New American Library, 1977, p.1.

9. Toni Morrison. *Song of Solomon*. New York: New American Library, 1977, p.5.

10. Marilyn French. *The Women's Room*. New York: Harcourt Brace Jovanovich, 1977, p.17.

11. In Marilyn French's new novel, *The Bleeding Heart*, the central issue is: How can I live without pain?

Carol Burr Megibow *teaches English, including courses on Women in Literature and Women's Nontraditional Literature. Her Ph.D. is from Case Western Reserve, where she did her dissertation on the novels of Jane Austen, Charlotte Brontë, and George Eliot.*

CHARACTERISTICS OF WOMEN'S DREAMS

Johanna King

The study of dreams allows a fascinating glimpse into the individual and collective psyche and has been the subject of interest for thousands of years. In this chapter I shall first review some basic notions on the meaning of dreams, then review the psychological literature on differences between women's and men's dreams, and finally discuss how these differences are related to waking-life sex-role differences.

Before the 1900 publication of Sigmund Freud's *The Interpretation of Dreams* questions regarding the meaning of dreams were the domain of religion or mysticism; afterward they became the legitimate subject matter of science, particularly psychology. Freud's belief that the dream was an accurate and unique, if disguised, mirror of the inner world of the dreamer, and would yield, if properly interpreted, wonderful insight into that inner world, was truly revolutionary in his time. His ideas, as those of any revolutionary, were not readily accepted, and, to his great and bitter disappointment, it took nearly ten years to sell out the first edition. Nevertheless he felt this work was his best; he wrote in 1931 that *The Interpretation of Dreams* "contains, even according to my present day judgment, the most valuable of all the discoveries it has been my good fortune to make. Insight such as this falls to one's lot but once in a lifetime" (Freud, 1965, p.xxxii).

Freud used the dreams of his patients, most of whom were women, in his writing, but he also used many of his own dreams to illustrate his points. But this posed a dilemma for him:

> But if I was to report my own dreams, it inevitably followed that I should have to reveal to the public gaze more of the intimacies of my mental life than I liked, or than is normally necessary for any writer who is a man of science and not a poet. Such was the

> painful but unavoidable necessity; and I have submitted to it rather than totally abandon the possibility of giving the evidence for my psychological findings. Naturally, however, I have been unable to resist the temptation of taking the edge off some of my indiscretions by omissions and substitutions. But whenever this has happened, the value of my instances has been very definitely diminished [Freud, 1965, p.xxiv].

Like any revolutionary, Freud was rigid and uncompromising and tried to account for all of the contingencies of dream content in his theoretical system. Some of his ideas, notably that all dreams are the disguised fulfillment of a repressed wish, and that the dream intentionally distorts and disguises its true meaning, have not stood the tests of empirical verification and clinical usefulness. Others, notably that the dream can only be understood in relation to the unique life experiences of the dreamer, and that a great deal of meaning can be condensed into a specific dream image, have achieved the status of accepted assumptions in schools of psychotherapy as diverse as Jungian, phenomenological, and gestalt.

Jung credited Freud with the first significant attempt in practice to discover the true meaning of dreams and took an essentially Freudian view when he called the dream a "spontaneous self-portrayal, in symbolic form, of the actual situation in the unconscious" (1974, p.49). He took issue with many other of Freud's ideas, most especially with the notion that the dream is a façade, concealing its true message. He said:

> But the so-called façade of most houses is by no means a fake or a deceptive distortion; on the contrary, it follows the plans of the building and often betrays the interior arrangement. The "manifest" dream-picture is the dream itself and contains the whole meaning of the dream. . . . What Freud calls the "dream-façade" is the dream's obscurity, and this is really only a projection of our own lack of understanding [Jung, 1974, p.97].

The phenomenological therapist Medard Boss (1977) also notes the pioneering nature of Freud's work and especially appreciates his realization that dreaming is not a disturbed state of mental existence. However, even more adamantly than Jung he denies the distinction between "manifest" and "latent" dream content, and insists that there is no need to interpret the dream. Rather, he claims, appropriate work with dreams involves "explicating, opening, and revealing the meanings and frames of reference that belong directly to concrete elements of the dreaming world, [and] to the way the dreamer conducts himself toward these elements . . ." (p.32).

Perls (1969), the foremost figure in gestalt therapy, felt that Freud's greatest contribution was his investigation of fantasy, which Perls called the intermediate zone between the self and the outside world. Perls's basic assumption was that all of the different parts of the dream are fragments of our personalities, an idea that both Freud (1965, p.358) and Jung (1964, p.52) believed to be true for some dreams.

None of these theorists assumed that the relationship between dreams and the waking experience of the dreamer is one-to-one; that is, the dream does not represent the waking experience either totally or literally. The dream instead filters the waking experience through the dreamer's unique system of needs, desires, hopes, and fears, expressed in terms of basic life themes. An individual dream, then, can only be fully understood in relation to the individual dreamer.

Yet various sex, age, and ethnic/cultural subgroups share many aspects of their waking experience and might be expected to share their dreamscapes in corresponding ways. A good deal of research has been done looking for dream themes that distinguish women's and men's dreams, based on the assumption that the waking experience of women and men vary in some significant ways. I have reviewed twenty-one studies of this type and conclude that women's dreams are unique in four ways:

(1) Women's dreams are characterized by themes of intimacy, personal relationships, and family concerns, while men's are more often characterized by themes of separateness, isolation, and movement through fluid, risky, and unfamiliar surroundings.

(2) Women's dreams are characterized by less aggression than men's, and aggression that is expressed is less intense.

(3) Women's dreams include less overt sexuality than men's.

(4) Women dream about women and men in about equal proportions, while men dream about men more often than they dream about women.

Intimacy

Women's dreams often revolve around themes of intimacy, connectedness, and familiarity. The importance of interpersonal relationships is paramount in women's lives; they are concerned and preoccupied, in sleep as in waking life, with the nature, intensity, and condition of these relationships.

The characters in women's dreams are more likely than those in men's dreams to be familiar (Brenneis, 1970; Brenneis and Roll, 1975; Brenneis and Roll, 1976; Fletcher, 1980); close to the dreamer in waking life (Husband, 1936); and family members (Colby, 1958, 1963; Brenneis, 1970). Already by the age of seven or eight, little girls are dreaming more about familiar people, especially females, than are little boys (Foulkes, 1977). Spaces in women's dreams are more likely to be enclosed, small, and/or familiar (Brenneis, 1970; Brenneis and Roll, 1975, 1976; Fletcher, 1980). Up until thirteen or fourteen both boys and girls have the home as a significant setting in their dreams; after that age home remains a frequent setting for girls but not for boys (Foulkes, 1977).

The following dream of an unmarried woman in her early twenties illustrates many of these points:

> I'm visiting someone who lives [in a house]. She's a good friend. She tells me that Jim is dating Alison. There's a pang of jealousy. Neither one is there. Jane lives there and I'm talking to Pauline. She points to the house across the way where they are building onto the two-story house making the top larger. It seemed the popular thing to do. I questioned the support and that the structure and the one I'm in could shake down in an earthquake. Pauline showed me through the house. It was all fading out. I do remember seeing a kitchen, bedroom, and a sparkling, bright, clean bathroom.

One can clearly see that the dreamer's attention is focused on close personal relationships, both between women and between women and men. All the characters except the "they" who are building across the street are familiar to the dreamer. Her feelings about these relationships are expressed both clearly and directly, when she experiences the pang of jealousy about Jim and Alison dating, and indirectly and symbolically, when she expresses her concern about the stability of both the structure across the street and the one she is in. Her yearning for a stable, orderly, "clean" domestic relationship is expressed in the last line. Both her concern about the "structure" she's in and the fact that the house is "all fading out" indicate that some aspect of her current relationship pattern is unsatisfactory.

In the following dream the themes of intimacy and familiarity are seen:

> Keith and I are getting ready to go to bed. I go in the bathroom; Keith is in there. There are small spiders all over a shelf by the sink he is standing in front of. He brushes the spiders away. Then we go in the bedroom. There is a huge king-sized bed. We have blankets or sleeping bags in our hands. The relatives arrive now; my Mom and Dad, my Aunt Louise, and an old friend of mine, Rose, and

her boyfriend. My Aunt Louise comes into the bedroom, then my Mom and Dad come in. Keith and I have to go to another bedroom. Now we are all in the living room. I talk to Rose, whom I notice has something wrong with her legs. She wears flesh-colored braces on her legs. Rose and her boyfriend begin to talk.

The domesticity of this dream is striking. The entire dream takes place in a familiar indoor setting. All of the characters are known to the dreamer, in this case a married woman who has one child. In fact the scene is so crowded with characters that there hardly seems to be room for her relationship, specifically her sexual relationship, with Keith, her husband.

An additional theme, one not noted in the research reviewed but one that is commonly seen in women's dreams, is the attribution of power and coping ability to men, and the perception of women as relatively weak. In this dream the dreamer's husband is able to deal easily with the disturbing spiders by merely brushing them off the sink. The dreamer's friend Rose, however, needs to be braced up in order to stand up for herself. In associating to the dream the dreamer comments, "I am projecting my fear onto her . . . I need braces to hold up my part. . . ."

In another instance the dreamer poses two alternative social relationship styles, "doing some dancing" and "being with" someone. This dreamer is in her late twenties and recently divorced. Notice the indoor setting and the familiarity of the main characters.

> There were a bunch of people in a room, and Sharon was one of them. We were having a drink. She decided to go to the next building to do some dancing. I stayed where I was. Then I left with Bruce to go there. I was with Bruce. We were walking across some muddy land, and he was holding both of my hands—like square dancing style—very gently, though.

In associating to the dream she notes that her friend Sharon is also divorced, and back in the social swing of things at the time of the dream. She acknowledges that Sharon is having a good time and adjusting well to her divorce. She sees herself as in transition, neither wanting to socialize much nor wanting to enter into another exclusive relationship. "I seem to be afraid to commit myself to either one at the moment," she says.

The attribution of strength to maleness is again seen in this dream. She describes Bruce as strong, intelligent, independent, and loving in waking life. She needs his support "to go there" (to the dance), and comments, "He is supporting me (emotionally or physically?). . . ." It appears at first that she chooses the relationship and Bruce over the carefree unattached life of Sharon. However, in her waking associations she wonders, "Perhaps he represents what I would call the 'best' of my male side, and the two of us, together crossing the muddy land, holding hands, represents the two parts of me cooperating."

Men's dreams are less likely to include familiarity-intimacy themes and are more likely to involve the less well known, the less social, and more movement across physical space.

The following dream of a married man in his late twenties illustrates some of these differences.

> I approached one of three automobiles, a green one with a woman on the passenger side. She is wearing a Russian hat and fur coat. Before getting to that car, I had stopped at another one and asked if I might be of any help to them. A man very sternly replied, "No, you may not!" Then the woman at her car said, "Yes, we can use your help. We just came from Russia; we've been there six years." So I got in the car between two men in the back seat. I felt trapped. As we were driving, they said they wanted to see America. So I said, "Great, we'll go to Las Vegas, Hollywood and Beverly Hills and Disneyland." Then further down the road, they pulled off to a very strange place like a deserted ranch with big shade trees.

The total dream, about twice the length of this excerpt, includes five single characters and a group of men. Not a single character is known to the dreamer. The setting is also unfamiliar. While the authenticity of some aspect of his life experience seems to be at issue in this dream, if we take the reference to "tinsel" America at face value, it does not seem to have to do with an interpersonal relationship. Also of interest is the attribution of powerlessness and the need for help to the single female character in the dream.

The following dream includes a known character, but the theme is clearly one of distance and barriers between the dreamer and others, rather than closeness. The dreamer is unmarried and in his early twenties.

> I was deer hunting with Joe somewhere around Scotia. Walking through the woods, I was lugging a cedar log on my shoulder that was approximately six feet by two feet in diameter. There seemed to be little difficulty carrying the log even though it was an uphill climb. I came upon a fenced-in area that was a surprise to me, and the fence had frequent signs saying "Keep Out" and to the effect of even staying far away from the area. At a distance there was a gate with a large, stout man guarding the gate. I pondered the reason for such a secured area and decided it had to be a private club of some kind and probably a nudist colony to account for the strong need to keep outsiders at a distance.

Women are much less aggressive than men in their dreams. The difference is not only in terms of the frequency of aggressive behaviors depicted in dreams but also in terms of the intensity of the aggression depicted. Women are less likely to use weapons (Colby, 1963), and less likely to employ physical violence (Colby, 1958; Paolino, 1964; Brenneis and Roll, 1975, 1976). The aggression in women's dreams is more likely to stop at the verbal level, with arguing, accusations, backbiting, shouting, and yelling the more typical modes of expression. The onset of these differences is early. Foulkes (1977) finds that five- to six-year-old boys are more preoccupied with conflict in their dreams than their female peers and that by eleven or twelve the boys have more aggression in their dreams.

These findings are of course consistent with how women express aggression in waking life. Women are typically very uncomfortable with their own outbursts of aggressive behavior, even if it remains at the verbal level. For women, to be called "aggressive" is an insult; for men, to be called "lacking in aggressiveness" is the insult. Women fear and avoid such labels as pushy, bitchy, demanding, and manipulative. If a woman wins in an aggressive battle with a man, she is said to be "castrating."

Eron (1980), in the course of twenty-five years of research on the antecedents of aggressive behavior in children and young adults, has demonstrated that these female-male differences are substantial, and already clear by the age of eight. In a sample of four hundred nineteen-year-olds aggression scores of the high-aggression young women were about equal to the scores of the medium-aggression young men, and the scores of the medium-aggression young women were about equal to those of the low-aggression young men.

Other of Eron's data support the notion that the dream differences reflect waking-life differences. Using a scale developed by Erica Rosenfeld, he measured three daydream styles in children: fanciful, in which the child daydreams about fairy tales and implausible happenings; active, in which the child daydreams about heroes, achievement, and intellectual pursuits; and aggressive negative, in which the child daydreams about fighting, killing, and being hurt. He concluded: "There is no evidence whatsoever in our data that fantasy has a cathartic effect! Especially in the case of boys, children who fantasize about aggressive *acts* tend to *act* aggressively. Girls, who in general do not score as high as boys on any measure of aggression, also do not daydream much about aggressive themes" (p. 250).

In the following dream one can see how difficult it is for the young female dreamer to express and follow through on her negative feelings:

> Jon and I are on the beach [doing some kind of work]. Upon
> getting the last batch of sand, I find that Jon is [just] sunbathing. I
> get angry and he ignores it by suggesting lunch. I go to lunch with
> him and begin feeling better. We are both stuffed and walking
> down the boardwalk when I suggest we go back to the beach. He
> says no, he has a date with Molly.... I get very upset and con-
> tinue walking and feel very alone even though we are together.

Her anger is easily co-opted by Jon's invitation to lunch, which "stuffs"
her and makes her feel better. The issue that instigated her anger, his
not doing his fair share of the work, is never dealt with. Later she does
not even express her negative feelings, perhaps fearing Jon's lack of
response.

When physical aggression does occur in a woman's dream, it is often
projected onto the male characters in the dream:

> [I am] perched on a ledge.... A big fat man rows up in a bird
> cage. He points a rifle at me and tells me to get in. Naturally, I
> comply.... At this point [men come] and they get his rifle from
> him but the fat man gets shot in the face. There is blood all over
> everything.

Though the intensity of the violent aggression is dramatic, the dreamer
experiences herself as an onlooker, not responsible in any way for what
happens.

This tendency to project the aggression onto a male figure is beautifully illustrated in another woman's dream:

> [Some] turtle-like bugs crawl very fast and fly and snap at people. I
> think one bites me and I get real mad and try to catch one. I
> succeed... and I twist its head off. I enjoy doing this. The turtle
> body goes running around still. Then I trap another one and sit on
> it. Someone is with me watching and calls to a man inside who is
> dressed in white, to come out and dive-bomb this turtle. He does
> it. He flies up in the air and comes down and punctures the green
> part of the turtle which then deflates like a balloon.

Though the dreamer enjoys her hostile and aggressive act, it appears
that someone else does not think it appropriate and calls for a man to do
it. In her waking association the dreamer converts her physical aggressive act, twisting the turtle's head off, to a verbal act. She says, "This is
revenge. I often get revenge verbally, by 'biting someone's head off.'"
With regard to the man in white she says, "One of my associations was
that I needed someone powerful to get rid of [the nuisance]. He can do
my dirty work and I don't have to be faced with responsibility for
it... he is seemingly a clean, white hero but the task he carried out and

the motives behind it are evil and dark." In one image the dreamer has projected both power and responsibility for aggressive acts onto maleness.

The following series of dreams of a forty-year-old woman, a university professor, married with one child, demonstrates a fascinating interplay between aggressive impulses and socially defined norms for behavior. In the first dream she assures herself, right in the dream, that she is not being aggressive:

> I decide to go to a store like Walgreen's . . . and I do some shopping. I get one thing. I remember someone getting in front of me and me saying, "excuse me, I was in line first"—very nicely, not aggressive at all.

In the second dream she expresses aggression verbally in an indirect and ineffective way and projects real anger onto a male figure:

> We're going to have a big party, and no one will give me much help cleaning up the house. . . . I keep nagging people, but it gets me almost nowhere, and I have to do most everything myself. People begin arriving before I get the vacuuming done. There's junk under the table in the kitchen, and I make some snide comment to my father about not picking it up—he gets angry.

Her concern for appearances and doing what is viewed by others as proper is revealed in comic form in the third dream:

> Suddenly [a woman supervisor] comes up behind me, and sort of hustles me off to the side. I say, "Oh, I'm sorry, do you have people with you?" She says yes, would I mind going a different way so they wouldn't know I was on her staff. . . . I start back up the hall, rather sedately so as not to draw attention to myself, and I see that the book that [a senior faculty woman] has given me is titled "Guidelines for Faculty Behavior."

The day before having this dream the dreamer had written a long and fairly vociferous memo regarding some perceived sexist policy on the part of an administrator, but she had not (and never did) send the memo. The dream makes fun of her vulnerability to "appearances."

The fourth dream illustrates two points that many women will find familiar; the need on the part of the dreamer to explain or justify her aggressiveness, and the displacement of her aggression from the source of the frustration onto a weaker victim.

> I stop and ask a [policeman] if I can turn around. It's a woman, but she has a heavy growth of beard. . . . I want to just make a U-turn, but she won't allow it. I see other people—a whole line of them—making U-turns and point that out. . . . I'm very irritated

and drive off angry. [My daughter] is sitting on my lap obstructing my view, and I ask her three or four times to get off. She won't, and finally I push her off to the right. She starts to whimper. I finally get [to my friend's house]. I start telling him the whole story. I tell him I haven't even had the chance to go to the bathroom yet, and go off to do that. There I notice I have started my period, and realize that is the explanation for my irritability.

The reader will also notice how the dreamer masculinizes the source of her frustration.

In the final dream in this series the dreamer reveals the conditions under which she will behave aggressively.

After a while [of being away], I come back [to a park] to get [my daughter], and find her sitting on the lap of some prototype dirty old man. I realize he had been feeling her genitals. Someone is with me. I pick [my daughter] up and put her down quickly, then grab the man by his shirt front and start to shake him and yell at him. My friend runs to call the police, and I continue to shake the man as brutally as I can.

The dreamer is outraged and rises to the defense of her child with all the energy of the proverbial she-bear.

This series of dreams makes it clear that this woman is not incapable of expressing aggression, but that the circumstances must be unusual for her to feel justified in doing so.

In men's dreams the personalization of aggression is much more common, and the dream ego more readily takes responsibility for aggressive acts. Easy identification with aggression is seen in the following dream of a man just turned twenty:

I could see in the distance that the Hell's Angels were rioting and raising general havoc. I had to get my father's .357 magnum so I could rescue the people. I crawled—dragged myself up to this yellow vw with three women sitting in the back seat. They . . . were very still, although it seemed clear that they were frightened and hiding. They were afraid of me at first, but I told them not to be afraid, I was going to help them . . . the next thing I knew I had the gun. I then crouched down into position using the vw as a partial shield, and aimed the gun at the area where the general havoc was taking place.

The dreamer also ascribes weakness and fear to the female characters in his dream.

In another dream, that of an unmarried man in his mid-twenties, a little more concern about effectiveness is revealed, but the acceptance of the aggressive act is clear, nevertheless.

> I am in a sword fight with a large human-like man wearing a uniform. We are fighting in the kitchen of my childhood home. I try to cut him up, but he still keeps fighting. He is strong but my sword has some kind of magic that should defeat him.

In a third man's dream, though he accepts responsibility for his aggressive act in the dream, he does not do it without suffering:

> At the outset of this dream, there is a feeling of guilt because the corpse of someone I have killed has been discovered. . . . After only a few days, the internal pressure is so great I want to confess. On the other hand, by the responsibility I would accept by confessing, I also want desperately to think of another way around confessing. I wish [I] had buried the body deeper.

Sexuality

Sexuality, involving explicit erotic themes of mutual or autostimulation and/or intercourse, is much less common in women's dreams than in men's (Husband, 1936; De Martino, 1953; Colby, 1958, 1963; Brenneis and Roll, 1975). Of even greater interest is the finding that when explicit sexuality does occur in women's dreams, and the dream ego is involved, the partner is usually known to the dreamer and is often an object of sexual interest in the dreamer's waking life. This is consistent with the findings of King and Sobel (1975), which indicate that women are more concerned with the affectional context of sex than are men. While men have traditionally been able to separate sex and love, women tend to want, value, and feel good about sex only if it occurs in the context of an ongoing intimate relationship.

A young unmarried man who had recently broken off a long-term relationship with a woman reported the following:

> I awoke recalling some details of two dreams, each involving two very different women and both suggesting sex or a high degree of intimacy. Both women seemed very attractive to me and I recall the details of one of the encounters—we were embracing on a bed, rolling over on each other, fully clothed. Suddenly we were at least half nude and as I kissed her breasts, her nipples seemed extremely hard and erect.

Neither the identities of the women or the particulars of the location are evident to the dreamer. The erotic nature of the contact is quite specific.

The following woman's dream includes the common elements of interpersonal intimacy:

[My husband] and I walked into an auditorium—we were going to watch some sort of football game on TV or something. He had his arm around me—we were giggling and hugging up. He stuck his hand inside my blouse. I tried to get him to stop by saying that someone else would see, but he said no one would notice.

Sex of Dream Characters

A most interesting finding was reported by Hall and Domhoff in 1963. They tabulated the sex of all the characters who were identified by sex in 6,939 dreams of 2,817 dreamers. The dreams had been collected in eleven different studies, and the subjects ranged across several cultural subgroups. They found that women dream about equally of men and women, but men dream more about other men than they do about women. This finding has been corroborated several times (Colby, 1958; Grey and Kalsched, 1971; Munroe and Munroe, 1977), and contradicted once (Urbino and Grey, 1975).

What can this finding mean? Hall and Domhoff interpret the findings in a straightforward way: they say that dreams are primarily concerned with the preoccupations, anxieties, conflicts, and unsatisfied wishes of the dreamer and therefore conclude that the unresolved problems of males center more around their relationships with men than with women, and those of females are focused on their relationships with both sexes about equally.

An extension of this interpretation may lie in the differences in women's and men's dreams discussed earlier. Women dream of interpersonal intimate relationships more often than do men, and these relationships likely involve both sexes. Men have more aggressive themes in their dreams, and aggressive interactions more often involve male dream characters than female ones.

Another possibility is that women have contact with both sexes about equally in their waking life, while men spend more of their waking time with other men, and both sexes recreate this aspect of their waking experiences in their dreams. This hypothesis receives support from Grey and Kalsched (1971). Their data, collected in the United States and in India, on the whole support Hall and Domhoff. However, they also got information on their Indian subjects on the extent to which they lived a traditional sex-segregated life. They found that, for both women and men, the more traditional the dreamer, the fewer opposite-sex characters appeared in their dreams, and the less traditional, the more opposite-sex characters appeared. Further research relating the waking experience and the dreams of specific dreamers is necessary before this finding can be understood fully.

Summary

What do these data mean for persons who would like to get a clearer view of themselves through their dreams? Several points can be made.

(1) The sex differences in dream content presented in this chapter reflect significant sex differences that exist in waking life. These differences need not be viewed as innate or inevitable, or even reflective of every woman's or man's experience. Rather they may be viewed as typical differences, reflective of cultural norms, and normal socialization to those norms. They clarify how these norms provide the sexes different prescriptions for behavior and also how people feel and react toward violations of these normative prescriptions.

(2) The differences discussed here bring into sharp relief the issues that are central to sex-role conflict in our culture. It is not just that these are differences in inner perspective between women and men but that the differences may set the stage for conflict over priorities, interests, and values.

(3) Because dreams are such an important and insightful source of information about the dreamer's waking life, they should also be expected to reflect, both at the individual and collective levels, changes in sex roles.

(4) The dream-theme differences reviewed here highlight positive and prosocial themes in traditional women's sex roles; low aggression, interpersonal intimacy emphasizing the relational context of sex, and interaction with both sexes. Rather than being seen as negative characteristics of the role-restricted woman, these may be viewed as positive and laudable characteristics and as goals for the truly androgynous person, whether female or male.

References

Boss, M. "I dreamt last night. . . ." New York: Gardner, 1977.

Brenneis, B. "Male and Female Ego Modalities in Manifest Dream Content," *Journal of Abnormal Psychology*, 76 (3) (1970), 434–442.

Brenneis, C. B., and S. Roll. "Ego Modalities in the Manifest Dreams of Male and Female Chicanos," *Psychiatry*, 38 (1975), 172–185.

_____. "Dream Patterns in Anglo and Chicano Young Adults," *Psychiatry*, 39 (1976), 280–290.

Colby, K. M. *A Skeptical Psychoanalyst*. New York: Ronald, 1958.

————. "Sex Differences in Dreams of Primitive Tribes," *American Anthropologist*, 65 (1963), 1116–1122.

De Martino, M. F. "Sex Differences in the Dreams of Southern College Students," *Journal of Clinical Psychology*, 9 (1953), 119–201.

Eron, L. D. "Prescription for Reduction of Aggression," *American Psychologist*, 35 (1980), 244–252.

Fletcher, D. "Age and Sex Differences in Dream Content." Unpublished master's thesis, California State University, Chico, May 1980.

Foulkes, D. "Children's Dreams: Age Changes and Sex Differences," *Waking and Sleeping*, 1 (1977), 171–174.

Freud, S. *The Interpretation of Dreams*. New York: Avon, 1965. (First published in 1900.)

Grey, A., and D. Kalsched. "Oedipus East and West: An Exploration Via Manifest Dream Content," *Journal of Cross-Cultural Psychology*, 2 (1971), 337–352.

Hall, C., and B. Domhoff. "A Ubiquitous Sex Difference in Dreams," *Journal of Abnormal and Social Psychology*, 66 (1963), 278–280.

Husband, R. W. "Sex Differences in Dream Contents," *Journal of Abnormal and Social Psychology*, 30 (1936), 513–521.

Jung, C. G. *Dreams*. Princeton, N.J.: Princeton University Press, 1974.

King, M., and D. Sobel. "Sex on the College Campus: Current Attitudes and Behavior," *Journal of College Student Personnel*, 1975, 205–209.

Munroe, R. L., and R. H. Munroe. "Sex of Dream Characters in East Africa," *Journal of Social Psychology*, 103 (1977), 149–150.

Paolino, A. F. "Dreams: Sex Differences in Aggressive Content," *Journal of Projective Techniques and Personality Assessment*, 28 (1964), 219–226.

Perls, F. S. *Gestalt Therapy Verbatim*. Moab, Utah: Real People, 1969.

Urbino, S., and A. Grey. "Cultural and Sex Differences in the Sex Distribution of Dream Characters," *Journal of Cross-Cultural Psychology*, 6 (1975), 358–364.

Johanna King *is a counselor and teaches psychology at California State University at Chico. Her Ph.D. is from the University of Colorado.*

V. RELIGION

FEMINIST THEOLOGY

Gayle Kimball

Western religion employs male images and symbols, such as God the Father, the Son, and the "brotherhood of man." American spokeswomen for at least two centuries have sought to establish a place for women in religious terminology, imagery, and values. The reaction of women was first to build on a primary female function—motherhood. Harriet Beecher Stowe and Charlotte Perkins Gilman were representative women who conceived a religious value system based on motherly virtues of love and self-sacrificing service. Later thinkers, such as Mary Daly, rejected an emphasis on motherhood, substituting egalitarian sisterhood. The search for women's values defined them as life affirming, joyful, accepting of the body and the earth, communal, and sisterly.

Harriet Beecher Stowe was the most widely read novelist of the nineteenth century and was a member of the prominent Beecher family of popular preachers. Her outpouring of thirty books reflected and shaped the nineteenth century's glorification of the saving power of women as mothers. Mothers were like Christ in their loving self-sacrifice—a theme that was first developed by her older sister, Catherine. Catharine Beecher explained that theories about religion are "especially to be examined and decided on by woman, as the heaven-appointed educator of infancy and childhood."[1] Stowe added that mothers had a mediating power; as one of her typical male characters said, "Mother, if I ever get to heaven it will be through you."

In her Protestant Mariology Stowe stressed the role of the mother of Jesus. In fact, since Mary was the only earthly parent of Jesus, Stowe concluded that he had more of the feminine than any other man. She spoke of Mary as the teacher of Jesus, neglecting mention of Joseph.

Reprinted, with revisions, from *Women and Religion* (Missoula, Montana, 1975), courtesy of Scholars Press.

Mary was also more insightful than the disciples, understanding more calmly and clearly what Christ's purpose was; and she stood by him at the cross when his male disciples had deserted him.

Stowe told her readers that without a good mother, and the wife who takes her place, a man is lost; for, "We all need the motherly, and we must find it in a wife," who guides, cares for, tactfully teaches, and catechizes her husband.[2] No altar is higher than the home; a serene home heals those who come to it for succor. The home is a mother's shrine, throne, and empire, "more holy than cloister, more saintly and pure than church or altar."[3] Stowe believed that women were special instruments of God's grace. Their physical beauty is an inspiration to men and their love has redeeming powers, for women are finer, more tender and devoted, and less open to temptation than men. Love is a sacrament and women are best able to love; therefore, "In matters of grace God sets a special value on woman's nature and design to put special honor upon it," and Stowe urged the clergy to enumerate woman's influence among the means of grace.[4]

In the twentieth century Aimee Semple McPherson and Kathryn Kuhlman perpetuated Stowe's identification of women as oriented to the heart rather than to the mind and saw women as closely tied to the role of nurturing loving mother. McPherson defined herself as a "little mother evangelist" preaching love and joy rather than the "mazes of man's theology."[5]

McPherson's contemporary, feminist Charlotte Perkins Gilman, disapproved of "modern motherolitry," but as a transitional figure she retained much of the emphasis on motherhood, which she believed caused women to be altruistic, loving, and concerned with social progress. She explained that "the desire of the mother soul is to give benefit rather than to receive it." Women see the word "life" not as a noun but as "living," an active verb. (This is also the theme of Mary Daly.) Gilman advocated that mothers who carefully selected their mates could "send forth a new kind of people to help the world," instead of being servants and pseudomothers to their husbands. She hoped for "the mother who is uprising, whose deep, sweet current of uplifting love is to pour forward into service." She saw motherhood as the "supreme power of the world...."[6]

In opposition to female emphasis on love, joy, and service Gilman condemned men for projecting a God of violence, wrath, vengefulness, pride, and judgment. She believed that religion suffered from male domination and that men's views were shaped by their experience as hunters, which caused them to focus on death and the afterlife. She faulted male-oriented religion for stressing obedience and submission, which is what men wish women to practice.

Present feminist theologians also react to male values, what Sheila

Collins calls the "demon of patriarchalism" or what Mary Daly calls "demonic phallic morality," destructive machismo. Daly and Rosemary Ruether find that male dominance leads to hierarchical dualities, splits between I/it, we/them, God/Devil, good/bad, humans/nature, and feminine/masculine. Patriarchal religion emphasizes guilt, judgment, and death rather than the love, joy, and life-giving attributes of God. Women from Stowe to Ruether agree on this observation of the grimness and duality of male religious expression.

Current feminist theologians still touch on the theme of motherhood. Women have searched for historical models and images. They focus on the Virgin Mary as one of the few female symbols in Christianity. The Virgin must symbolically free and "save" the Son, writes Daly. While the Virgin was traditionally important only in her relationship to her son, "The New Being of antichurch is a rising up of Mother and Daughter together, beyond the Madonna's image and beyond the ambivalent Warrior-Maiden's image [of Joan of Arc]."[7] Daly advocates that women draw on the potential strength of Mary and Joan as important women, that women bond together with their new sense of strength and leave the Church that perpetuates women's subordinate position to men. The keynote is no longer self-sacrifice for women but affirmation and acceptance of self.

Daly points out that the Church honored Mary and motherhood, but no mortal woman could duplicate the feat of a virgin birth and that the Church usurped mothers' functions. Male priests, wearing skirts and caps, substituted baptism for birth, communion for feeding, baptism for washing, and extreme unction for consolation. The Church honored the motherly qualities of service, self-abnegation, humility, charity, and meekness but expected them actually to be carried out by women and not by its male leaders. Thus Daly explains that "the traditional morality of our culture has been 'feminine' in the sense of hypocritically idealizing some of the qualities imposed upon the oppressed."[8]

Reverend Letty Russell also utilized the theme of motherhood, noting that God is called mother or wife in the Old Testament and described as a mother bird with sheltering wings in the Psalms. She suggests that a new model of ministry should include the role of mother, advocate, and layperson. Both men and women would learn to "specialize in this nurturing, enabling and mediating role. . . ."[9] The Virgin Mother, the ancient goddess who had no need of a consort, is an image also used by Penelope Washbourn and by Beatrice Bruteau. The former explains that women can use the model of the goddess as independent and complete in her own being, and the latter sees the Virgin as a symbol, for unity and oneness coupled with the concept of the Mother as creative multiplicity.[10] The Virgin Mother provided a complementary image to God as the Father.

The notion of motherhood also appears in feminist liturgies, such as the worship service "Motherhood Reborn" celebrated at Graduate Theological Union in Berkeley, which focused on grounding, creating, and delivery and defined God's presence as "birthing that occurs within and among us."[11] Another feminist worship service referred to God as the "Lady of Birth."

For the most part, however, feminists have dropped the search for a female identity in the qualities arising from motherhood and have replaced it with the theme of sisterhood. A new mythology is being written, such as about the sisterhood of Eve and Lilith. Sisterhood stands for the opposite of male hierarchies and power structures of dominant and subordinate. It is associated with communal egalitarian values.

Sisterhood is a major theme for Mary Daly. She defines it as the revolutionary "bonding of those who have never bonded before."[12] She believes that sisters must form an exodus community to depart from the patriarchal Church, which offers no hope of reform. Women must form an antichurch, she states. Instead of artificial polarization her aim is diarchy, of a "sisterhood of man" resulting in androgyny (although she later disavowed the usefulness of androgyny). Wholeness and androgyny are frequently reiterated feminist themes. To merge feeling and thought, the personal and political, to develop women who are full persons, adds to universal human becoming and thereby fulfills the biblical promise that men and women are made in the image of God. That will be the Second Coming and is a transcendent spiritual event, Daly believes.

The Christa, the Coming of Women into actualization of their potential, is also looked for by Elizabeth Farians.[13] Letty Russell and Sheila Collins concur that women's liberation partakes of the numinous, as conversion to the women's movement is "structurally similar to conversion to a new religious consciousness."[14] The liberation of women from their childlike status, their growth into maturity, is a happening of such import, with such charge of new energy, that it partakes of an awesome power and evolution. Women are experiencing a "new way of seeing reality, which might be likened by some to a conversion experience."[15] These changes in the lives of women are signs of the Holy Spirit at work, "*subverting the church into being the church.*"[16] The community of support that frees women sends sisterhood on the way to servanthood, Letty Russell believes, in the sense that newly maturing women are providing service to humanity. That women are developing a new communal process is also asserted by an editor of *Women in a Strange Land.*[17]

A new humanity is rising out of the woman's movement, observes Ruether. The Judeo-Christian split between body/soul, humans/nature, and self/other is being overcome. Women have traditionally cultivated a communal personhood, she notes, and are bringing about a new social ethic that involves reconciliation with the garden earth and reconciliation of spirit and body.[18] Optimism about the ability to change the human condition is part of the feminist ethic.

In order to develop as persons who can manifest their egalitarian values women must search for their "stolen identity," for past sources of strength and identity on which to build. They are questing in many disciplines and turning old images around. Traditional images of degradation for women are reversed: women find strength in Eve's and Lilith's assertive acts and celebrate the "liberation of the apples" in liturgy. They find delight in witches' healing powers and rejection of the patriarchy.

Sifting through the history of religions women find such images as the Hindu female Shakti as personification of dynamic power and life-giving energy. The Old Testament and Gnostic imagery of Wisdom as female, the Patristic view of celibate female virgins as spiritual beings who formed communities of women, and Shaker Ann Lee's and Mary Baker Eddy's dual Mother-Father godhead are other examples of what women find useful in self-definition. They return often to the ancient mother goddess, who Sheila Collins finds has "transformative and integrative powers . . . equal to that of the Christian Christ."[19]

Because there is such a paucity of female imagery in Western religion feminist scholars must be far ranging in their pursuit for models, symbols, and definitions of female values. Literary images are a rich source, as in the Heroine's quest for meaning in *Surfacing*, by Margaret Atwood, or Doris Lessing's *The Four Gated City*. Images in political theory are found, such as the nineteenth-century French St. Simonian expectation of a female messiah to redeem Western society from excessive rationalism and sexual repression. Themes from psychology are garnered by such women as Christine Downing, former president of the American Academy of Religion.

Women are also thinking about the importance of their own personal experiences as the source of definition of female values. The consciousness-raising discussion group is the vehicle for sharing experiences. From these communal discussions emerges a theme for women's theology, which is the need for regaining the lost self: "The theme of liberation and self-actualization which is found in the concrete experiences of women thus forms the content of feminist theology."[20] Not only is there the richness of past history for women to draw from, but also the content of their own lives is now seen as important.

In feminist worship services and liturgies women act out the new imagery, as in the passing of the apple from which a bite is taken in commemoration of Eve's search for knowledge. *Sister Celebrations* is a collection of liturgies that includes such worship services as "Sisterhood Service on Mother's Day," combining nineteenth- and twentieth-century feminist images. In their rituals women are utilizing their sensuality and acceptance of the body, in dance, song, poetry, drama: these creative transrational activities have been described as right-hemisphere-of-the-brain functions, which are more developed in females.

In addition to finding new sources of female imagery women are asking for nonsexist language. Use the feminine pronoun for the Holy Spirit, says Letty Russell, for it is the Comforter and Reconciler. Search for the forgotten name of God, she asks, such as the plural meaning of Elohim. Mary Daly calls for the castration of language. She suggests that the word "God" may just be inherently oppressive, but that, on the contrary, the concept of the Goddess is "loaded with healing associations."[20]

In conclusion: nineteenth-century women used the traits of loving self-sacrifice projected on women by men to try to develop a sense of worth for subordinate women. Their strategy of giving pious women responsibility for converting souls was not realistic. Twentieth-century feminist theologians are still attempting to rectify the problem of low status for women in the Church. Some perhaps continue to make the error of exalting women as different from men in a female democratic cooperative spirit—which may only be a result of being oppressed. The concept of androgyny is an exciting one, in which women will be socialized, for example, to be assertive and men to be open with their emotions. The solution is, however, to have women's actual presence in religious leadership, not just female imagery. If change does not occur more rapidly, other conscious women will continue to follow Daly in her exodus from the patriarchal Church, leaving it one-sided in its expression of spirituality.

Notes

1. Catharine Beecher. *Commonsense Applied to Religion*. New York: Harper and Brothers, 1857, p.25.

2. Harriet Beecher Stowe. *My Wife and I*. New York: AMS, 1967, pp. 94–98. (First published in 1871.)

3. *The Minister's Wooing*. New York: Derby and Jackson, 1859, p.566.

4. Harriet Beecher Stowe. *Dred*. New York: AMS, 1967, Vol. 1, p.357. (First published in 1869.)

5. Aimee Semple McPherson. *In the Service of the King: The Story of My Life*. New York: Boni and Liveright, 1927, p.89.

6. Charlotte Perkins Gilman. *His Religion and Hers: A Study of Our Fathers and the Work of Our Mothers*. New York: Century, 1923, pp.92, 277, 279, 294.

7. Mary Daly. *Beyond God the Father: Toward a Philosophy of Woman's Liberation*. Boston: Beacon, 1973, p.130.

8. *Ibid.*, pp.100, 195.

9. Letty M. Russell. *Human Liberation in a Feminist Perspective—A Theology*. Philadelphia: Westminster, 1974, p.180.

10. Penelope Washbourn. "Differentiation and Difference—Reflections on the Ethical Implications of Women's Liberation"; and Beatrice Bruteau. "The Image of the Virgin Mother," in *Women and Religion*. Missoula, Mont.: Scholars Press, 1975, pp.93, 127.

11. Arlene Swidler, ed. *Sister Celebrations*. Philadelphia: Fortress, 1974, p.11.

12. Mary Daly. *The Church and the Second Sex*. New York: Harper and Row, 1975, p.265.

13. Elizabeth Farians. "The Coming of Woman: The Christa." Pittsburgh: KNOW reprint from *Seminarians for Ministerial Renewal*, April 1971.

14. Russell, p.124; and Sheila D. Collins. *A Different Heaven and Earth*. Valley Forge, Pa.: Judson, 1974, p.42.

15. Collins, p.202.

16. Russell, p.159.

17. Clare Fisher, Betsey Brenneman, and Anne Bennett, eds. *Women in a Strange Land: Search for a New Image*. Philadelphia: Fortress, 1975, p.lx.

18. Rosemary Ruether. *Liberation Theology*. New York: Paulist, 1972, p.124.

19. Collins, p.143.

20. Mary Daly. "The Qualitative Leap Beyond Patriarchal Religion," *Quest*, 1 (Spring 1974), 35.

More Recent Bibliography Includes

Christ, Carol. *Diving Deep and Surfacing: Women Writers on Spiritual Quest.* Boston: Beacon, 1980.

Daly, Mary. *Gyn/Ecology: The Metaethics of Radical Feminism.* Boston: Beacon, 1978.

Goldenberg, Naomi. *Changing of the Gods: Feminism and The End of Traditional Religions.* Boston: Beacon, 1979.

Starhawk. *The Spiral Dance: A Rebirth of the Religion of the Great Goddess.* San Francisco: Harper and Row, 1979.

Washbourn, Penelope. *Becoming Whole: The Quest for Wholeness in Female Experience.* San Francisco: Harper and Row, 1977.

GODDESS WORSHIP IN WICCE

Interview with Z. Budapest

Z. *Budapest is a high priestess of the Susan B. Anthony Coven Number One, which she founded in 1971. She was the first to establish a strong connection between witchcraft and feminism as allied thought forms. She teaches about Goddess worship on campuses as well as in classes. Her tradition is the Dianic tradition, which emulates Diana the soul of nature, who never consorts with men. Therefore she practices women's mysteries. Z. Budapest is the author of* The Holy Book of Women's Mysteries: Part One and Two, *which included her first revolutionary book,* The Feminist Book of Lights and Shadows. *She wrote a children's story about courage called* Selene *and a play called* The Rise of the Fates. *She is the editor of* Themis, *the voice of the feminist witch, and frequent contributor to* Womanspirit.

GK: *Please comment on the origin of your involvement in Wicce, worship of wise women, or what the patriarchy calls witchcraft.*

ZB: My tradition comes from middle Europe; it is called the Dianic tradition because it centers on Diana, whose name means Holy Mother, and Aradia, the first female avatar, her daughter. Dianic witches were in my family something like eight hundred years. My family tree goes back to 1270. Mostly what my family tradition is about is cures and herbs. We traditionally had an herb shop, which then developed into a pharmacy. My grandfather used to sew back on the cut-off ears of peasants when they fought, and cure diseases; he was a pharmacist, an herbalist, acting as the town doctor.

My grandmother was an herbwoman who took herbs around visiting friends and people who were sick in the community. She was one of the first suffragists in my country and established trade schools for women, where they were taught millinery, basket weaving—things that brought in immediate money. She was also an orator who became a Congresswoman. I have a good psychic connection with my grandmother, who died during the war. I think that she is with me and is my guiding spirit.

My mother is a spell caster and a medium. She used to belong to psychic groups where she was put in trance and would talk in ancient Egyptian, which only university professors could understand. She reads palms, and she does spontaneous fortune telling, just by being exposed to someone. And she is also a ceramic artist who makes her living making Goddess images. In 1977 she raised a pagan temple in a modern museum in Budapest which consisted of a very large room; in the middle was a Great Goddess, very stylized, very peasant. She called her "the Source"; all around were icons on the wall and Dianic totem poles.

My education consisted of observing my mother, who has crumbled buildings with her curses and prophesied the end of the war and her own marriages; I watched her read palms and cards. She taught me how to read cards, which is what I'm using as a means of psychic counseling. That's essentially my background. I added to that whatever came from my family, my own scholarship, which is considerable. In my astrological chart in the tenth house, at the mid-heaven, I have Neptune; I'm totally into mythology, symbols, and higher vibrations from Venus. I taught myself about other Goddess traditions around the world and blended that with feminism, which was the last step to make my craft powerful. And when that happened, I developed my own life work, which is priestessing a feminist community.

GK: *What is the organizational nature of The Sisterhood of the Wicce?*

ZB: We incorporated The Sisterhood of the Wicce in 1975. We are now incorporated as the Susan B. Anthony Coven Number One, as part of the Convenant of the Goddess. The Covenant of the Goddess was created after The Sisterhood of the Wicce because the Sisterhood created so much patriarchal backlash. We let go of it and went with the Covenant because we had to fight a criminal case about fortune telling for three years. We are the very first women's religion incorporated in this country with a female diety. With this historical step we have fulfilled mythical importance.

There are many covens now: the Elizabeth Cady Stanton Coven in Orange County, the Sojourner Truth Coven in the Catskills, the Jane Addams Coven in Chicago. We have the Mother Goddess Church in Florida and the Matriarchy Foundation in New York. When I was at the Witches and Amazons Spirituality Conference at Indiana University (June 1978, organized by Gloria Kaufman), I told everyone to incorporate. Locally incorporated feminist spirituality groups are going to be everywhere. I planned, for 1980, a giant ecumenical conference in Los Angeles, sponsored by the Susan B. Anthony Coven Number One. I do not advise, however, women's religion to be a centralized religion with a Pope, with Ten Commandments, and with a unified policy. I'm strongly for versatility, diversification, reveling in differences. That way we stay strong, we keep growing, and nobody can squelch us.

GK: *Is there any kind of network that allows the covens in different parts of the country to communicate and share ideas?*

ZB: In fact there is a spiderweb of communications amongst covens. Our own is *Themis*, the voice of the feminist witch, now in its sixth issue. That goes out to three thousand women internationally. There is *Homebrew* (which is more like a journal), *Elevenstone, Circle,* and many more. Pagans always liked to communicate. Since we are part of COG, The Covenant of the Goddess, that too has a newsletter, which arrives on the Full Moon.

GK: *What about* The Holy Book of Woman's Mysteries?

ZB: *The Holy Book of Woman's Mysteries* is out, but the money we raised was only enough for Part One. It is a unique book because my own mother's art is included in it. Masika Szilagyi raised a pagan temple in Budapest, and all her statues we run as covers on *Themis.* Her imagery is very important and expressive. *The Holy Book of Woman's Mysteries* costs six dollars and can be obtained from our coven. Part Two and Three needs funds. I often wonder how come women help with their monies the male gurus, the Moonies, etc., and I don't even know one woman who has money enough to invest.

GK: *In all those goddess traditions what are some of the characteristics that you find?*

ZB: There are quite a few overlapping features. First, the big feature is that the Goddess is seen as Mother, including both the male and the female. Not that she is androgynous, but that she is female and can create the male. She is all female, but she can make the same, and she can make the different. In her services both sexes are seen as her children, and therefore they are both divine and sacred to the Goddess. So the most significant feature of Goddess worship is a complete inclusivity; as the mother includes all her brood, the Goddess religion includes all of her children.

What's also overlapping is that she is that which gives life. Her definition is "I am she who binds hearts together." She is seen as Love, and as a Force; she is seen within and without, she is *not* seen as a person. She is nature, and the secretness of nature. She is someone whose worship is in a circle, instead of separation of clergy and people in a square. She is miraculous, prophetic, powerful in cures, protector of childbirth, and protector of things that grow. She is prayed to most of the time under the full moon in all the cultures. The full and the new moon are her times.

GK: *Another quality that seems to come up over and over again in women's religion is joy, life affirmation, sensuality. . . .*

ZB: "All acts of love and pleasure are my rituals." That's in the *Great Charge* of the Star Goddess. She has no taboo on anything that feels good. She has one taboo, and that's "No one shall be harmed or destroyed in all my holy mountains." Her holy mountain is the planet.

GK: *In* The Feminist Book of Lights and Shadows *you mention the "female principle of the universe." How do you see that as being different from a male principle?*

ZB: The difference between the Mother concept and the Father concept is that the Mother includes both sexes, and the Father does not. The Father is exclusively male; the Mother always includes both sexes. The Mother-oriented religion has the innate ability to include both sexes, both of her children, those that she creates the same (the female child), and as different (the male child). They both are sacred to her. That kind of mentality allows for an inclusive religion.

The Father concept is a male homosexual religion of the Father and the Son. It is an incestuous male homosexual concept that excludes the Mother, the female principle of the universe, and the creator. And of course the entire semen theology of the Pope, barring ordination of women, is completely supporting this—that they are unable to include *all* of humanity because they have an inferior religious concept. A religion is only good if it works for everyone—that's a superior religion. An inferior religion is when you are unable to open up to the entire humanity: they can't figure out a way how to work with the entity of human life. What they have is a militaristic concept, as all the religions that have male gods grow out of military hero worship. They are all related to that, and they support a militaristic society.

GK: *That's what Charlotte Perkins Gilman wrote about in* His Religion and Hers. *An early twentieth-century feminist, she believed that the male experience is traditionally that of a warrior, which has to shape his world view.*

ZB: Unfortunately it has been shaping the world view for the past five thousand years, but before that men were very happy doing other things. There is more to life than making weapons and killing each other. There are other occupations men could do.

GK: *When you talk about women's values, it's being inclusive and. . . .*

ZB: And treating life with reverence, and making life a priority, not seeing divisions between people from the point of view of this family, this name, this country, this border. When women look at the world, they see their children. They do not see the divisions that men impose, that these are the Johnsons and the Millers. They do not see it as possessively.

GK: *Do you think that comes from women's experiences being mothers?*

ZB: Yes, I really do. I think that biology, in this case, is theology, and Genesis is always at the crux of all religious concepts. The ability of women to create from their own bodies the same and the different enables women to have farther vistas. And man, who has not included in his body anybody, was kind of expelled, is unable to include all of humanity. They are not the natural mystics of the world. Women are.

GK: *You say that this is all biologically based. Do you think that there is any hope for men, or are we doomed to the dominion of the patriarchal viewpoint?*

ZB: There is only one hope for overcoming it, and that is that the planet that is his already is in crisis; and through understanding, men could come to see this, through much education and dispelling of ignorance, which is what we see as evil. Arduous experience of hardship and disasters would be a hard lesson. The problem is that women get pulled with it because at this point men run the world.

In times of great crisis the female principle is more visible. The female principle always comes up; it's unorganized, it's a phenomenon. I think what's happening now with the Goddess movement is part of that. Mother Nature somehow acts through the females when a species is endangered. What's happening with humans is that we have not only endangered ourselves through polluting what we need to survive, but we have also wiped out quite a few other species. We are essentially pests. The biological definition of human life is we fit in the category of pests, because we eat everybody, and nobody eats us.

The female principle exhibits leadership through women. Man cannot lead us out of here; under no circumstances will men save the world.

GK: *But the question is, will they listen?*

ZB: I have a female strategy; I'm advising people and telling my witches to aim for lowering the birthrate of males. The female principle can do that. The collective unconscious can do miracles. Even if we had a ten-year gap in bearing male children, we could start over again and take it from the beginning and train them differently. But indiscriminate breeding is crucial for male power. When women are controlling breeding, they usually choose a sire, but when they have no alternative, like the abortion right being taken away, then overpopulation creates cheap labor, cheap labor creates cheap life, cheap life creates devaluation of female life, and cheap labor and cheap life is only good for war. That has to be stopped, so it's absolutely important that women control their breeding, and try not to have male children for awhile. Twenty-five years of moratorium on male births would be worth it. In twenty-five years we could turn the world around. It would be such a generation gap, and such an overwhelming female image around, that it would do it. All we have to do is discontinue the line for a little bit, and then we can go back to it. It is a utopian solution, but it could be done.

GK: *It would be fascinating to see what that female energy would create. When you think of Diana, the Goddess, is that a symbol for you of female power, or is it a reality? Do you think that there is a higher spiritual entity that is Diana?*

ZB: Diana, the Holy Mother, is the soul of nature, in which we partake as being part of nature.

GK: *It's the essence of nature?*

ZB: The soul of nature. It's not a person, in other words.

GK: *But She listens. You can call on Her and get a response?*

ZB: Yes.

GK: *What kind of response and contact have you had with the Goddess? In terms of ritual practices, what happens when the coven is worshipping?*

ZB: The Goddess is experienced as the Life Force, she is within *and* without. Her presence in nature is expressed in omens. Something that's very unusual; for instance, after an invocation to the Goddess the wind wakes, a wind will come. Or an owl would fly into the circle. That happens often. Another time, under a full moon, the entire coven (thirty-eight women) experienced a spinal heat shooting up from their backs, at different intervals, but each of us got it. That was received with shrieks and great excitement. Just the fact that when we are naked in the middle of the night, and are warm; nobody catches colds by being naked in the middle of winter, dancing on a mountain. Other times it takes a month to see if something worked. Most of the time what people ask for at sabbat they get by the next sabbat. This is something also pretty dependable.

GK: *What if they ask for something that may not be ethical? What do you think about the morality of asking for specifics?*

ZB: You can't stop people from praying. Christians pray for specific things. They pray against gays, for instance. They pray against the Jews. Witches don't pray against anybody. I think there is nothing wrong with asking for what you want if you know specifically what you want. The Goddess movement prays for ERA, welfare for each other. I advise women also to leave their spells open, because that particular thing might not be the right one, or something else would be much better; one should never close the door and see the Goddess as a dingbat. That never works. But people do ask for specific jobs, people ask for help to move, people ask for the Goddess's help to finish a project for the ERA.

It's okay to ask for what you want, but the Goddess has veto power.

GK: *What about spells that harm people?*

ZB: If you attack the innocent, it returns tenfold. This is the Law. If you don't attack the innocent, if somebody actually harms you, you can return that harm. Women are not saints. Nobody is running for Pope, or saint. Women can be formidable enemies. Again I would always advise people to put an open end to it, saying that "if this person actually did me harm, then reverse it." Endorse reversals of psychic attacks to divert harm. That has been pretty dependable.

GK: *I'm interested in the way that women organize their groups. The way that the coven works is that there are ideally thirteen, with a high priestess. Is that right?*

ZB: No. That's classical witchcraft, which we don't do. *Lights and Shadows* is my book about classical witchcraft, but what we actually practice in a grove with whomever shows up is the congregation; it's usually a magic number. It's organized around the Nymph, Maiden, and Crone. Sometimes each of these jobs can be shared by three women. These women take part in evoking the corners, drawing the circle, taking care of music and entertainment (that's a Nymph's job in particular). I've seen and heard from witches' covens in the Midwest which run their meetings on the trinity concept. The Maiden would be the woman who would have the agenda and would chair. The Nymphs would have the refreshments, and the Crone would make sure that everybody gets heard and no one is left out. This trinity leadership concept is a very healthy one for people.

GK: *You aim for a "socialist matriarchy"; does the trinity idea fit into that?*

ZB: Yes. The matriarchy is innately socialist. Communal interests are highlighted as good for the individuals. The order of birth is observed as a hierarchy.

GK: *So age is given respect; to be a Crone is a position of honor.*

ZB: Yes, the Crone is revered as the carrier of wisdom, the expression of the Goddess in the coven. When the Crone speaks in a circle, one knows that the Great Goddess often chooses her to speak through her. Crones are more mediumistic. The crone is anyone who feels like it; it doesn't have an age limit on it. Ideally it should mean someone who is no longer menstruating, but people have hysterectomies in their twenties. It is a state of mind, and a feeling of maturity. The Crones are listened to; in disputes the Crones are asked for judgment. In fact, in old times, a group of Crones could stop wars. For instance, in Germany there is a record of this, that a group of older women interfered with the warriors and sent them home, and they didn't dare to go against them because they came in their capacity as the elders. And they threatened them and said that the Goddess's wrath would be on every one and each of them if they didn't listen, and they didn't want to mess with that.

GK: *What are you focusing on currently?*

ZB: *The Holy Book of Women's Mysteries*, which is the first such very large and comprehensive book. The first book, *Lights and Shadows*, is kindergarten compared with what I am putting together now. Spells include how to raise storms, how to still the winds, how to free political prisoners, and the witches' marriage called Trysting. Part One of the Holy Book gives us the Women's Festivals, such as the Haloa (celebrations of free speech for women). The last chapters talk about understanding Aphrodite, the Goddess of Love and Death, and Aradia, the only female avatar, who came to the oppressed and taught the art of Witchcraft. I have a whole section for men in it as I would like to see a rebirth of Goddess worship among our sons. That's a good way to change the world, to give them a different spiritual focus.

GK: *Are any of them doing it?*

ZB: Yes, there are a lot of male witches.

GK: *But aren't they Satanists?*

ZB: No! Satanists have gotten such great publicity. There were something like four of them. Satan is a Christian concept. It has nothing to do with witches. It's a very new thing. It's one hundred fifty years old, and it was born as a backlash to the witch burning, totally invented by priests and sadists.

GK: *Do the men who worship have their own covens, or are they integrated?*

ZB: No, men worship with women, but there are men's mysteries. They perform initiations for each other, but there should always be a high priestess present. The men cannot have a complete spiritual experience without the representative of the Great Goddess who created them. Women, on the other hand, do worship with themselves only. They may take their children with them, but after puberty, boys are not allowed in women's mysteries.

GK: *Which are. . . .*

ZB: Women's mysteries are celebrating female energy, getting in touch with nature. There are eight major sabbats, on the Wheel of Life, and some wonderful women's festivals, such as Thesmophora (first fruits offerings), Haloa (celebration of free speech), and a handful of other greats.

The Goddess movement will emerge because the world is in trouble. The world is in trouble, not so much warring with nations, but this time polluting the sacred earth, air, water, which threatens the entire ecosystem. Male energy without the redeeming quality of the female principle is toying unchecked. The worshipping of death culture is insane. If the world was not in trouble, the female principle would not bother to be this visible. But it will be now; it's amazing how that occurs. The male churches are our real enemies. They are the ones who are fighting the ERA with their church money, and they are the ones who absorb a lot of sisters to do the volunteer work. And, indeed, women hold up both ends. Women are something like 90 percent of church-goers. So our real field of conquest is on the religious front. If we want women to listen, we have to reach them on the religious field. To interact with the divine is always a woman's wish.

GK: *Are you finding that happening, that you're making contact with the women out in the suburbs, the middle Americans?*

ZB: No, I think what happens in this first ten years is that I will reach feminists with a book that's distributed very well, and includes men. What is presented in the *Women's Mysteries* is from the five continents, and relates many things to include men. You see, women would not really buy into a religion that does not include all their children. On the other hand, women have been convinced that it's okay if they themselves are excluded. When the connection is made by women that religions need not exclude anybody, that women have a spiritual contribution to the welfare of the earth, that in fact women's values are life-affirming values, women will ask for their own heritage, for their own temples back, their own Femineries, their own divine souls.

And it is going to be the real revolution, changing the spiritual focus of our species from death worship into life worship, Goddess worship.

Blessed Be!

VI. ORGANIZATIONS

FEMINIST THERAPY

Ellyn Kaschak

Once, some ten years ago, in a land called America, there was no feminist therapy, for the women of the land, Sleeping Beauties all, slept. But no Prince Charming could bestow the magical kiss, for, to the princes of the land, these women appeared to be quite awake. Not as awake as they, the princes, of course, who were men and whose business it was to tend to the affairs of the world, but certainly awake enough to tend to their tasks as wives and mothers. Even more surprising to those of us now looking back at this time was that women themselves did not know that they were asleep. Of course, many noticed that something was wrong, wrong with each of them as individuals. They did not know its name, so they called it depression or anxiety or penis envy. They called it many names, but did not call it sleep. For, after all, how could they who slept know that they did?

Because the women slept, there was as yet no feminism in the land, for feminism is the business of women who are awake and women who are awakening. There was no feminism, but there was psychotherapy, for psychotherapy was then the business of men.[1] In those days psychotherapy helped women to adjust to their proper roles, to sleep their sleep and to dream the proper dreams, dreams that only princesses should dream.

Erik Erikson:

> For the student of development and practitioner of psychoanalysis, the stage of life crucial for the understanding of womanhood is the step from youth to maturity, the state when the young woman relinquishes the care received from the parental family and the extended care of institutions of education, in order to commit herself to the love of a stranger and to the care to be given to his or her offspring... young women often ask whether they can "have an identity" before they know whom they will marry and for whom

they will make a home. Granted that something in the young woman's identity must keep itself open for the peculiarities of the man to be joined and of the children to be brought up, I think that much of a young woman's identity is already defined in her kind of attractiveness and in the selectivity of her search for the man (or men) by whom she wishes to be sought.[2]

Bruno Bettelheim:

... as much as women want to be good scientists and engineers, they want, first and foremost, to be womanly companions of men and to be mothers.[3]

Joseph Rheingold:

... woman is nurturance ... anatomy decrees the life of a woman ... when women grow up without dread of their biological functions and without subversion by feminist doctrines and therefore enter upon motherhood with a sense of fulfillment and altruistic sentiment, we shall attain the goal of a good life and a secure world in which to live.[4]

Then slowly in the mid- and late 1960s, and more rapidly in the seventies, a change occurred; nothing less than a social revolution swept the land. Following the Civil Rights movement and hand in hand with many ethnic minorities who were demanding their rights, women began awakening. Sleeping Beauties began awakening themselves. This was an awakening that no Prince Charming could accomplish, for the truth is that these were not princesses at all, but ordinary and extraordinary women. The feminist movement was born, and nurtured by women it grew and produced its own offspring, feminist therapy.

I do not wish to tease you, the reader, any further with this parable, because, I am sorry to report, the expected happy ending is not, at least not yet, forthcoming. Everyone is not off in a castle in some beautiful land living happily ever after and never growing old. We are all living and struggling and growing older and wiser and younger and happier.

But I have gotten ahead of my story. My purpose in writing this chapter is to explain just what feminist therapy is, who is doing it, why, and how. Feminist therapy grew out of the second feminist movement of the late 1960s. More specifically it is based upon the consciousness-raising or C-R group as a model. By this time literally thousands of women throughout the United States, and in many other nations as well, have participated in C-R groups and have discovered for themselves that *feminism is therapeutic*. For each woman who learned that her deepest and most hidden feelings were not hers alone but those of women in general, that there was not something wrong with her as a woman but with all women in our society, there was another awakening. Each woman's experience was validated as the experience of Everywoman.

Society is replete with "double binds" for women. Perhaps no example is more striking than the results of the well-known study of psychiatrists, psychologists, and social workers by Broverman et al.[5] These therapists were asked to choose the qualities that they felt characterized the healthy adult, the adult male, and the adult female. Both male and female clinicians described male behavior as highly correlated with that of the healthy adult. Females, on the other hand, were considered to be less aggressive, more emotional, less independent, and so on. It is thus apparent that in these terms it is impossible to choose to be both a healthy adult human being and a healthy adult woman. In fact, according to such a definition, *there can be no such thing as a healthy adult female person.* Needless to say, males are not faced with this no-win choice. Society's definition of women has apparently been reflected and supported by just those practitioners who are supposed to be "above" such discriminatory and biased viewpoints, who are supposed to be the experts in "mental health."

It was becoming increasingly obvious that broader social problems had in many cases been mistakenly identified as individual maladjustment by psychology in general and by psychotherapists in particular. Many critics of traditional psychotherapy, among whom are feminist therapists, believe that it has served as an agent of social control,[6] enforcing traditional values and sex roles. One way in which psychotherapy has prevented broader social change is by stressing the uniqueness of individual symptoms and emphasizing individual responsibility and individual solutions. It has perpetuated incessant talk, rather than action, as a means to bring about genuine change. Feminists have also criticized traditional psychotherapists for having shortsightedly ignored the oppressive and discriminatory social context in which we all must live and function. Feminist therapists know what traditional psychotherapists did not, that the personal is also political, that one can not do psychotherapy without also doing sociotherapy.[7] Women's problems—people's problems, in fact—are obviously a result of both psychological and societal stress.

As women and feminists many psychotherapists were becoming increasingly aware not only of the antifemale and intrapsychic bias of psychotherapy but also of the discrepancy between their own experience as women and the psychology of *man*kind that they had been taught in our universities. In the early 1970s several groups of feminist psychologists and mental health professionals in such areas as San Francisco, Los Angeles, Boston, New York, and Chicago began to form small groups to discuss and develop a nonsexist and sociotherapeutic approach, whose goal would be *change rather than adjustment.*

One of these groups, the Women's Counseling Service of San Francisco, of which I was a founding member, began meeting regularly in the summer of 1972. From the very beginning we had several purposes. Before we could do anything else we had to provide, for ourselves and each other, support and validation for our own perceptions and experiences, which were not recognized by the larger psychological systems with which we each dealt every day. Second, we were faced with the enormous task of creating and developing a feminist therapy, one that would replace the traditional personal and intrapsychic focus of psychotherapy with a combined social and psychological perspective, one that would recognize oppression as a reality and involve us as women-psychologists in action leading to its change.[8]

At the time we struggled and stumbled often. We saw clients and they struggled with us. We learned together and from each other. We had no theory to define and guide our practice. We had no psychology of women, for no psychologist knew who women were or who they could be. Our group and others began to develop feminist therapy.

Having learned from the consciousness-raising experience that participation in small groups helped women to overcome their isolation and alienation from themselves and each other, we employed groups as a preferred mode of treatment. Of course, while the group experience provides support and validation of a kind and amount that cannot be offered by the therapist alone, individual sessions permit a degree of depth and intensity that may have to be shared with others in the group. Thus individual therapy is offered by most feminist therapists, although often as a transition until a client feels enough support and strength to enter a group setting. Paradoxically, of course, she must often come to this point before being able to enter a group that will, in most cases, offer her even more strength and support.

Within such a group each client seems to progress through several similar stages. Entering therapy with the belief that "there is something wrong with me," that "my unhappiness represents a personal failure" (*Stage 1*), she soon becomes aware, through the combined skills of the therapist (or preferably therapists, since we too need support and validation) and validation of her experience by other group members (*Stage 2*), that her problems are both personal and social in nature. With this awareness (*Stage 3*) in virtually every case comes a tremendous amount of anger at others, at society, and sometimes at herself for having "been blind" for so long (*Stage 4*).

Exploring and working through this fourth stage to some constructive resolution really represents the heart of feminist therapy. By the term "working through" I do not mean to suggest that all anger disappears but rather that it is channeled constructively into action and change (*Stage 5*).

A major aspect of this five-stage process involves helping each client first to identify and then to reclaim and reintegrate lost parts of herself as a woman. These parts are lost to all members of our society, regardless of gender, as a result of the rigid and artificial division of human characteristics known as sex roles. Traditionally each individual in our society has been able to function as only half a human being. *He* could be active, *she* passive. *He* could be intellectual, *she* emotional. *He* could deal with the outside world, *she* functioned within the home. Together they made up one fully functioning human being—named the Couple. No one could stand on her or his own two feet. People could only lean on each other as a way to survive. In feminist therapy clients learn to stand and then to walk. Having learned to walk on one's own, one can then go far, visiting many places previously unknown or out of reach.

The image I wish to present here is one of an integrated, whole human being, an androgynous one. One way to describe what is meant by androgyny is perhaps a maximal flexibility, an ability to respond in terms of the demands of a situation and one's own needs rather than in response to prescription and proscription. The androgynous person is able to be both active and passive, independent and dependent, emotional and intellectual. Let me emphasize that the androgynous individual is absolutely not a caricature of a member of her own or the "opposite" sex but a new synthesis, an individual free to choose and change roles, an individual not confined by arbitrary psychological restraints.

Obviously, and I cannot emphasize this point enough, this is only one half of the change needed. An androgynous person can only function in an environment that affords an equal opportunity to all people, one that does not assign tasks, roles, and lifestyles on the basis of kind of genitals, color of skin, and so forth. Thus feminist therapists also actively facilitate and are involved in working toward the elimination of societal constraints. Let me emphasize that this is not to advocate an impossible Utopian ideal, such as total freedom for all. In fact many feminist therapists believe that traditional therapies, particularly the more humanistic ones, have duped their clients by offering the illusion of total freedom, the possibility of self-actualization in an oppressive and discriminatory environment. Only with the abolition of arbitrary sex roles so that each person can choose the roles that she or he will play on the basis of her or his own needs and abilities, along with the needs of a receptive social environment, will androgyny be possible, will feminist therapy have provided a "cure."

Perhaps the most essential difference between feminist therapy and the more traditional forms of psychotherapy is the rejection by feminist therapists of the necessity or desirability of the extreme power differential between the therapist and client. "Freud believed that the psychoanalyst-patient relationship must be that of 'a superior and subordinate.' The psychotherapist has been seen, by his critics as well as by his patients, as a "surrogate parent . . ., savior, lover, expert, and teacher. . . ."[9] Feminist therapists, on the other hand, believe that such a power differential is only a mirror image of the inferior position in which women in our society find themselves and as such can only maintain and reinforce the status quo. Very simply, such an unequal relationship can only serve the needs of the psychotherapist and is, at best, antitherapeutic.

Thus feminist therapists have dedicated themselves to the elimination of the power differential within the therapeutic relationship. Such a radical change in the nature of psychotherapy requires nothing less than a redefinition of the actual process of psychotherapy itself.

In feminist psychotherapy the consumer or potential consumer is encouraged to shop around, to interview several therapists until she finds one whose personal manner, therapeutic style, and values are congruent with her own. Making such information available to prospective and current clients requires a willingness on the part of the therapist to make herself more transparent, more "known" than the traditional therapist. In other words, the protective garb of professionalism is shed. The general process of psychotherapy, as well as more specific techniques, and the personal values of the therapist may be discussed and explained to the client. For, while the therapist is a skilled and experienced expert, she is not a witch, a magician, or a goddess.

In keeping with the principle of equality clients are invited to choose when and on what they want to work in therapy. A choice not to work on a particular issue yet or at all is respected and not considered unconscious resistance to be "broken through" by a powerful, omniscient therapist. Feminist therapists generally consider their fees to be negotiable and based upon the ability of the client to pay, as well as on the needs of the therapist. As a result feminist therapy is available to women of all classes and not just to the affluent. Many feminist therapists and clients choose to conduct sessions in the homes of the therapist and/or clients as a further step toward genuineness and demystification.

Such a process obviously tends to preclude the development of classical transference, upon which much traditional psychotherapy is based. Rather than deal with the client as an infantile, regressed, and powerless individual, therapist and client meet as equals, as women who have both experienced pain and discrimination and who both have decided to do something about it. The therapist has certain skills and experience and a greater awareness of "double binds" or traps through which she can guide them both.

At this point I would like to present some case histories in order to illustrate some of the principles that I have discussed and to highlight issues that are of major impact within feminist therapy. I hestitate to present cases, to objectify or in anyway dehumanize the experiences of these women. I believe, however, that many women will recognize themselves in these descriptions, for these truly are many women. As such they should be read not just as cases but as examples of who women today are and who they can be. Each case is in fact actually a composite of several clients with whom I have worked and many whom I have not yet met.

Let me describe the members of a "typical" feminist therapy group conducted by the Women's Counseling Service.

(1) Linda, a twenty-seven-year-old woman, entered psychotherapy because she had felt "depressed and worthless" ever since being rejected from medical school. Her boyfriend, with whom she lived, had been accepted and was at the time attending a medical school in San Francisco. He was very busy, needless to say, and unable to spend the amount of time with her that he had previously. To add to her feelings of worthlessness, Linda had been unable to find any work in the over-saturated job market of San Francisco, although she had been a practical nurse in Missouri before coming to San Francisco. Her days seemed empty and aimless.

A feminist, she finally chose to call a feminist therapist. She found the name of our group in a central listing at the Women's Center and called for an appointment. After an initial interview she decided to join an available group. During her first session she explained that the school to which she had applied accepted only five women in a class of over one hundred and that she actually had better grades and admission test scores than her boyfriend, but that she still felt worthless and inferior to him now that he had been accepted. She stayed home every day, read, brooded, and cried. She had no plans for the future, except that she knew that she would never be a physician.

Although she realized intellectually that she was the victim of discrimination, it took several months before Linda could acknowledge and feel that there might not be something wrong with her personally. However, even at that point she still felt helpless to do anything about it, insisting that sexism was beyond her control. She did become increasingly angry, particularly at her boyfriend, whom she began to see as "her enemy." He responded by withdrawing and becoming even more involved in school, which only served to increase Linda's anger. Their relationship became increasingly distant. Linda blamed herself and as a result felt even more lonely, worthless, and depressed.

Paradoxically, although she blamed herself for just about anything that happened in her life, she also felt totally helpless to make any constructive change, for which she also blamed herself. Through the support and validation of the rest of the group and the continued clarification of the "double binds" confronting her, Linda eventually began to see the possibility that she could affect her own destiny, perhaps not totally, but certainly much more than she was doing.

Although her boyfriend was sympathetic, he was less than supportive, instead focusing his energy on his own academic career. Linda felt that he didn't care about her. He felt that his career should come first to both of them and that she was being selfish in putting herself first. A stalemate.

Meanwhile Linda joined a group that was attempting to form a women's health collective in order to pursue her medical interests in an alternative manner. She soon became involved in writing a grant proposal, as a result of which the group was funded. She began to feel more confident and self-assured, for which the group members offered reinforcement. She became actively involved in alternative health delivery systems and in working for legislation that would prevent medical schools from discriminating against women.

Linda had become increasingly confident and now was almost never heard to whine, sigh, or act the martyr. She had slowly become a strong and competent young woman. This change in her continued to cause problems in her relationship and finally led her and her boyfriend into therapy together. Unfortunately he was unable to accept an equal relationship and continued to feel that both his wishes and his career must be primary. Although Linda had never accepted his definition of a relationship, neither had she so openly resisted it. They could not compromise and finally separated.

Linda eventually formed a more equal relationship with another man, who was also a physician, interestingly enough. She continued her work with great enthusiasm. Slowly, ever so slowly, she was able to give up her self-deprecating behavior, to realize that she and all women were worthwhile human beings and, when justifiably angry, could respond constructively rather than destructively.

(2) Jean, a forty-two-year-old wife and mother of nine, also entered the group with that women's disease, depression. She had originally married because she had gotten pregnant and came from a rather strict religious background that seemed to offer her no alternative. Her husband, at the time a nineteen-year-old garage mechanic, did "the honorable thing." Although they both felt unhappy and trapped, they continued to have children at frequent intervals as a way to avoid confronting their plight.

During the last year both she and her husband had formed other relationships and were contemplating divorce. He would remarry and wanted the children to live with him. She wished to live alone and to become a musician. Although she did not really wish to have the children with her permanently, she felt that as their mother she was obligated to do so.

Jean entered the group one week after separating from her husband. She was living in San Francisco while he remained in Chicago with the children. In addition to overwhelming and incapacitating depression she felt tremendous guilt at having been "a terrible mother, who deserted her own children."

Although the other group members could readily support and even share her feelings, they had a great deal of difficulty in supporting her decision to allow her husband custody of the children. Jean was angry at everyone, including the other women in the group, and frequently threatened to quit. However, while acknowledging her right to do so, the therapist pointed out that running away from situations in which she felt trapped by misunderstanding was a pattern that she had followed all her life and that only left her even more trapped by her own guilt. Jean decided to "stay and fight," as she put it. She struggled to convince the other group members, as well as herself, that she had a right to choose for herself. Her depression alternated with anger, but her guilt remained constant. Eventually she, as well as the other group members, began to see that there was no one way to be a mother that was necessarily right for all mothers and children or absolutely different from the role of a father.

Slowly, ever so slowly, she began to feel more alive, less guilty. She began to write music, which was frequently published. When she finally felt freer to choose, she then realized that—without the demands that society and, therefore, she had placed on herself—she was able to care for and miss her children rather than just resent them. Jean eventually arranged with her husband and his new wife that the children would spend three months of each year with her. She spent many honest, painful, and joyful hours talking with her children, helping them to understand her choice and eventually letting them know, in a way that she was unable previously, that she loved them very much. Today her relationship with her children is closer and better than ever, and her career is flourishing.

(3) Fran, a fifty-eight-year-old woman, joined the group because she was faced with a new problem. She had married her husband when she was thirty years old. Although she hadn't loved him, she had feared, because of her age, that this was her last chance for marriage and security. Since he traveled extensively in his work, they saw comparatively little of each other in the years that followed. They were strangers.

Now he was to retire. Although her husband looked forward to settling in at home, Fran dreaded having him around all the time. On the other hand, she still wanted the security that his income and his existence seemed to provide her.

In the group she began focusing on the societal and personal pressures that had made her feel insecure and worthless as an unclaimed, unmarried woman, illegitimate without a man. She also confronted her own exploitation of her husband. She had merely used him.

Predictably despair turned to anger and self-blame. After continued and repeated confrontation she began to realize that her self-blame was another means to keep her helpless and immobilized.

Fran eventually agreed to explore the possibility that she and her husband might become friends, might achieve mutual respect and caring, or else might agree to part. She approached him, and after much pain and honest confrontation they agreed to visit a marriage counselor to work out a relationship or a separation. Although the risks were greater, the possibility of each of them becoming a more genuine, less fearful, and less crippled person seemed to excite them both.

This case particularly involves and highlights the mutual exploitation and oppression of both sexes. Both Fran and her husband had been cheated and had cheated each other. If they dared, they might now begin to find two people hiding behind a frightened couple.

(4) Harriet, a twenty-six-year-old woman, had known that she was a lesbian since she had been sixteen. At that time she had rather naively shared the information with her shocked parents, who immediately brought her to a traditional Freudian psychiatrist, who eventually had her institutionalized in a state hospital for several months. Since that time she had continued in therapy with that same therapist, who had encouraged her to develop relationships with men. Although she had tried, she felt little for them either sexually or emotionally. In all this time she never even approached another woman but remained isolated without friend or lover. She felt that she had no right to burden anyone else with her presence. She really had no right to be alive and had actually tried suicide twice, once right after having been hospitalized. Like the others, she experienced frequent depression and intense loneliness, which she blamed on her own "sickness and perversity."

Finally a friend suggested that she contact the Women's Counseling Service, since she had obviously made no apparent progress in the many years of her therapy. In desperation she did so. It was months before she felt able to join the group, to "confess" what she considered and had learned in therapy was her "sickness" to a group of women. (Ironically enough, this occurred during the same year that the American Psychiatric Association voted homosexuality out as a disease, an interesting method of determining illness, to say the least, but one that came too late to alter Harriet's damaged self-image.)

The other group members were sympathetic and supportive of Harriet. For her part, however, she could not tolerate such acceptance and continued to try to prove to them and to the therapist that she was a worthless and sick human being. Although she repeatedly accused the therapist of just being "therapeutic" rather than genuine, Harriet could not dismiss the support and acceptance of the group members as easily. Eventually she began to feel that she might be a worthwhile human being, one who had a right to be alive and even to be happy.

As she realized the role that the oppression of society and of the psychiatric establishment had played in creating her unhappiness, Harriet began to change even more. She began to approach people in a new way, to make friends and to form relationships. Her new, more positive self-image was reinforced even further by these contacts. As her isolation gave way to meaningful and intimate relationships, Harriet herself seemed transformed into a relaxed, self-confident and joyful young woman. She had almost no time for anger. She was truly alive for the first time. Although she, as did the others, became aware of the need for society to change, her own struggle continued on a more personal level. She would be a pioneer in a newly open and increasingly accepted lifestyle.

(5) Louise was a practicing attorney, a wife, and a mother of two young children. She felt that she should be able to perform each role perfectly, as they are traditionally defined. Needless to say, she entered the group thoroughly exhausted, blaming herself for her own imperfections, and depressed. She did little but cry during the first few sessions that she attended. She berated other group members for being even a few minutes late for a session, expecting and fearing perfection from them as well. She acted superior to other women, considered herself "as good as a man, maybe better."

Gently confronted again and again by group members and by the therapist, Louise finally became aware that she, like most members of our society, considered men to be "better" than women and was trying very hard to prove that she was as good as and even better than a man. As a result she had to dissociate herself from women, those inferior beings. Whether she blamed herself, men, or society for this state of affairs, she still found herself trapped. And she was, just as much as any of the other women described. Blaming is a closed system; only its target varies. It allows its user not to act or change. It allows its user to become depressed (feminine) or angry (masculine) or even paranoid (crazy). Louise, as all the other women in the group, had to become aware of society's injustices and then struggle to move beyond depression and anger to action and a constructive personal and/or societal change. And she did.

Louise began to realize that she lived in a society that defined women as second-class citizens. She could try to be a superwoman, but she was still "just a woman," and an exhausted and isolated one at that, trying to fill both sex roles to perfection. She soon separated from her husband in an attempt to clarify her own goals for herself.

After a year of separation and of painful self-examination for both of them they came together again to try to form a new and equal relationship. Each would try to be one flexible human being, not two and not one half. Even with their heightened awareness of the potential traps they continue to struggle every day not to fall back into taken-for-granted and familiar sex roles. Some days they succeed.

The cases that I have described serve to illustrate the absolute necessity of dealing with both psychological and societal proessures upon all women, whether or not they are participating in the process of psychotherapy. The distinction is an arbitrary one, because virtually all women in our society are subject to the very same attitudes and restrictions. Only the solutions may vary. Even the means of accommodation to this situation are remarkably similar and themselves a function of society's definition of appropriate ways for women to behave and to view themselves.

These cases will probably convey that, in my experience and that of feminist therapists with whom I have spoken, most women in our culture are quite susceptible to depression and its handmaiden, self-blame. It would be surprising to find any other state of affairs in a society that itself deprecates women and devalues "women's work" or at best considers it secondary to that of men. The struggle away from this immobilizing self-definition to a more positive and active one, though at the core of feminist therapy, does not generally end when the therapy is terminated but continues and will continue as long as our arbitrary definitions of people remain.

These group members are examples of the many ways in which women are changing themselves as a result of their involvement in feminist therapy. The group that I have just described is a fairly heterogenous one, but many feminist therapy services, among them the Women's Counseling Service, also offer more specific issue-oriented groups dealing with such areas of concern to women as motherhood, relationships, sexuality, assertiveness, psychological and physical rape, and the unique problems of ethnic- and sexual-minority women, to name a few. In addition issues of particular concern to women are their need for external approval, fear of the consequences of success or achievement,[10] competition, and sisterhood as a reality rather than an abstraction.

I have spoken of men, in this chapter, only in relation to women because that is the most typical way in which men come to a feminist therapist. Although there is no reason that men cannot be clients of feminist therapists, they have not yet chosen to do so in large numbers.

Feminist Therapy   261

Those who have, in my experience, are themselves attempting to overcome restrictive socialization processes and to develop more equal nonsexist relationships in their own lives. One hopes that more women and men will have the opportunity, whether through feminist therapy or by other means, to become more fully functioning, androgynous, free human beings.

Although I have been speaking generally in this chapter, I certainly do not pretend to speak for all feminist therapy groups, which can range from collectives, which share responsibilities and income equally, to group practices, which share only office space and consultation. Then what is feminist therapy? To many it is exactly what I have described in this chapter. To others it may vary slightly with regard to technique or political philosophy. To everyone who has been seriously involved in its inception and struggle to survive and to grow, feminist therapy is the only nonsexist, profemale alternative to traditional methods, which reflect and reinforce a social system in which "normal" feminine behavior is, at the same time, considered "sick."

Feminist therapists can also agree that ideally there should be no such distinction as feminist and nonfeminist therapy. All good therapy should be feminist and nonsexist, just as it should be nonracist. It is a clear contradiction to call any other process therapeutic.

Feminist therapists can further agree on certain goals, such as the actualization of ideals and images in a real sense by real women. Women must learn to take pride in themselves as women and in women in general. Finally feminist therapy teaches women to value help-seeking and change rather than to be ashamed of sometimes being dependent in much the same way that they have had to fear being independent.

Although I left the tale of the Sleeping Beauties without a happy ending, perhaps it does have a happy ending after all. True enough, most women are not princesses and most men are not princes. However, once little boys grew up to be men and little girls to be bigger girls. Now every little girl can grow up to be a woman—and that after all, may be even better than being a princess.

Notes

1. Phyllis Chesler. *Women and Madness.* New York: Doubleday, 1972.

2. Erik H. Erikson. "Inner and Outer Space: Reflections on Womanhood," *Daedalus*, 2 (1965).

3. Bruno Bettelheim. "The Commitment Required of a Woman Entering a Scientific Profession in Present Day American Society," in *Women and the Scientific Professions,* MIT Symposium on American Women in Science and Engineering, Cambridge, Massachusetts, 1965.

4. Joseph Rheingold. *The Fear of Being a Woman.* New York: Grune and Stratton, 1964.

5. I. K. Broverman, D. M. Broverman, F. E. Clarkson, P. S. Rosenkrantz, and S. R. Vogel. "Sex-Role Stereotypes and Clinical Judgements of Mental Health," *Journal of Consulting and Clinical Psychology,* 34, 1 (1970), 1–7.

6. Nathan Hurvitz. "Psychotherapy as a Means of Social Control," *Journal of Consulting and Clinical Psychology,* 40, 2 (1973), 232–239.

7. Ellyn Kaschak. "Sociotherapy: An Ecological Model for Therapy with Women," *Psychotherapy: Theory, Research and Practice,* 13, 1 (Spring 1976).

8. *Ibid.*

9. Chesler, *op. cit.*

10. Matina Horner. "Toward an Understanding of Achievement-Related Conflicts in Women," *Journal of Social Issues,* 8 (1972), 157–175.

Ellyn Kaschak *has been actively involved in the development of feminist therapy since 1972, when she helped form a feminist therapy center in San Francisco. She currently teaches psychology at San Jose State University in San Jose, California. She continues to practice feminist therapy in San Jose and in Oakland. Her Ph.D., in clinical psychology, is from Ohio State University.*

FEMINIST WOMEN'S HEALTH CENTERS

Interview with Dido Hasper

Dido Hasper is the president and coordinator of the Federation of Feminist Women's Health Centers and a founder and director at the Chico Center. She discusses how a feminist organization integrates personnel issues and politics and how its delivery of health care is different from traditional practice.

GK: *How did the Feminist Women's Health Centers get started?*

DH: In the late sixties and early seventies there was a group of women that was working very hard to legalize abortion on demand. The Health Centers started out of that group. The first Feminist Women's Health Center was built out of the concept of self-help. Carol Downer was the first woman to see her own cervix and then show it to other women. She realized that self-examination was a basic tool to regaining control over our reproduction. Working as an advocate for women getting services at a hospital, she saw women's cervixes when they got abortions or pap smears. She wanted to be able to see her own, so she took a speculum home from the hospital. Once she saw her own cervix she realized she had had six kids and a yearly pap smear but the only person to see her cervix was her doctor. She went to the group she was working with to legalize abortion, got up on a table, inserted the speculum, looked at her own cervix, and showed it to the other women. This was the first self-help group and the beginning of a movement to regain control of our bodies.

    The self-help groups realized from doing self-exam and watching abortion that the technology of abortion was a simple, safe technology that women could learn themselves. They talked about different methods they had used to cure their vaginal infections and stay well. This group continued to fight for abortion on demand and also continued with self-help.

In 1971 Carol Downer and Lorraine Rothman took a trip across the country visiting abortion clinics and learning more about safe abortion. They returned and started the Women's Abortion Referral Service in Los Angeles. This referral service was set up to ensure women the least expensive abortion using the best technology. They would go with the women to the hospital and be an advocate for her to ensure the quality of care she received. The Women's Abortion Referral Service had enough women calling them so they could make demands on hospitals about the kind of abortion technique used. Women could have a local anesthetic instead of a general, the physicians started using more flexible instruments, and finally they stopped dilating the cervix so much. In 1973 the Supreme Court legalized abortion on demand, and so they opened a clinic themselves.

GK: *That was fast.*

DH: Yes, it was. They opened the first women-controlled clinic, where they provided the services they had been fighting for in the hospital. The clinic provides a more relaxed situation; women did not have to have an IV before their abortion or have extensive medication if they didn't want it. They hired physicians and trained them to do the least traumatic abortion procedure.

At the same time the clinic was starting menstrual extraction was also developed. Lorraine Rothman invented what we call the del'em. It consists of a canning jar, aquarium tubing, a one-way air valve, a syringe, and a canula (which is what's put into the uterus to do an abortion): it was all relatively readily accessible to women. The self-help group started doing their own women-controlled research; so while we were providing abortions in our clinics, we were also learning the technology ourselves to ensure that if the legislature made abortions illegal tomorrow women would still have that technology.

GK: *The other advantage of menstrual extraction is just to get it over with.*

DH: Right. Menstrual extraction is not designed solely for pregnancy. Women have used it to limit their periods. Some who have really painful cramping would prefer to have a menstrual extraction, have the contents of their uterus removed on the first day and get it over with right then.

GK: *So the clinic in L.A. got started, started doing abortion procedures and teaching self-help. Maybe you should first define self-help; then, second, how did the other centers get started and affiliated?*

DH: Self-help in the Feminist Women's Health Centers is the process that we use in health care and in many of the ways we work. Self-help groups are groups where women get together and use a plastic speculum, a mirror and flashlight, to look at their cervixes to better understand their bodies. By having this better understanding we are able to take care of many of the things that have sent us to our gynecologist. Self-help groups are able to relieve simple vaginal infections or overgrowth of certain kinds of bacteria in our vaginas without having to use medicine. One of the things, for example, that came out of the self-help group was using yogurt to control yeast overgrowth. And that's been very successful. It's a commonly known thing now in the women's health movement.

GK: *You might mention the "yogurt conspiracy."*

DH: In 1972 a self-help group in Los Angeles included both staff people of the Los Angeles Feminist Women's Health Center and women from the community. It also happened to include an undercover policewoman. It was an ongoing self-help group. The women got together one night a week for six weeks to discuss their health care. They learn how to fit diaphragms, talk about vaginal infections, prenatal care, anything that the group decided to discuss. One woman had a yeast infection and asked Carol to spoon some yogurt into her vagina.

On the fifth week of the group the Health Center was raided. Two woman were arrested (Carol Downer and Colleen Wilson) for practicing medicine without a license. The yogurt in the refrigerator—which happened to be people's lunches—was seized as evidence of this illegal activity. Carol was charged with several counts of practicing medicine without a license and Colleen Wilson was charged primarily, although there were other counts, for fitting diaphragms. At the time Colleen and the group decided that she was not in the position to go through a trial, so she pleaded guilty to a lesser charge. Carol went to court, had a jury trial, and was acquitted of all charges. We saw it as a great victory for self-help and for women taking control of their bodies.

GK: *You were elaborating on the self-help principle.*

DH: The self-help concept has been the basis of our clinics. There are Feminist Women's Health Centers in Los Angeles, San Diego, Orange County, Concord, Oakland, Chico, Tallahassee, Atlanta, Detroit, and West Berlin, Germany. There are other women-controlled Health Centers all over the United States. Many are based on self-help, and health care is delivered by lay health workers. We do work with medical professionals, but as far as any routine well-woman health care we believe that most of it can be taken care of outside of the medical profession.

GK: *How does a lay health worker learn what the sign of a yeast infection is or what cervicitis is?*

DH: The basis of our training program at the FWHC is self-help, learning by experience. Women have so much information about their own body that is never validated by a physician. We have never seen what we do as medicine, rather as health care. The major points of being a lay health worker are being a self-helper and knowing when to get back-up. In the Health Centers, especially in California, we have a completely documented training program because of our extensive battles with the State of California, Department of Health Services, over the unlicensed practice of medicine.

I think we've taken the self-help concept and expanded it to the way we work in the Health Centers. All the people who work in the Health Centers have a much greater control over their workplace than traditional workplaces, whether it be the receptionist, the clinic records keeper, or a full-time staff person. The Health Centers were created with the idea that we could put our minds together and figure out a solution. That is exactly what self-help is about, using our common sense and experience.

GK: *Let's talk about the development of the health centers.*

DH: After the Los Angeles clinic started Lorraine Rothman and other women started the Orange County FWHC. Women who had worked at the L.A. FWHC moved to Oakland to help start the Oakland FWHC. That summer Los Angeles had a summer institute; they invited women from all over the country to come and train at the Health Center for the summer to learn self-help, health-worker skills, and how to start a Feminist Women's Health Center. Women did come from all over the United States to the Summer Institute, and out of that the Tallahassee FWHC started in 1974.

At this time there was a women's clinic at night at the Free Clinic in Chico, in northern California. They referred all the women that wanted abortions to the Oakland Feminist Women's Health Center. Oakland had so many referrals from Chico it suggested a clinic start here. They did a self-help group for us and showed us menstrual extraction and we got very excited. We opened in February 1975. Since we opened Feminist Women's Health Centers have started in Atlanta, Concord, and San Diego. Originally Oakland, Orange County, and Los Angeles were all incorporated as one Health Center with three branches. They used to rotate between those three Centers. You'd be two weeks in your own Health Center, one week in each of the other Centers. This structure was good for communication, but very exhausting. So the structure was changed in late 1974. All the Health Centers incorporated separately at that time.

There's a Federation of Feminist Women's Health Centers. That includes Los Angeles, San Diego, Orange County, Concord, Chico, and Atlanta. The Federation is founded on the principle that we agree on our political strategy, our goals, and our internal workings. We are accountable to each other. I think we've gone farther than we ever expected to because of our ongoing fight with the State. For instance, we standardized our clinics. Now you can go into any of the FWHCs in California and get the same health care. If you're a health worker in one, as soon as you get oriented to where the supplies are kept, you can work at another clinic without noticing much difference. So in that way we are very similar and we have a lot of communication among Federation Health Centers. In fact my job now is coordinating the Federation.

GK: *How do you keep in touch?*

DH: There's a lot of telephoning. I send out reports on an irregular basis and make sure that I'm talking to people constantly. These reports go into the staff reports at each Health Center. We have Federation meetings also.

GK: *How often are Federation meetings held?*

DH: About once a year because it's so expensive to get everyone in one place. We rotate to each others' Health Centers, work on projects together, and attend conferences together.

GK: *Is there some kind of formal leadership within the structure? Does Carol Downer chair the meetings? Are there agendas?*

DH: Our meetings are pretty informal; we don't use Roberts' Rules of Order or traditional Board of Directors meetings. Our agendas come from the needs of the Health Centers. Carol is definitely recognized as the leader of the Federation and of the Health Centers. There's a lot of input into our direction from every level of the Health Centers. Very little happens without a lot of people talking about it first, and I think that that's most of the time to our benefit. Some of the time it's really slowed us down, as I'm sure any collective process does.

GK: *Let's say there's a Health Center that's doing a procedure that other centers don't think is proper. What can they do?*

DH: Believe me, there's been disagreement in the past over many different things that the Health Centers are doing at different times. It usually gets talked about when we rotate. There's a lot of rotation within the Health Centers, where women will go to different Centers for different reasons: sometimes for training, sometimes because that Center is short-staffed or because a person's expertise is needed at another Center. Many times someone has come to a Health Center where something is happening that is very different than in theirs. That will immediately start a discussion.

There isn't really a hierarchy in determining what the end result is going to be. I know that when I've been to different Health Centers it's not only changed their Center, it's changed Chico too. Whenever somebody has a better way of doing it, we'll try it. Where it's come down to political differences, it's been a lot harder. When there have been political differences within the Feminist Women's Health Centers, we have done everything we could think of to work it out. We've met and met and struggled to try to come to an agreement. If it's something that's big enough, it generally means that somebody may decide not to work with the Federation.

GK: *Is that what happened to Oakland?*

DH: Yes. We had some basic disagreements about feminism and capitalism. I really hesitate to expound on it at this point because we have a lot more agreements these days than we have disagreements, but at the time that it happened there was bitter disagreement that has resulted in Oakland and the rest of the Health Centers not working together.

GK: *It was a money-making kind of issue?*

DH: Yes. At the time they were pooling their resources with the Feminist Federal Credit Union and Diana Press to buy a women's building which had been a women's club in downtown Detroit and we just couldn't see eye to eye on that. I think that there's a lot of other things that were evolving at that time that separated Oakland from the general course that the rest of the Feminist Women's Health Centers were taking. Something that I think we've learned over the years is that Health Centers are going to have different priorities at different times, that Centers seem to have a growth pattern. Initially it has been important for a Health Center to get grounded in its community.

GK: *It usually involves a battle with local doctors.*

DH: It very often has. All the Health Centers have experienced some amount of harassment. In some communities all the physicians have been against the Center's existence. The Tallahassee Feminist Women's Health Center filed an antitrust suit in 1976 against the local physicians who were boycotting their clinic and forcing doctors to not work with them. They just recently settled the case.

GK: *Will doctors work for them now in abortion clinics?*

DH: Yes, that was part of the settlement. They have local back-up now.

GK: *So the Federation is mainly for information sharing?*

DH: And for pooling our resources, money, and expertise. To achive our political goals we manage to be able to spread our resources almost as well as housewives spread their resources.

GK: *Your book is a good example of that information sharing.*

DH: I have good news about that. We have two books now. One, *Women's Health in Women's Hands,* is a comprehensive guide to women's health care from a self-help perspective. The other, *A New View of a Women's Body,* is a shorter book of the illustrations and pictures from *WHWH.* We started writing a book in 1975 about women's health care. We wanted to put down our own experience and be able to share that with other women. WHWH has been a mammoth project. It's five years later, it's written, and it's very complete. It's the best health resource I can ever imagine a woman could have. Suzanne Gage has done wonderful drawings of how to insert a diaphragm, what a cervix looks like, the structure and functions of the clitoris and different reproductive organs. We have extensive photographs of cervixes at different stages in a women's cycle. These drawings are being published separately from WHWH. They will have captions and cover all that is in WHWH in a more condensed and less detailed way. So finally our work is going to be available for any women who can go into a bookstore and buy a book. Women will have some idea of the things that we've learned.

WHWH was written collectively. I believe there are fifteen authors. They came from Chico, Orange County, San Diego, Los Angeles, and Tallahassee. All participated in research gathering and financing; it's really been an all–health-center project.

GK: *What are political concerns that you are working on as a group?*

DH: Of course, we all define ourselves as feminists first and foremost. That's getting to be less and less of a commonality these days, as you're probably experiencing yourself. It seems like the women's movement isn't as active or as popular as it once was. We very much are trying to regain control of our reproduction. We see that as being one of the most important parts of feminism and being a woman. Because we're feminists, our politics we see encompassing all aspects of our lives, our personal relationships, the way we interact with each other and with the rest of the world. Over and over again it's been said in the Health Center that if you're not doing it in your own life (like confronting sexism), you're not going to be able to do it out there any better.

We've expanded our political perspective over the years. We've started talking more and more about imperialism and how it affects us as women, as feminists, and as people who live in the United States.

GK: *Like testing birth-control pills on Puerto Rican women? And sterilization of Third World women?*

DH: That's something that we've always pretty much known about. I think we've been well aware of imperialism since 1975, when we went to Mexico City and were appalled at what happened with International Women's Year and how they could have a government-sponsored women's conference with poor women starving in front and not notice it. We've taken the step from seeing it to fighting it, working with international struggles against imperialism and working to ensure feminism isn't dropped. I've seen so many political organizations in the last few years drop feminism from their principles of unity. We've always seen that we had to fight patriarchy and capitalism hand in hand. Every step of the way the partriarchy and capitalism hit us daily in the medical community. I think the big change over the last years has been that we have started expanding to an analysis of imperialism, the super powers, and imperialistic forces.

GK: *Rita Mae Brown said, what good is it if you have a feminist ideology and the multinationals pollute the environment, etc.?*

DH: Yes. To expand on that, what good is it to have an analysis of revolution without having feminism as part of the analysis? We see it as necessary to have both daily change as well as to fight for the future, however distant or close that is. We do see our work in our clinics as being reformist. We have been part of discussions about patriarchy and imperialism and how imperialism hurts us as feminists, how it benefits us, and how we can fight it. I don't think we can fight imperialism individually, like throwing out your TV or not driving a car. I don't think that that's the answer, I think it's much more broad-based than that.

One of the things that we have done is try to be in contact with people of other movements. I think Carol Downer going to Iran in 1979 was a step that helped us to better understand both the struggle in Iran and also the one in the United States. So little information is available in the United States about liberation struggles around the world that I feel like we are kept dumb by the lack of information. We have made a commitment to get this information. Right now there are women from Nicaragua who are training in the FWHC in Oakland. Any time that we can share any of our resources (like our clinic skills), we will. We're not a highly monied organization so our contribution to other movements can rarely be financial.

GK: *What about in the internal structure as in the Chico FWHC? You talked about having to live the principles of feminism, not just talk about them. What input does the receptionist have?*

DH: You picked the right person. Our receptionist is a self-helper and a very active participant in most all of the political activities that the Health Center does. Our goals were to have everyone be full-time, do everything, everyone agree and have the same commitment. As a matter of fact we started out that way. Over the years we came to see that that was a pretty exclusive position. It left out women who had different pulls on them that didn't allow them to plug in the way we could. Then we tended to swing the other way; at times in our own Health Center we've been inclusive to the point of sometimes having people working in our Center who actively disagree with us. That is just plain liberal, there's no two ways about it. Our goal is to have women work in the Health Center who basically agree with feminism, controlling our reproduction, fighting patriarchy and capitalism, and those women work to what capacity they can. It's not an easy task. We have a lot of personnel problems all the time.

GK: *But there are directors, how many?*

DH: They've ranged from twenty to seven; now there are six directors and nine full-time staff. We consider that we have an open-ended hierarchy in the Health Centers. People can plug in to it whatever degree they can and are encouraged to always plug in more, from having a limited commitment and a very defined job to being in a leadership position. Of course, you're not going to be in a leadership position unless you have many of the qualities of leadership. People who are in leadership positions usually have experience in political activities and have some kind of vision of the direction of the Health Center.

When you come to work at the Health Center, if you come to work as a full-time staff, you start by having a two-week orientation at the Center where we try to show the range of what the Center does and believes. It's a fifty-five–hour per week orientation, which is not unusual for our hours; in fact fifty-five is pretty good a lot of times. After that you go through a four- to eight-week training period. The length of that training is figured on your own and the group's evaluation of your progress.

At the end of that training you can evaluate with group input to be a full-time staff person who is a member of the internal working collective and has an area of responsibility. Of course, we want everyone to become directors.

If you come to work at the Health Center and you can't make a full-time staff commitment, your training will probably go somewhat differently. You would probably have a specific job like receptionist or an assistant to a particular area: Medi-Cal billing, bookkeeping, accounts receivable and payable. Some of the training is the same because everyone goes through a self-help group who works at the Health Center, but you wouldn't go through eight weeks of training to be a receptionist. What we're trying to do right now is to make all the political activities be as open to everyone's input and participation as possible. Though we know people can't plug into the fifty to seventy hours a week of administration, clinics, and meetings, we do think that people can plug into the outcome of that work, which is political events, discussions, and political education.

GK: *As I understand it, there's some feeling that the people who are part-time feel left out of things.*

DH: Oftentimes that's true. Sometimes we have arguments about it. I've never fully understood why people feel that way because it is a self-determined limitation. We have never to my recollection forced anybody into a lesser position than they wanted. We push awfully hard to make sure people keep going forward, but I don't remember ever pushing anybody back.

I really disagree with a division being made around hours worked. I think division should be made around politics and political beliefs. I really support those kind of discussions. But in a feminist workplace if the divisions are all around hours worked, it doesn't really get to the root of the problem. In my experience I've often found that some of the people who were talking the loudest about the division around the hours worked really did have disagreements with the politics. But I'm speaking as a full-time staff person and a director too.

GK: *What about the time involved in making decision on a consensus basis in meetings?*

DH: I think the book would have gotten written three years faster if we hadn't been collective. I think that we'd probably be at least twice as rich, or half as poor, if we weren't collective. When I was working on the book, we used to joke that if we really wanted to give it to somebody we'd make them write a book collectively. It was the hardest process. For example, when we were writing the book, the book ended up without a single joke in it because no one could agree on what was funny. It was the most dry material because what was funny to some was offensive to someone else and stupid to a third person. Naming the book, that was hell.

A lot of times the most amount of our time is spent ensuring that everyone has all the information. There's no way that every decision that we make can be a collective decision. Sooner or later you have to delegate a certain amount of responsibility to different people who have the information. Most of our time is spent sharing information that we've gotten or need input on. That is really the bulk of our communication, both internal and with other Health Centers.

GK: *What about the principle of self-criticism and criticism? How does that work in practice?*

DH: In the Health Centers people feel very strongly about what they believe in. I think a lot of our criticism comes through having disagreements, having the argument and fighting it out. Also criticism and self-criticism is another principle like feminism that's becoming less and less popular, in my experience. A lot of the different community groups where I'll attend meetings are less focused and make less demands on people to state their disagreements or agreements. On a day-to-day basis it mainly works through somebody disagreeing with someone else and then coming to the end of that disagreement of who's right and who's wrong.

GK: *Kind of dialectical?*

DH: Right, very much so. When people really believe in what they're working on, it seems to come a lot easier and a lot freer and be taken in that way too. Some of the most productive disagreements I've ever had have been with people who felt as strongly as I did about what we were working on and disagreed. At least that's the way it works for me and that's the way I've been able to further develop my own politics. Especially if the criticism is given with a big dose of nonjudgmentalism. I think when it gets really hard is when you're criticized with a judgment.

GK: *You're a bad person if you don't think this.*

DH: Yes, right. Being judgmental is something we've discussed, talked about, fought over, and really tried to criticize ourselves about.

GK: *Are there other ways that the FWHC is different from a patriarchal business or medical establishment?*

DH: Right from the minute you walk into the doors of FWHC it has to hit you. If you look at the surroundings, it's put together by women for women, it's comfortable. You don't have to have your examination on a table with stirrups in it and you don't have to be draped, you get to know right away what's happening to your body and why. You get to stop if you want to stop. That manner of health care delivery is because we're women and because we're feminists. We ask ourselves if we could do it any way we wanted, how would we do it? From there we go to the practical.

I think that our views of fairness are very different than traditional patriarchal structure. A good example is our salary scale. People who have been here longer get a higher base pay than people who have been here a short time. We do feel strongly that commitment, time, and the work that you've done needs to be recognized. But we're also in a position where we don't always get our full salaries. We get percent salaries when we don't make enough money to pay ourselves and pay our bills. The way the salary scale works is the people who make the most money take the biggest cut. I've never heard of a patriarchal capitalist business that works in that way.

Another difference is the way we view the work we do; no one has ever been above cleaning the Health Center, no one has ever risen above working the clinic or doing the billing or adding up the checkbook. We don't have executives in that respect. We talk about our relationships, our families, our living situations, we get input from each other on how to make them better.

G.K: *What about bringing children to work?*

DH: Every woman who works at the Health Center has childcare. The way we prefer to do it is we have our own childcare program where we can have some input and go and see the children. The kind of childcare we offer depends on the number of kids we have. We do bring our children to work whenever we can, whenever it's practical for them and us, and we take care of women's children who come into the clinic.

It's not always the best situation. I know that two years ago we had a political education among the Health Centers and everyone was pregnant. We said, "Oh God, can you imagine what it's going to be like next year when everybody has kids," and a year and a half later there were seventeen kids. This is a group that four years ago had Carol's children and Lorraine's children and maybe a smattering of others. There were seventeen kids; it really changed the nature of political education.

We do think that childcare should be provided because we want to do everything we can to make as many different kind of women as possible to be able to plug into our Health Centers and not to leave mothers out. We've done some amazing things too. We've changed people's statuses, we've redefined their work around their families, we've given them different hours. My hours now change on a daily basis, it's not *my* hours—it's my daughter Carmen's.

It's important to say that we're not profit motivated; the amount of money that we bring in and the amount we need to operate don't always balance. Our goal, of course, is to pay ourselves what we're worth, which we haven't ever succeeded in doing. But we try to pay people enough to live on, make sure that we have the supplies we need, and we don't charge much over that to the women who use the Health Centers.

GK: *You charge on a sliding scale?*

DH: Right, we have sliding scales for all of our services.

GK: *What about the lunch program and the health club membership?*

DH: We have some unconventional benefits. We have the conventional ones too: we have health insurance and a retirement program. Over the years we've become more and more health conscious ourselves, and we all now have a lunch program where we serve healthy food for low cost to people who work at the Health Center. We strongly encourage exercise, have memberships in local gyms, try to support each other to get the exercise and take the time out of our day. Any reproductive health care that we need is of course provided by the Health Center.

We have feminist personnel, which is something that's very different from ordinary businesses. Our personnel department is not concerned with maximizing output as much as it is concerned with ensuring that the output that we do put out is working toward our goals. Personnel makes sure that we have childcare when we need it, that we have days off before we're ready to drop, and that we have discussions on the agenda about conditions that are affecting people's work.

People don't always understand that we're not antimale and we're not separatists. We have women of all sexual preferences. That's another real benefit about working in the Health Centers. You can be open about your sexuality. We have women who aren't married to men, we have women who are in relationships with women, with men, women who are mothers, single women, and women who aren't in relationships with anybody.

We try to encourage ourselves to talk about it as much as we can to better understand what we're doing and why.

GK: *You're providing an alternative, and that's an assault on the patriarchy.*

DH: Not in itself. I think that providing the alternative gives us better lives right now, but I don't think that it changes anything in and of itself. But the better lives we can have the more we can do to get at the heart of fighting patriarchy and capitalism.

GK: *That's always the question—how does one get this kind of radical change?*

DH: I wish I could answer that one. We see certain aspects of what we do as being revolutionary; we have always seen self-help as being a direct assault and directly regaining control. Whenever we are in a position where we've seized technology, such as developing menstrual extraction, we see that as being revolutionary. We also provide alternative workplaces that do make our lives better right now. If I didn't work at the Health Center I would have a regular job forty hours a week and then I would spend at least twenty hours a week on political work. Being at the Health Center has enabled us to have a working situation where we can more directly do our political work for a lot more hours than if we had to work for General Motors or IBM.

GK: *What about future directions? Where would you like to see your energy go as a FWHC and as a Federation?*

DH: As far as overall goals, we want to have more contact with Third World liberation movements, with women in those movements, and be able to share resources on that level as well as on the inter–Health Center level. We're all trying to learn Spanish in California because we felt like we've been effectively cut off from a big portion of the population. If you go into any of the FWHCs everything has the word for Spanish written on it as well as the word for English. Some of the FWHCs in San Diego and Los Angeles have been doing self-help in Tijuana, Mexico, to expand beyond our own groups. A lot of our energy is used to broaden our base, getting bigger, including as many women as want to be included, and expanding in that way.

I would love to see a more united women's movement. Now its you there and me here and so and so over there. The way that we are represented to the rest of the country and the rest of the world is in the conferences like IWY and State Department Women's Conferences. Their existence has looked like they were purposely put up to sort of derail the women's movement. One of our basic goals is changing power relationships: on an individual level, on a group level, and in the big picture.

INSTITUTIONS OF
WOMEN'S CULTURE

Interview with Ruth Iskin

Ruth Iskin is a leading force in the women's art movement on the
West Coast. Trained as an art historian, she works in the areas of
feminist art criticism, curating exhibitions, teaching, and organizing.
Since 1972, when she moved to Los Angeles, she has been a leader at
Womanspace, the first alternative art space for women artists in
California; Womanspace Journal, an early magazine devoted to
women's art; the Feminist Studio Workshop, a college-level school for
women in the arts; the Woman's Building, a public center for women's
culture; and Chrysalis, a magazine of women's culture. These
institutions are monuments to women's culture of the 1970s. Their
organizational style is perhaps as significant as their being showcases
of women's creativity. In this interview Iskin analyzes the workings
of these women's institutions and discusses women's culture.

GK: *I'd like to talk with you about* Chrysalis *and the L.A.* Woman's
Building *as women's institutions. Working in an all-woman envi-*
ronment, what have you seen that is different about feminist
organization, structure, leadership, environment, and style?

RI: The women's movement in general and alternative feminist organizations in particular have had an enormous influence in
developing new structures and modes of relationships in the work
environment. One of the deepest differences I have experienced
in working in alternative feminist institutions is the fact that everything from goals and priorities to procedures and modes of interaction is all wide open for reevaluation. They are constantly
being determined, questioned, and reformulated. There are no

prescribed patterns to follow. The inherent goal of the feminist alternative is not only to accomplish certain tasks, like mounting an exhibition or publishing a magazine, but also to figure out in the process how to do such projects in a different way according to feminist principles, so these institutions can be models for a different kind of order. Our institutions can be viewed as labs for experimentation with feminist politics. They are the concrete environments where we can apply feminist philosophy with a great deal of freedom and where we can recreate feminist theory by learning from practice.

Feminist institutions have tended to create structures which are essentially nonhierarchical and allow for rotating leadership of groups rather than individuals. These institutions have encouraged collaboration and cooperation as primary working relationships. The alternative feminist institution functions as a learning environment and training ground for individual and collective growth for women, both in regard to learning skills and in regard to a more general personal development. Last but not least, the women's movement has encouraged us to incorporate our feelings and personal experiences into our work and working environment. In fact the first structure to be invented by the

Feminist Studio Workshop,
Woman's Building

women's movement was the consciousness-raising group, and we have incorporated it into our working relationships at feminist institutions here.

GK: *Do you, for example, structure the consciousness-raising format into the workings of* Chrysalis *magazine or the Woman's Building, or do you do it when it seems to be needed?*

RI: At the Woman's Building and *Chrysalis* we tend to use consciousness-raising techniques when it seems needed. In the Feminist Studio Workshop School we have structured C-R into the schedule; the students meet regularly once a week in ongoing C-R groups.

GK: *Do you go around the circle, and each person expresses her viewpoint with an exchange following?*

RI: Yes. Each person gets her turn going around the room and later on there is usually discussion. Often it happens spontaneously in meetings. Someone makes the suggestion, "Let's go around the room about this issue." Frequently it's not a clear separation between feelings and beliefs or opinions; usually they are very mixed.

GK: *What are the effects of incorporating personal feelings into the work environment?*

RI: People can function more fully and humanely with each other by relating on different levels. It creates more meaningful relationships among people who work with each other; the working relationships are tremendously important in our lives and create a strong bonding. Yet there are also drawbacks. We've learned that just as repressing one's feelings can undermine the wellbeing of people in their work environment, a great deal of focus on feelings and interpersonal problems can become destructive. The personal level can take up a large segment of energies, sometimes to the extent that it undermines doing the necessary work.

GK: *What about leadership in feminist institutions?*

RI: Alternatives to hierarchy and traditional leadership have been primary concerns in feminist institutions. These institutions encourage women to develop their full potential and emerge into leadership; the assumption is that leadership is not something

Susan B. Anthony Day,
Woman's Building

reserved for a few but attainable by anyone. The structures are fluid and the roles aren't fixed.

GK: *And that has happened in the Feminist Studio Workshop, that students became teachers, right? Is Suzanne Lacy an example?*

RI: Yes, it happens all the time, it's part of the process. Suzanne was a student at the feminist program at Cal Arts in the early seventies and now is on the faculty of the FSW with some of her former teachers. Many of the women who have emerged into leadership in the Woman's Building began as students in the FSW. The FSW school provides women with the opportunity of taking on large-scale projects in which they involve many other women in a guided collaboration. It functions as a training ground for assuming larger responsibilities and leadership. The FSW school also deals with this process in a focused way involving all the range of feelings that come up. Emerging into leadership is a gradual process; it takes developing of self-confidence, experience, and counteracting a lot of women's conditioning. It's a slow and painful process. At the FSW we've called it the "feminist process."

GK: *What about the anger that seems to accompany that process?*

RI: The anger and frustration are feelings that accompany the recognition of one's own powerlessness. Often that anger might get turned on to another woman who is perceived as embodying the desired goals and aspirations, the role model. Dealing with these feelings is part of the "feminist process" at the FSW. When a woman becomes a leader, she essentially assists other women in making the same transition. It's like being a midwife for women giving birth to their own power, which in turn enables them to make more of a contribution to others.

GK: *What about the collective as an organizational structure in the institutions you are involved with?*

RI: We don't identify ourselves as a collective, in any of these groups, although at one point we did see ourselves as the FSW collective, referring to the core faculty (including Sheila de Bretteville, Arlene Raven, Deena Metzger, Suzanne Lacy, Helen Roth, and myself). On an organizational level these women's institutions have adopted or adapted certain structures from the mainstream. For example, the Woman's Building has a board of directors. Nevertheless, when you examine the reality of the working relationships, it is much more in tune with the idea of the collective, in the way decisions are made and in the sense that the input of those individuals who shoulder the responsibility for the institution are the ones whose input makes the difference.

One of the most important characteristics of feminist institutions is that openness and constant invitation to the community to become active, and thus determine the direction of the institution. At various times different people are ready to do that. Since 1973, when the Woman's Building was founded in L.A. (by Judy Chicago, Sheila de Bretteville, and Arlene Raven), there have been hundreds, perhaps even thousands, of women who have participated actively in the institution and affected it. Of course, on the level of audience participation there have been many more. One of the most valuable and probably innovative characteristics of alternative feminist institutions is that people can easily make a transition from outside spectator to active participant.

GK: *It seems like it's a fine line; Jo Freeman pointed out the problem of "the tyranny of structurelessness." Radical feminist groups, like the Redstockings, found that their downfall was the problem of mistrust of leadership. So it is necessary to build a cooperative framework and still identify people with responsibility.*

RI: It's always changing; at various points there have been more recognizable leaders than at other times, but there are always people who are in positions of responsibility. It's all very fluid, with a lot of openness for people to come in. As opposed to a certain amount of ambiguity as to who does what at the Woman's Building, at *Chrysalis* magazine the roles have been more clearly defined.

GK: *What are some of the job descriptions at* Chrysalis?

RI: There is an editorial board which founded the magazine: Kirsten Grimstad, Susan Rennie, Arlene Raven, Sheila de Bretteville, and myself. (Debra Marrow is currently also on the editorial board.) The board makes all decisions about the direction of the magazine and which manuscripts are published. More recently we've added another body—the publishers—which makes all business decisions. There is some coincidence between people on the editorial board and the publishers group.

GK: *A lot of the time it seems that women's organizations are like mushrooms; they proliferate and die. I wonder if that has anything*

"Women in Architecture" show
being installed, April 1978

to do with the structure of feminist organizations or if it's just lack of money and support from the establishment. Do you want to comment on that, especially in terms of the L.A. Woman's Building?

RI: One key factor certainly is money. So many women's projects and institutions were founded on idealism, a commitment to implement ideals in the world and fill urgent needs, without taking into serious account whether the creation of an institution or a project would support itself financially. That was certainly the case with the Los Angeles Woman's Building.

The Woman's Building and the FSW were founded because needs of women in the arts and women's culture were not fulfilled anywhere. These ambitious institutions were founded with enormous enthusiasm and much volunteer work. The financial planning to cover rent and administrative overhead was minimal at the beginning. As years went by more and more experience was gained.

When we founded *Chrysalis* in 1976, we brought three years of experience at the Woman's Building with us. At that point, after several years of working very, very hard under constant pressure to raise money for the Woman's Building so its doors could remain open (with no salaries or minimal salaries and each of us holding additional jobs), we realized that we wanted to create the new endeavor of the magazine so as to be financially feasible.

GK: *What did you do differently with* Chrysalis?

RI: We wanted to provide a national publication of women's culture—culture defined in the broadest sense to include politics, psychology, history, etc., in addition to the various arts. From the beginning we wanted to make it an effective magazine, and that meant attempting to reach a broad audience (relative to other feminist publications at the time). We made a decision to incorporate as a profit-making organization (rather than a nonprofit organization like the Woman's Building and the FSW). After producing a few issues we approached people for capitalization. But unlike mainstream magazines, which do not begin publication before raising significant funds (a quarter of a million was at the time considered minimum), we started out on a shoestring, with a $2,500 donation from a feminist poet and two hundred advance subscriptions. (The advance subscriptions came from an announcement in Grimstad and Rennie's *New Women's Survival Catalogue*.) With those funds we started the magazine and printed the first issue. In an attempt to ensure the viability of the magazine we engaged the services of a computer company specializing in magazines. With them we devised a four-year plan of numerous promotions meant to increase the circulation of the magazine gradually to the point of financial self-sufficiency.

GK: Chrysalis *is called a "journal of women's culture," and the Woman's Building is called "a center for women's culture." How do you define women's culture?*

RI: Women's culture as it has emerged in the seventies is the expression of women's experiences, ideals, and goals for themselves and the world. When feminism reemerged in the seventies, it brought to the forefront a recognition that Western culture mostly represented a partial point of view dominated by men's experiences in a role-divided culture and society. Although women certainly have made many significant contributions to culture over the centuries, those have either not been attributed to women or not been recognized as important. One example often used is the quilt as an art form. It's a complex and beautiful tradition passed along from generation to generation, practiced by women in their homes as a functional art, yet it wasn't until fairly recently that it, along with other "crafts," has been recognized as art. Its aesthetics are closely linked to women's lives. The way women have pieced together small parts to create a whole has been likened to the way women's lives are a structure made up of many fragments and interruptions.

Simone de Beauvoir discusses how women's lives, with their mindless daily chores, do not provide for the kind of daring and adventurousness necessary for exploring and creating important innovations. It certainly has hampered women from contributing fully. On the other hand, women's traditional way of life has had a positive impact in providing a nourishing source for women's creations. For example, the fact that women generally were more involved in human relationships—with children, other women, and with men—has provided women with an easy access to their emotional lives, an important source for any artistic creation.

It is not accidental that much of women's culture focuses on autobiographical aspects, renders personal expressions, and uses collaboration and participation as a foundation for the artistic process. Women's art and culture have not been looked at as a body until feminism came around. The question of a women's aesthetic is a field of investigation which is just a few years old. Previously women artists were seen as unique and special cases. Now the question of a women's aesthetic can be asked, and certainly we're still groping for answers. Yet I think we need to be careful

Suzanne Lacy and Leslie Labowitz
"In Mourning and in Rage"
(performance project)

not to assume that women's art has to subscribe to one particular style, just as it would not occur to us to demand a stylistic coherency of all male artists.

GK: *Please elaborate on characteristics of feminist education at the FSW.*

RI: Feminist education, as we've developed it in the Feminist Studio Workshop, exists within a larger context of women's culture by virtue of the fact that it is in the public center of the Woman's Building. It's sheltered but not isolated. Feminist education assists women in developing their full potential while developing new form and content in art, form and content which are related to their experiences and lives as women and to feminism.

GK: *Like cooperative work and diaries. . . .*

RI: Cooperation is a very important aspect, yes. Another important goal of feminist art is to have effect on culture at large. Suzanne Lacy's and Leslie Labowitz's performance projects are a good model for this direction. Their work is usually done in collaboration with many others: artists and nonartists, politicians, grassroots organizers and educators. And in this respect their work is very directly influenced by the Woman's Building and the Feminist Studio Workshop. By making the use of mass media integral to their performances they have been able to reach a truly mass audience and thus have a direct impact on a large scale. Affecting people's thinking and the social structure are important goals of feminist art. Ultimately it boils down to creating real change.

GK: *What would you like to see for the future of the L.A. Woman's Building, if money wasn't a problem?*

RI: In my fantasy vision the Building would be an institution that integrates women's culture—the realm of the intellectual, artistic, and creative—with both the physical and the spiritual realm. In addition to gallery spaces, a graphics lab, performance spaces, and offices (all of which exist at present) the building would include spiritual nests, spaces for meditation and ritual, and a healing center based on integrating the spiritual and physical. The Building would also have a mass-media access, perhaps by featuring a cable station specializing in programming for women's audiences. So much for fantasy. In reality I think the important role the Woman's Building has played is in acting as a nucleus spurring the development of a new women's culture—a radical feminist culture.

GK: *There is nothing comparable with the L.A. Woman's Building since the Chicago Women's Building in 1893, right?*

RI: There are a lot of alternative art spaces around the country; most of them focus on gallery show spaces.

GK: What is the scale or magnitude of women's culture?

RI: When we look at what has been produced during the 1970s—the number of books published, the enormous amount of art produced, the films and music, the institutions that have been created, and the new forms of organization and relationships within those institutions—it is clear that there is an enormous wealth of material produced by feminists which has great vitality and constitutes a new body in our culture. Women's culture has become, in a matter of several years during the seventies, an alternative culture. As time goes on its impact can widen as more and more people have access to it. Women's culture has introduced new ideas and new forms and is having a growing influence on women as well as men. The women's art movement has been the most vital movement in the art of the seventies and has had a large impact on the focus of content in art of the later seventies. Nevertheless I think we need to be aware of the fact that the influence of women's culture and art, and of women's institutions, has not been fully acknowledged. But the changes are occurring.

GK: *And I think the impact is not just on alternative spaces, it's begun to infiltrate corporate offices too.*

RI: It's begun to have impact everywhere.

INDEX